The
Round
World

The Round World

Life at the Intersection of Love, Sex, and Fat

Printed in the United States of America

ISBN 978-0-9972802-0-3

Library of Congress Control Number: 2016907678

First Edition

The Antrobus Group
8424A Santa Monica Blvd.
West Hollywood, CA 90069

www.antrobusgroup.com

At the end of the day,
it isn't where I came from.
Maybe home is somewhere
I'm going and never have
been before.

—Warsan Shire
Somali/British poet

TABLE OF CONTENTS

LIST OF FIGURES

ACKNOWLEDGMENTS

To Rebecca Ward for her enthusiasm and sound advice about my early, inchoate drafts,

To Gisela Enders for graciously inviting me to speak at her international conference and giving me my first opportunity to speak to a wider audience,

To Russ Turk for inadvertently launching me into the public eye of talk shows and news media,

To Jennifer Morales for her sober and fair criticism of various drafts of the manuscript, as well as for her endlessly helpful edits and insights,

To Cliff Lamb-Rosas for his constant friendship, insight, and inspiration for the title of this book,

To Kari Pope for her fellowship and good conversation, allowing me to ask questions that proper folks shouldn't ask,

To Edward Mellen for creating community and bringing the Round World together in a way that is so powerful and necessary,

To Brian Lieske for his many decades of friendship, allowing me to see beyond my world and into his,

To Fiona Holland for her passion and inspiration, which kept me going more than she knows,

To Philip Barragan, my dear friend and colleague, who for so many years has listened to me espouse and theorize, and reined me in with the gentlest of wise criticism,

To Trevor Kezon, my best beloved, who supports me unquestioningly and helped me forward when I felt I was in a ditch,

To Kevin Clarke for his beautiful design of this book and his guidance in helping it become a physical reality,

To the many people in this book who have taught me so much and contributed so profoundly to my life.

WHAT'S IN THIS BOOK

The Round World is the first book to explore what it's like for those of us who see fat people as powerfully erotic and beautiful, and who seek them as romantic partners. In coming to terms with the nature of such desires and relationships, we'll look at issues such as body image, self-esteem, prejudice, health, sexuality, identity, adoration, and objectification. I'll share stories about myself and others who live in the Round World in a conversational style. I'll also propose models for the way we see the world and our relationships—how we succeed and why we sometimes fail at them. Our relationships face unique challenges because they operate inside a taboo where the standards of beauty, power, and attraction seem upside down.

The Round World is presented as a sort of travelogue, recounting a journey to a place where the inhabitants find that obesity enhances love, sex, and relationships. Our trip comprises five parts:

In Section 1, "The World Is Wide," I talk about what it's like to have an attraction that is at odds with a taboo, and my own journey toward helping people embrace their bodies and their desires. We'll also start to look at the stereotypes of man/woman relationships and how they get collapsed with fat/admirer stereotypes. Though everything in *The Round World* applies to people of any gender or sexual orientation, we can sometimes see the issues of fat/admirer relationships more clearly by looking at same-sex relationships, which are free from the bias of male/female gender politics.

Section 2, "You Don't Know Fat," focuses on what we think about fat individually and as a society. It examines the facts, prejudices, and medical issues around obesity, and gives the reader a chance to locate his or her perspective on the Fat Map. I don't think you can fully appreciate what being with a fat partner means to someone like me until you distinguish what fat people mean to you.

In Section 3, "Love and Sex in a Big Fat World," I describe the various dating scenes in the Round World, along with the unique challenges faced by fat people and their admirers. We'll examine exactly what so-called chubby chasers find sexy about Fat and the roles in which fat people and their admirers find themselves. We'll see how these interactions often revolve around shame, guilt, and objectification, and how to avoid these pitfalls to create successful relationships.

Section 4, "Fat Kink and the Drive to Get Fatter," journeys into the kinky side of Fat and the sexual ecstasy that many men and women find in becoming obese or in helping a partner attain their goal of obesity. Again, their hearts and relationships are explored through personal stories, and given shape in psychological models that offer freedom from judgment and new insights into sexuality in general.

Finally, in Section 5, "Life Beyond the Round World," I talk about what life in the Round World has to say to people who aren't fat and don't share a sexual attraction to obesity. Some of us live in a taboo conversation, whether it's the taboo of obesity, race, gender, religion, money, or any other taboo topic. We'll talk about our stories, our monsters, and how conversations about any taboo share common elements that keep us from connecting with people. In understanding how the Taboo Conversation works, we can begin to have authentic conversations, discover new allies, and form deeper bonds with the people who matter most to us—in or out of the Round World.

1

The World Is Wide

We all come from a single source.
Everything that lives has its genetic
code written in the same alphabet.
Unity creates diversity.

—Jonathan Sacks
The Dignity of Difference

BELLY UP TO THE BAR

I'm sitting in a bar in an affluent, gay neighborhood. It's a fashionable part of town where beautiful men flirt, cavort, and seduce other beautiful men. Some people think you have to be beautiful to come here—that gym cards are checked at the border and ugly people get deported. That's not true, of course. I'll admit though that "average" here is a little above average. Like the men around me in this bar, I go to the gym (often, by some standards). In fact, to make sure I can fit it into my schedule, I belong to three gyms in different parts of the city. I am highly knowledgeable about the nutrients in the food I eat and overly particular about how it's prepared. But so are most of the guys around me in this A-gay bar in West Hollywood. I live in this neighborhood, and the other denizens perceive me to be one of them. But the similarity is only superficial. While they're aroused by each other and sometimes by me, I love fat men.

What is it like to be attracted to a characteristic that is taboo? How do you deal with being desired for a characteristic that you may actively dislike about yourself? How does that affect relationships? Dating? How does a person deal with family, friends, even a whole society that thinks his body is wrong? Or that the desire for such a body is wrong? But maybe bodies and desires are simply the domain of lust, and true love comes from the union of like minds. Is it mind and body that draw the line between love and lust? Adoration and objectification? When does that line get crossed? These questions and others are the territory of this book as we venture into the Round World, a world that spins on a different axis than the world most people live in.

I've been attracted to obesity for as long as I can remember. It's been the same for most of the people who share my attraction, whether they're gay or straight. As we'll see, gender and sexual orientation are not necessarily primary in the Round World, even though they may be a strong or even exclusive orientation for most of us. *Fat, big, blubbery, bulky, round.* We describe it in accordance with our tastes and self-acceptance of it. Whether we identify as gay or straight, male or female, our affinity for Fat seems to have been with us as long as we can remember.

I was fascinated by obesity as early as kindergarten. I can remember straining to hear a conversation across the playground that included the word *fat*. The words still ring in my ears though it happened decades ago. How do you remember something like that, so trivial yet so vivid? I knew at five years old that I was into fat, but I didn't figure out I was gay until I was 20. Even though my family lived next door to a gay couple, and I lived in an arts dorm in college with more than its fair share of gays, it never occurred to me that I was gay.

It kind of makes sense, actually. Have you ever picked up a gay men's magazine? Seen the cover of a gay novel? Gay media is populated with pictures of beautiful, slim, athletic men. But I never got a sexual urge from guys like that. So in my mind, I wasn't gay. I wanted to look like one of those guys, sure, but so do most men, don't they? Not look gay, but look fit and chiseled with six-pack abs. Beautiful. At least we're supposed to look like that, right? So putting together that I was gay took me longer than most. As I talked to more and more people like me—chubby chasers, or just *chasers* in the gay world, *fat admirers* or *FAs* in the straight world—I discovered that my feelings and experiences shared a common thread with theirs. I began hearing similar stories and seeing similar difficulties in dating, sex, and relationships. I fell in love, but realized that love was not enough to sustain a romantic relationship if we didn't share a fundamental sexual compatibility.

Today I give seminars about what lies at the intersection of obesity and sexuality. I mentor men and women in my community, and I've been featured on talk shows and in documentaries dealing with obesity and sexuality. Because of my visibility and experience in the matter, men and women from all over the world email me and seek my perspective. They're looking for more than just connection. They're in search of a sense of where they fit in the world of what their feelings mean. Most especially, they look for a way to resolve the apparent contradictions of their sexuality. I've been described as a sort of Sherpa of fat love. How did I get to be a Sherpa? I spent decades being lost on a mountain, bumping my head on the same trees and rocks over and over again, talking to fellow travelers, until I got to know that mountain so well that I could sketch it accurately and guide others along its trails. I call it the Round World. It's my name for a domain where fat people interact with the people who find fat people attractive. It has physical locations, like dance parties and bar nights. It has cyber-locations, like websites and chat rooms. It has everyday locations, coexisting with the regular world, like in a coffee shop when two people of opposite sizes seem to be coincidentally smiling and no one else knows why.

My (Not So Tiny) Tribe

This book is a travelogue. When you visit or read about foreign lands, you learn a bit about the place and the people there, but mostly you learn about yourself. For example, I think if you were raised in the United States, the best way to learn what it means to be an American is to go to France. By contrast, if you are from France, you will never feel more French than on your first trip to the U.S. In my experience, there is nothing more astonishing than finding out that what you thought was logical and universal behavior is simply a matter of culture or prejudice. It works the other way, too. Things that you might think are "so American" are actually not uniquely American at all. When you're reading this book, imagine you're visiting my tiny tribe in our tiny country—a place where attractive people with slabs of muscle or long, lean lines, or average Joes and plain Janes, are sexually turned on by a fat partner. Bring snacks.

No subculture is a monoculture. The Round World is just as diverse as any other community of people you could meet. This is even truer when we include all four parameters: gay, straight, male, and female. However, I believe that there's no point in segregating gender and sexual orientation when it comes to Fat. Seeing fat people and the desire for a fat partner as a unifying characteristic brings us to a more powerful understanding of ourselves and our lives.

I remember leading my most popular seminar, called "Love and Sex in a Big Fat World," at an annual convention of fat gay men and their admirers many years ago. As it happened, some straight women and a lesbian couple were also there, listening in the back. After the seminar, one of the women approached me to say how much she enjoyed my talk, and she invited me to speak at the annual conference of the National Association to Advance Fat Acceptance (NAAFA), a social and political organization that "seeks to build a society in which people of every size are accepted with dignity and equality in all aspects of life." Another of the women invited me to lead a seminar at an annual event that she produces for fat women and their male admirers. Although I was grateful for both invitations, I had never spoken to groups of women, so I asked them how their experience was different and how I should adapt my seminar to address the concerns of straight people. Their advice was simple: "Change nothing." They told me that everything I had said resonated with their experience of fat/admirer dating and relationships.

Since then, I've spoken in front of all sorts of people in the Round World—different ages, genders, ethnicities, nationalities, sizes, and sexual orientations. None of these characteristics matter as much as the one overarching theme: Fat. All of us in the Round World have the same fears, challenges, and delights. We differ only in what's most urgent to a particular person or group. Also, people who are not part of the Round World tell me that what I have to say is very useful to them in dealing with other stigmas and prejudices that have nothing to do with being fat. We'll get into that more in the last section of this book.

Round World Culture Shock

Has anyone ever admired a characteristic about you that you actively dislike? What if someone adored a characteristic that you actually loathed about yourself? Your temper? Your crooked nose? Your scars? Your limp? Now imagine that this person confessed to you that this quality—this part of you that you've done your best to deny, downplay, correct, or forget—actually turned them on. Sexually. Would it bother you? Amuse you? Disgust you?

And what if there were a whole community of people who all liked this supposedly undesirable quality about you? Actually meeting them, you might experience culture shock. Imagine, a whole community of people who think that what you've hated about yourself for your entire life is not only desirable, but also pleasurable and even highly erotic. Would you avoid these people? Deprecate their sexual interest as "just a fetish"? Could you marry someone who liked that about you? Would you be afraid that it was all they liked? In the Round World, this characteristic is obesity—perhaps the most hated, feared, and unspeakable of all physical traits. What does this do to relationships for those of us in the Round World? How does it affect our dating? Our sexual and emotional development?

> ### *Think of a part of your body you really like.*
>
> (If there's no such body part, think of a part of your body that you don't dislike.) Under what circumstances would it be acceptable for someone to compliment that part of your body? How could the compliment be phrased to make it palatable? Who could deliver such a compliment so that you wouldn't take offense? (A man, a woman, a lover, a relative, a child...?)
>
> **TRY THIS AT HOME**
>
> ### *Now think of a part of your body that you hate.*
>
> (If there's no such body part, think of a part of your body that you take some pains to cover or hide.) Imagine that the same person says the same thing to compliment this undesirable part of your body. How would you react? What would you think of them? How do the two situations feel different or alike?

Just like the regular world, the Round World revolves around a central axis, a line around which everything turns. The Earth has the north and south poles, the extreme points of that axis. The poles of our axis in the Round World are Shame and Guilt. Now, most of us don't live at such desperate and depressing extremes, any more than most people live at the north and south poles of the Earth. But the spin of the Round World about that axis affects us all, no matter where we live or what our size. If you did the exercise above, you have a glimpse into one half of the Round World.

I should say that most people I know are quite happy to live in the Round World. It's not a bad place. It is, however, a different place. And something becomes possible when you distinguish the context of the world you're living in. For example, I say in my seminars that if you're not getting the sex you want, if you don't have the love in your life that you want, I promise you that it has nothing to do with your body. That shocks a lot of people. People usually respond, "Sure, love can be separate from the body, but how could sex be separate? How could my body have nothing to do with the quality or quantity of sex I'm having?"

We'll talk a lot about that in this book, but for now just consider the case of Superman. Clark Kent and Superman have exactly the same body. They're both equally hunky and good-looking. What's more, they have exactly the same capacity for empathy, gentleness, daring, and selfless-ness—all great qualities in a lover. But I bet Superman is better in bed. Why? Because he's focused on his partner. Superman doesn't worry about being Superman. That's just who he is, and he's okay with that. So he's present and available to be with people fully—not only in the bedroom, but also in life. But Superman as Clark Kent is focused on being Clark Kent. His attention is on himself and holding his act together. That's why he naturally fumbles, doubts himself, and generally goes unnoticed. It's no wonder Lois Lane doesn't take him seriously, even though he's got the body and good looks of Superman!

What you have to gain

In this book, you'll meet people of all different sizes who are completely at peace with their bodies, and other people who are at war. Some want to lose hundreds of pounds; others want to gain hundreds of pounds. You'll see what dating might be like in a 500-pound body, and how dating at that size might bring advantages. You'll see what it's like to be attracted to a kind of beauty that others consider grotesque. You'll get a glimpse of what it's like for some people who are taken over by passions and desires that they'd rather not have. You'll learn what it's like to live in a body that responds viscerally, emotionally, and hormonally to Fat.

No Fat Chicks?

In this book about the Round World, this tiny planet you will visit, you'll notice that most of my examples are about gay men. This is not meant to be exclusionary. In fact, it's not only advantageous for the trip we're going to take, but in certain cases it's even necessary. Of course, there are a lot (really, a lot!) of straight men who love fat women—no doubt far more than the number of men who love fat guys; after all, straights outnumber gays in the world. What's more, I've encountered quite a number of women who prefer fat men or fat women (or both).

Almost all of what I have to say about gay fat/admirer relationships applies equally to straight ones, and trying to cover all eight possible combinations of man/woman, gay/straight, fat/admirer would make for tedious reading. Nevertheless, I've tried to discuss as many possibilities and combinations as needed for an accurate description.

Using examples from my tribe of gay male chubs and chasers rather than the straight majority has two particular advantages:

First, so much of fat/admirer love in the straight world is complicated by gender politics. All too easily, we see women as victims and men as aggressors. We also tend to see thin people as having more power than fat people. So when you set these two stereotypes—male/female and fat/admirer—on top of each other, you can't see either one clearly. It's like trying to judge the color of a car while wearing yellow sunglasses. You can't distinguish between the color of the car and the color of your filter. Of course, relationships are much more complicated. When I lead seminars in front of straight audiences, I often have to remind them that what they're dealing with may not be just a man/woman thing. For example, a straight fat woman in one of my seminars might say, "Most of the men who contact me just want to have sex with a fat girl.

Most women I know want more than that." Although the observation is perfectly valid, I remind people that many gay men have exactly the same complaint. In a dating environment of all men, many men have the same complaints about men that women have. So if the complaint arises in a same-sex environment, it can't be a man/woman thing. What is perceived as gender politics or gender differences is often not that at all. It's something I'll get into later in this book.

Very often when my straight participants look at their relationships, they can't tell whether they're seeing gender issues, or size issues, or just personality quirks. Neither can they discern how much of what they're perceiving is based on their own prejudices about the opposite gender. Presenting examples from a same-sex perspective obviates all this. So why the gay male perspective? Well, as I said, this book is a travelogue, and the gay male perspective is the route I travel in the Round World. It's what I know best. However, based on what I've heard from people on other paths, it seems my observations and psychosocial models apply pretty well to any gender or culture, given a bit of tweaking. (I'll discuss this in the first part of the next section, in fact.) In cases where the straight side may differ markedly, I'll mention that, too.

The second advantage that arises from focusing on gay men is that we can learn how people consider masculinity or femininity independent of their partner's gender. For example, in the absence of women, what is masculine? As we'll see, one answer is that masculinity can take the form of obesity. Fat can be an emblem of power or beauty. In fact, for some people, their attraction to the power or beauty of fat can even supersede their attraction to their partner's gender.

In talking to groups of gays and straights all over the world, I've found remarkably few significant differences in the obstacles that fat people and their admirers face. So even though you may not be a fat gay man, or a man who's attracted to fat gay men, I think you'll find this book just as useful as if the examples were about you. In fact, you might find them even more useful since many people feel confronted and defensive when examples are made of them. But gay or straight, male or female, we're all in this together when Fat is concerned.

Your Body of Evidence

I get asked all the time, "You're so fit. How can you like fat guys?" Or sometimes people actually blurt out, "What! Why!?" as a flummoxed co-worker demanded one day when he found out what I like. It's a fair question, especially since I'm an amateur bodybuilder. I'm a very muscular 220 pounds on a six-foot frame.

I suppose I could just say, "Everyone likes what he likes." I mean, why do you like—or dislike—chocolate? Try explaining that to someone with the opposite point of view. At first it seems sort of pointless. Some-

FIGURE 1: The author at a chub/chaser event in Oklahoma City. Photo by HeftyBear.

one who hates chocolate will never gain more than an intellectual appreciation of why you like it. But ultimately, if you pursue the conversation far enough, I think you'll find that it begins to reveal how you each experience the world differently. You may come to see that attached to chocolate are other tastes, experiences, and even prejudices that you never suspected. In learning about your friend's distaste for chocolate, you may learn something about yourself.

People have all sorts of ideas about fat people—what they eat, what they do or fail to do. It doesn't stop there. The body of a fat person elicits opinions about what kind of person they are, what sort of character they possess, or even how their childhood may have been.

I think it happens to anyone whose body stands out from the norm. It happens to me. I'm very muscular, and people come up to me all the time with their assumptions about what I eat, how often I work out, the reasons I work out, what sort of guys I like, what interests I have—even how intelligent I am. For example, the biggest contradiction for people seems to be how I can take such obvious pains to be fit and muscular and yet be sexually attracted to obese men. Actually, I don't see any contradiction at all. In fact, it took me a long time to figure out why my attraction puzzled people so much. To me, having one sort of body and liking the opposite seemed as normal as short people liking tall people. Sometimes people ask, "If you like fat so much, why aren't you fat?" That never made any sense to me either. To me, it's like asking a heterosexual man why he doesn't want to be a woman since he likes having sex with women so much. Curiously, the FAs (straight fat admirers) whom I've talked to seldom get asked this question. No one wants to know why they don't want to turn themselves into fat women.

Finally, someone was able to articulate the specific source of their confusion: "Well, you have an obvious commitment to health and fitness [and obviously your fat boyfriend has none]." Ah hah...mystery solved.

It had honestly never occurred to me that this concern with health might be the basis for their puzzled questions because it's based on two mistaken assumptions.

First, I do not have a commitment to health and fitness. Really. Okay, sure: I have a healthy fear of dying, just as everyone does. But I don't bang out my body at the gym so I can die later rather than sooner. I don't get my body fat percentage measured. In fact, I don't even do cardio. Many people assume I build muscle to keep people at bay, using my size to intimidate people or to avoid intimacy. Or they project their own insecurities onto my body: "Wow, I wouldn't want to get into a fight with you!" (Why would I want to fight?) A little later in this book, I'll talk about the true commitment that my body expresses—why I spend so much time building muscle and eschewing body fat. But for now, I'll just leave you with the idea that people make assumptions about my body that are not accurate. And of course, this also happens to fat people.

Second, the reverse side of the assumption that muscularity implies a commitment to fitness is that obesity implies no commitment to fitness. In fact, you (or someone you know) may regard this assumption as a fact. The collision of these two false assumptions, and trying to reconcile them, is what seems to bake everyone's noodle. So when folks discover that a guy who looks like me wants to date a guy who looks like that, they make up all sorts of explanations. It's about power, it's about pity, it's about money, it's about self-esteem, it's about objectification, and so on. But no one ever seems to question the underlying assumption that muscle is always good and fat is always bad.

People's sexual attractions and assumptions about the body are part of what we're going to explore in this book. If I'm to be of any use to you as a guide, these will be *your* tastes and assumptions you get to examine. By understanding what my community sees as beautiful and sexual about the world of Fat, I invite you to discover some of your own assumptions and challenge some of your perceptions about people's bodies—maybe even your own.

Writing the *F* Word

You may have noticed that I use the word *fat*. A lot. (More on my reasons later.) I also write the word two different ways, sometimes with a capital *F* and sometimes with a lowercase *f*. For example, "Some women like fat guys." When I talk about fat as a characteristic or as adipose tissue, I use fat in lowercase. But when I talk about deeply held beliefs, stigmas, preferences, and desires, then I'm talking about Fat with a capital F. For example, "People rarely examine their beliefs about Fat." As we'll see, there is a vast difference between fat as a substance or characteristic, and the ethical and political debate that people engage in about Fat. In many cases, my purpose is to point out how we have confused fat with Fat—confused a characteristic with our personal and societal opinions about that characteristic.

I'd also like to clear up the confusing and redundant nomenclature that we use in the Round World to designate ourselves and others. It's redundant because all the terms got invented twice. Later on, I'll talk a bit more about how these terms get applied and why they evolved as they did. For now, however, here's the whole taxonomy as we use these terms today in the Round World. It's not logical or even consistent, but it's what we've got.

PERSON	STRAIGHT MALE	STRAIGHT FEMALE	GAY MALE	GAY FEMALE
Is fat	BHM (big handsome man)	BBW (big beautiful woman)	Chub	BBW (big beautiful woman)
Wants a fat partner	FA (fat admirer)	FFA (female fat admirer)	Chubby Chaser	FFA (female fat admirer)
Wants to get fatter	Male Feedee	Feedee	Gainer	Female Feedee
Wants to help a partner get fatter	Feeder	Female Feeder	Encourager	Female Feeder

FIGURE 2: Terms used by people in the Round World

Inherent in these terms is the power dynamic I spoke of in male/female relationships and why I'm trying to separate that from the fat/admirer dynamic. Notice that for the straight columns, the default assumption is that the woman is fat or getting fatter—roles that are associated with weakness, disadvantage, or even victimhood. However, if the person seeking a fat partner or wishing to fatten her partner is a woman, then the term for her requires modification; the default assumption is that only a male would occupy this position. For example, an FA (fat admirer) is assumed to be male unless modified as FFA (female fat admirer). A person who wishes to subject themselves to being fattened is assumed to be a female (Feedee) unless otherwise modified (Male Feedee).

Lesbians in the Round World usually imply their orientation through context rather than terminology. For example, I once saw a personal ad that read, "BBW seeks slender gal for hot nights and good times." I don't recall ever seeing a term such as "lesbian feeder" or "W4W BBW."

Using all these terms all the time would be maddening. For simplicity's sake, I'm going to use *chaser* (short for *chubby chaser*) to talk about the people who are attracted to fat people, regardless of their gender or orientation. When this is too broad a net to cast, I'll let you know and get more specific.

We're All in This Together

My friend Mary recommended me to a couple of her friends who produce a podcast. The program promotes women feeling good about themselves and empowering them in their lives. Mary has known me for a long time and heard me talk about my work with groups, couples, and individuals. She thought that since so many women have concerns about how they look and what they weigh, I might be a good guest for her friends to have on their show. After Mary raised the idea with them, I followed up with an email explaining who I was and the issues I talk about.

One of the producers called me back. She was quite cordial, but her first question was "Is this some sort of fetish?" That's actually a hard question to answer. Liking fat men is not by definition a fetish. (In sexology, the term *fetish* is quite specific and denotes a type of sexual arousal that involves eroticizing a physical object.) Is what I talk about strange and sexual? Sure. Do I use the term *fetish*? Never. It's incorrect and, worse, pejorative or even pathological. In fact, you'll notice that when someone asks if you have a kink or if you enjoy kinky sex, they have a mischievous grin on their face. The connotation of *kink* is of an exciting sexual act that is weirdly fascinating. However, when people use the word *fetish*, they rarely smile. I find they set their jaw in an attempt at neutrality while they imagine something shameful or ridiculous. This is even true among people who have an unusual sexuality themselves. I get lots of mail saying things like "I don't want to give in to a fetish," or "If only I didn't have this stupid fetish," or "I don't want to risk my health for a fetish." On the other hand, I get other more positive notes that talk about "understanding my kink," "being high on my kink," or the joy of "having sex with someone who shares my kink."

So when the producer asked, "Is this some sort of fetish?" I knew the territory we were heading into.

"Well, I like fat guys," I said, "and I talk about what men see when they look at fat…at fat men and also at fat women. I talk about how it is for us." Somehow, this was interpreted by the producer as "how fat women should act and dress to please men." That took several minutes to clarify and ended with the woman saying that her partner, the other producer, was "overweight" and "had some insecurities about her body." She asked me why I used the word *fat* when it is so offensive to so many people. She told me that the "overweight" producer had a concern that the show not be some sort of Jerry Springer-style shock show where people come on and showcase their fetishes. She assured me that they were certainly not interested in such depravity.

I said, "Wow, I never thought Fat was so horrible that seeing it as attractive would be outside the bounds of good taste. Why don't I just speak with your partner since she seems to be the one who has these concerns?"

There was a long pause. Then she said, "I don't think that would be a good idea."

That's when the penny dropped. Suddenly, I got why we were having such a misunderstanding. The producer I was talking with on the phone was curious enough to check me out. But the other producer, the silent, fat one, saw me as just a monster. Only a monster could love something as monstrous as obesity—and only an exhibitionist monster would want to be interviewed about it publicly.

As you might guess, that was not the first time I've met with this opinion. In fact, interactions such as this one remind me why so many chubby chasers feel ashamed. And why straight men in particular find the label *fat admirer* (FA) or *chubby chaser* insulting and belittling. Many people—in and out of the Round World—react with disgust when they hear these terms. If you have experience with feeling insulted and belittled because of your body, then you have an insight into how it sometimes feels to be a chubby chaser. Imagine smiling at a good-looking man and having him sneer at the sight of you saying, "Sorry, I don't date fat-shits." (Yes, people actually say this.) Well, that's as crushing as telling someone who likes your fat body, "Sorry, I don't date fetishists." (Yes, people actually say this.)

We treat others no better than we treat ourselves. If I think my desire for fat men is unfortunate, then I'll treat every fat man as an unfortunate. If I think my desire for them is sick, then I'll treat their obesity as a disease, avoiding them and seeking my cure by dating normal men. If my desire is a dark secret, then so are my dates. But if I can find a way to be whole with my desires, then I can have a real relationship with a person who is part of the whole of my life.

I'm going to keep returning to different aspects of this principle, that we see others as a reflection of ourselves. It's a principle with many variations and profundities that affect every aspect of our lives. For now, however, let me just say that whatever animosity there may be between us or among us—chubs and chasers, gainers and encouragers, BBWs and FAs—there's not really a big difference. We're all in this together. Fat oppression doesn't hurt only fat people. It hurts all of us in the Round World. Perhaps you see how it hurts humanity as a whole any time that we make people lesser. But yes, it always hurts worse when the injury is inflicted by "one of our own," by someone we thought would be kind, appreciative, or at least understanding. What keeps some chasers in the closet is the same as what keeps some fat people from freely acknowledging that they're fat. What keeps some gainers and encouragers mired in shame and conflict is the same as what keeps some fat people in shame and conflict over their bodies. We're all in this together. We are better off together in community than alone in resentment and shame.

In a greater sense, this book is not just about Fat. This book is about people coming home to their bodies and their desires. It's about granting ourselves and others the freedom to be who we've always been, and the freedom to love what we've always loved.

FAT OUT LOUD

The path to understanding my sexuality has not been quick or straightforward. It's that way with a lot of people like me. For whatever reason, my attraction to fat men never caused me guilt or shame, as it does for many others. I've always been able to talk about it to the extent that I was aware of it. I should say that I was unaware of quite a lot when I started out. As I said earlier, I didn't even know I was gay until I was 20. However, people seem to confide in me easily, and I confide easily in them. I think that greatly enhanced and accelerated my psychosexual development and gave me a desire to help others find their way as well. That's what led to my appearance on MTV's Emmy-winning documentary series *True Life*.

Each episode of *True Life* examines the lives of young people in a particular subculture or circumstance. Each episode follows the lives of two or three young people grappling with the theme of that particular episode. Episodes have titles such as "I'm in an Interfaith Relationship," "I Hate My Plastic Surgery," "I Work in the Sex Industry," or "I Have Another Life on the Web." I appeared in an episode titled "I'm Happy to Be Fat." It followed three unrelated individuals who were fat and happy about their lives and bodies: a woman who was starting a Fat-positive club at her university; a woman who had gained 100 pounds and felt sexy and confident; and Mikey, a beautiful and intelligent man I had always wanted to meet. All 460 pounds of him.

Mikey and I had chatted many times online over several years. (This was in the days before Skype, when chatting meant typing.) However, we had never actually met since I lived in Los Angeles and he lived outside Memphis. One day, Mikey typed in one of our chats that he was going to be on MTV's *True Life* and that the producer of the show really wanted to show him out on a date with a guy, preferably a "hot guy." Mikey wanted to know if I'd be interested in flying out to Memphis to meet him and spending a weekend together on camera.

Now, I have to tell you that I was not Mikey's first choice. I wasn't even his second. I was somewhere down around fifth or sixth. He was taking a considerable risk having a nationally televised date with a relative stranger. The fact that I fit the bill as a "hot guy" didn't play much in my favor. All the guys who date Mikey are hot; he's even dated a model or two. But getting one of those guys to agree to fly to Memphis and appear on camera was what eliminated everyone above me on the list.

Why would I agree to do such a show in the first place? What need or purpose did it fulfill? In the end, it came down to the fact that the benefits outweighed the risks. When Mikey invited me to do the show, I told him I'd have to think about it. I knew something about how reality TV works, and I had heard the horror stories of fat people and their dates who'd been humiliated by such shows over the years. But I also saw that Mikey and I would be the main storytellers, barring any dastardly editing or entrapment. Mikey and I both felt that people like us could make a difference by being in front of the camera, just by people seeing us being normal. However, there was also something more personal at stake. I think a lot of chubs and chasers are secretly resentful that we never show up at the center of love stories. Even if the fat girl does land the hunk, she does so because her other qualities so outshine her supposed handicap—her weight. In our case, Mikey said he wanted to show that you can be really fat and still have an amazing life. I wanted to show that you can love what you love, and the sky won't fall down in disgust and shame.

The episode we filmed was fairly true to life—or at least as true as so-called reality TV can be. We were lucky to have a really great director. Nothing was staged; there were no retakes for the camera. So when you see me meeting Mikey for the first time at the Memphis airport, that really was how it happened. There was, of course, editing, which inevitably shapes events into a story. For example, I spent three days with Mikey and his family, but the time constraints of TV make it look like I parachuted in, had some fun with Mikey, and then was airlifted out. All in all, though, it was a good experience with a good result. Mikey got emails from all over the country from fat people saying how he'd changed what they had thought was possible for them and their lives. Some called him a hero. Of course there was lots of controversy and vitriol on the MTV website about the show, which is inevitable when you juxtapose Fat and sex. The episode was one of the highest-rated in the show's nearly 20-year history and continues to be rebroadcast.

The episode quickly came to the attention of Tyra Banks, who booked us on her talk show. We were subsequently contacted by various European production companies that all wanted to present their version of gay fat love for their audiences. Let's face it: They put us on TV because a muscle hunk smitten by a quarter-ton fat guy makes good television. But we went on TV because showing people how Mikey and I live our lives makes something possible for people that wasn't possible before. Years later, I still get emails from guys who tell me that they never believed that someone like me could find someone like them attractive. I got emails at the time from chasers who said things like, "That was so brave!" Still today, chasers email me to say, "You were the first guy I ever saw who liked what I like." I get other emails from people who say that until they saw that show, they had always assumed that fat/admirer relationships were based on desperation and low self-esteem. They say that today they see those relationships differently.

One of the most poignant emails was from a beautiful, young gay man in Colorado. He was a six-foot-one Adonis fresh out of college with stunning good looks and washboard abs. Moreover, he was out as gay to everyone, and all his friends were young, out, gay Adonises too—the kind of guys you imagine horsing around in an Abercrombie & Fitch ad. Anyway, this hot guy writes to say that he saw me on TV and totally relates because he's been attracted to fat guys his whole life. But no one knows. In fact, he's never even been with a fat guy sexually. Writing to me was probably the first time he'd ever expressed his desires to anyone. He wrote, "I loved that *True Life* episode. But dude, how do you deal with your friends?"

The question, of course, prompts the response, "Dude, who are your friends?" In talking with him, I found out that his friends were very focused on style and appearance. He was sure they would turn on him like jackals if he ever confessed to them that he liked anyone who didn't look like them. Consequently, this guy had never had sex with a fat guy; he'd dated only beautiful guys whom his friends would approve of. So this 24-year-old Adonis had never had sex with someone he found truly attractive. Think about it: This is a guy whom people look at and say, "Geez, he's gorgeous. He can have any guy he wants." The truth is he can have any guy *except* the guy he wants.

Another email was from a young man who lived in the wilds of the Bible Belt. As a fat gay teen in a small Texas town, he said he'd thought his life was over before it had even begun. Even if he had the courage to come out of the closet and suffer the slings and arrows of being known as the town faggot, what for? Who would date him at his size? He despaired of ever having sex, let alone a relationship. He said he had considered suicide. He wrote that after seeing the show, he saw things differently. He said, "Now I know that all I have to do is get out of Texas!" What I think he meant was that all he had to do was hang on until his eighteenth birthday and then find a community that would accept who he was, appreciate his body, and value what he had to offer.

I mention these two guys because the Adonis and the fat teen share something fundamental. They both believed that they could not have the relationship they truly wanted. The two men on opposite ends of the beauty scale both had the same problem: They saw no possibility of happiness because of the limitations of how they looked—one too beautiful to date what he liked, the other too fat to date what he found beautiful. They discovered that it was not their bodies that limited them, but merely the expectations of other people.

Being public with my tastes certainly does have its ups and downs, but the ups far outnumber the downs. I can tell that some people are clearly disgusted or even angry about the fact that I like fat guys. It's as if I've violated some sort of morality by condoning obesity or abetting size criminals. Some folks, however, are more blasé and find my tastes quirky. I'm sort of like a guy who loves to drink vinegar and is not ashamed to order a glass of it in a restaurant: "Weird, but...whatever." What's more surprising, perhaps, is that I get so many positive reactions from passers-by when I walk down the boulevard of my gay neighborhood with an enormous, handsome fat guy on my arm. Some people just break out in grins. Some even stop us and say something like, "You guys look so great together," or "I wish I could find someone like that," or sometimes just, "I love you guys." Why the kudos? Certainly they've seen gay couples before, especially in a gay neighborhood, and even guys walking holding hands is hardly remarkable in these environs. I think it's because, without meaning to, my date and I represent something everyone craves: Hope. We represent hope that you can be open about what you like. We represent hope that there is someone for everyone. We represent hope that maybe love does conquer all.

LABELS & IDENTITY

When I talk about chubby chasers, I'm talking about people who, on some level, prefer a fat partner because they find that characteristic attractive. Not something to look beyond, but something to look for. That's a pretty broad definition, but what we are is not complicated. Though the term originated in the gay community many years ago, it has become quite common in the straight community now as well. However, in the straight world, *admirer* or *FA* (fat admirer) is more often used. It's a label, and it applies to the degree that a person accepts the label and allows it to form part of his or her identity.

Fewer women than men identify as chubby chasers, and the label is seldom applied to women, for a couple of reasons. First, I think women's sexuality is often ignored or rejected, sometimes even by women themselves. So a slim woman who often dates fat men is not likely to be seen as having a sexual attraction to Fat. Her choice of partner is more likely seen as generous, open-minded, or tolerant. Or she may be seen as unconfident, slumming it, self-loathing, or just blind. To be fair, any of these descriptors may be true, but a sexual attraction to Fat seems conspicuously missing as a possible motivation for a woman to date a fat man. On the contrary, men are thought of as driven by our sexuality and as coveting what we desire. So terms like *chubby chaser* stick to us far more readily (and pejoratively) since our sexual desires are supposedly our sole motivation in dating.

Not for a moment do I believe that anything I've just said about male and female sexuality is actually true. Rather, I believe that these perceptions of sexuality are extremely common. Also, I should point out that many people actively dislike having the terms *chubby chaser* or *FA* applied to them, but others of us avidly embrace them.

We could quibble over the political correctness of using words such as *admirer, chaser, fat,* and *chubby.* However, the terms are useful, and no one has come up with anything better. So I'm afraid these are the best we've got at the moment. I'll be introducing some more labels as we go along. Some I've inherited from the community, and others I've made up because they're useful.

Many people are uncomfortable with labels; they find them confining, inhibiting, even divisive. In my seminars, however, I talk a lot about labels and why they can be good things if used consciously. Imagine going to the supermarket and finding all the labels removed. Imagine the chaos this would cause! The contents of every bottle, bag, carton, can or container would be a mystery. You'd never know what you'd bought until you got it home. Perhaps then you would avoid this consternation by moving to the fresh produce section. Here, you could see and smell the food's physical attributes to help you decide what to purchase. Perhaps this could inspire a culinary adventure. Maybe you'd combine food in ways you never thought of before because your preconceived notions of food categories and labels would no longer inhibit your creativity. Maybe you'd invent banana gazpacho or avocado caramel and be quite pleased with the results. On the other hand, there would be no way to ask for what you wanted or to articulate what you like: "These fruits you have here are very nice, but I'm looking for more of a purplish thing with tiny seeds that reminds me of my 13th birthday. Where can I find something like that?"

We use labels to make sense of the world and make sense of ourselves. They're not the Truth with a capital T. They're just useful. But when they're not useful, we should feel free to discard them. Returning to the grocery store example, it's not particularly useful for me in the grocery aisle to label myself as a gay man. My sexual orientation does not help me select better produce or check out more quickly at the cash register. However, if I'm selecting someone to date, or looking for advice on sex, or maybe choosing a news outlet on the internet, then identifying as gay might play a role. Actually, I think in some way it always plays a role because I consider being gay a significant part of who I am. It's just not *all* I am.

This is true of any label: man, woman, straight, gay, black, Chinese, left-handed, and so on. Labels mean both nothing and everything. On the one hand, these labels are insignificant parts of our being that fail utterly to capture the totality of who we are. On the other hand, they identify the undeniable, intrinsic parts of ourselves, and because of that, they filter the way we see the world. For example, when I look at the world, I have a white gay male perspective, and so the world looks a certain way to me. What's more, I'm never going to be able to get rid of that perspective. I can only add to it other perspectives. What really causes problems, however, is when I believe my perspective to be the right perspective.

So I am going to label things. In fact, I'm going to label everything; it's what humans do. But that's okay as long as I remember that the label

I'm using is a human creation—either I inherited it from someone else or maybe I invented it in my own head. In either case, it represents a view of reality, and that's not the same as reality itself. For example, the word *apple* is not the same as an apple. Try eating the word, and you'll see what I mean. The fruit is more satisfying to eat, but it's very difficult to ask for an apple if I can't label it. That's how labels give us access to things—things as mundane as apples or, as you'll soon see, things as lofty as love, sex, pride, joy, and intimacy.

HERESY & OUTRAGE!

In the trip we're going to take together into the Round World, we'll be talking about Fat and sexuality. Two big taboos. I have no doubt that at some point you may find what I have to say outrageous. The word *fat*— even the image of fat—is so taboo and repulsive to most people that it is literally unspeakable in polite company. On top of that, I'm talking about liking—even prizing—Fat, which some might consider irresponsible, sick, dangerous, or even immoral. Some of the people you'll meet on our journey are attracted to—even lust after—a characteristic that is linked with every negative idea people can think of: sloth, illness, greed, disability, victimhood, even death. Each of these traits triggers its own moral questions, such as "How can you love someone who is too fat to do things?" "How can you get turned on because someone is unhealthy?" "Isn't a man who pursues a fat partner just looking to lord his power over a victim?" (These questions may not have occurred to you, but trust me, I get asked them a lot.) So in wrestling with these questions, I may indeed present ideas or models that sound superficial, ill-conceived, or even immoral to you. You may find yourself having strong, visceral reactions to what I have to say, which may seem to go against common sense or even common decency. It may seem I have spoken a heresy.

So before we set out for the Round World, you'll need your shots. Let me inoculate you now so that you have a higher tolerance perhaps for the upsetting nature of this discussion. I hope that when upset occurs, you can spend less time cursing and throwing the book across the room, and more time investigating just what's made you so upset. Hopefully, you'll retrieve the book if only to see just how I could possibly justify writing such a thing.

My goal is that anyone will find value in this book, no matter what his or her point of view on Fat may be. In fact, the next section takes on just that: what you may or may not believe about Fat and about the people who are fat. Because of this, it may at times be necessary for you to tolerate and even enter into other people's points of view on obesity that seem ridiculous, unscientific, or even morally wrong. As a tiny example, I offer that thus far I've already used the word *fat* almost a hundred times. You might like that I have the courage to confront the word honestly. On the other hand, you may disapprove of my using such a rude and insulting term so flippantly. Or perhaps you think my use of the word is acceptable, but it makes you a little queasy; you wonder whether you should recommend this book to a certain friend because he or she may find the word insulting or cruel. The bottom line is that people agree on remarkably little when it comes to Fat. So in order to take you into the world of people who are aroused by Fat, you may find yourself nose-to-nose with ideas that repel you. You may find that facts you consider basic and incontrovertible are not taken as facts by other people.

But a fact is a fact, right? It's not subject to fashion or opinion, right? I mean…it's a fact! Well, a fact is often a matter of agreement at a particular time from a particular perspective. It seems perfectly obvious that the sun rises and sets, and so for thousands of years it was a *fact* that the sun went around the Earth. However, this is not a fact today. Today, the opposite idea is a fact. If I told you that smoking causes cancer, would you believe me? Would you ask me to cite a medical authority to prove it? I think most people would take the statement as fact and require no further proof or evidence. On the other hand, what if I told you that only one in seven smokers will actually get lung cancer? Would you believe me as easily? Would you accept that statistic as fact, or would you require evidence because it seems to question the established fact that smoking causes cancer?

Most of us accept or reject ideas based on the prevailing facts of our society. A good example of this is marijuana. Is it the drug of naïve wastrels and a gateway to increasingly dangerous drugs? It is if you come from a particular point of view. Or is marijuana a harmless recreational herb with medicinal applications? It is if you come from a different point of view. Or is marijuana the most insidious of all drugs, more dangerous and deadly than alcohol or even heroin? It is for a particular Egyptian pharmacist I once met. She assured me that countless medical studies have shown how marijuana ravages the brain far worse than does any other drug.

A WIDER VIEW

So what about Fat? We'll get deeper into the world of science and facts a bit later. For now, however, I'd just like to assert that the subject of Fat is an uncomfortable jostling of perceptions, statistics, experiences, and beliefs. One person's fact is another person's prejudice. Even doctors and scientists disagree quite markedly on the subject.

You might think that there's a fairly orthodox view among educated people about Fat. We take it for granted that there are objective standards to answer certain questions: How fat is too fat? How much adipose tissue is unhealthy? What's the proper way to lose weight? What's a good weight to be for your height? How come there are so many fat people today? How do people get fat in the first place?

Perhaps you think the answers to these questions are fairly settled. I'd like to suggest that people (including scientists) have radically different ideas about the answers to these questions. I'm not talking about the radical views of a few eccentric doctors or unruly fat activists. No. I'm talking about how you and your doctor, you and your sister, or you and your hairstylist all champion very different "facts" about obesity. I'll bet your best friend doesn't even agree on the same "facts" about obesity that you do—even the supposedly obvious facts. There are unseen divisions between folks in answering even a seemingly simple question like, "Why is that guy fat?"

I'm sorry to say I can't give you the definitive answers to any of those questions. That's not why I've asked them. But the answers to those questions point to a belief system about Fat, which turns out to be very important to people like me. You see, I've found that what a person thinks about fat people corresponds to what that person thinks of a person like me, a guy who finds Fat to be generally attractive. If I tell a person who is into health and fitness that I'm attracted to fat guys, he'll usually express concern about how I like something that is fundamentally unhealthy. If I tell my desires to someone who finds fat repulsive, my experience is that she will find me perverse and repulsive too. If the person I tell thinks that fat people are weak-willed gluttons or bottomless pits of emotional need, then I seem to be a scheming predator who seeks to exert my superior will over my poor, pathetic partner. However, if I tell my desires to a person who thinks that fat people are just people who are fat, then I seem like an interesting guy with an odd quirk. So if you want to understand why me and my tribe like Fat, a good place to start is by understanding why the rest of the world does not.

2

You Don't Know Fat

I find beauty in the grotesque, like most artists. I have to force people to look at things.

—Alexander McQueen
British fashion designer,
interviewed in March 2007,
in *Harper's Bazaar*

TOO FAT FOR THE ROOM

Though it's true he was a genius, there was nothing physically remarkable about my friend Glenn when he was a kid. He went to an ordinary public elementary school in Connecticut and looked like everyone else in his class. The only thing that seemed to distinguish him from his nine-year-old peers was an overly articulated interest in arcane subjects such as computer programming, magic, and astronomy. Classes were easy for him, but he wasn't exactly popular and had only a small group of equally nerdy friends. His parents were concerned, however, that Glenn's classes didn't challenge him enough, so they enrolled him in a private school nearby—a school that catered to the local prep school, which in turn catered to the nearby Ivy League schools, setting one up for a good position in life.

On the first day of classes at his new elementary school, Glenn got up, got dressed, and set out for the bus stop. What he did not realize, however, was that during the night he had become fat. It wasn't obvious to him at first; his clothes seemed to fit just as they had the previous day. However, when he got to the bus, his classmates told him in no uncertain terms that he was fat. He had never heard such a thing before. He'd been called a name or two at his old public school, but never "fat." It was a new experience for him, but his classmates seemed resolute, especially when the bus got to school and the agreement on his physical deformity seemed unanimous. He was fat. Perhaps he had been fat all along, but how could no one have noticed? On Tuesday, Glenn was normal. On Wednesday, Glenn was fat. The fact that no one in his nine years of life had commented on his weight before proved to be an ineffective rebuttal to his classmates. The fact that he had been a normal-sized kid only 24 hours earlier made no impression on them whatsoever. They knew what fat was, and Glenn was fat.

Glenn's new classmates knew they were right, just as we all do. *Others* may have a distorted view of what constitutes being fat, but *we* know the truth. We may not agree on esoteric things, but we're sure when it comes to something as obvious as what's too fat. Right? That's what this section is all about. We're going to talk about how reasonable people disagree on seemingly simple and self-evident things. We need to do this because in order for me to talk about why fat *is* attractive to some people, it would be very helpful if we could uncover why fat *isn't* attractive to most. People in general don't even agree on what constitutes being fat, but we seem to know it when we see it. That's all I'm trying to do in this section. I'm not trying to change your mind or evangelize. I just want to look at what it is that you see when you say someone is fat. Not what "society" sees, not what the A-gays see, not the Asians, not that obscure African tribe that fattens their brides before marriage. You.

"But I already know what I think about fat!" you might say. Well, in my experience, people mostly remember incidents and emotions. Sometimes we string these memories into a pattern. For example, perhaps you remember being disgusted or embarrassed or angry in connection with an event involving someone fat. If you're fat yourself, you may have a life filled with such experiences. But that's not the same as distinguishing a point of view, which we'll be getting to later in this section. Even fat people don't agree on perceptions of fat.

When I was first coming out of the closet as a chubby chaser, I would say things like, "I like big guys." (I should mention that among gay men, "What's your type" is not an uncommon opening line.) The statement seemed safe, polite, and accurate. The problem was that no one understood what I meant. I'm a bodybuilder, so when I said, "I like big guys," people usually assumed I meant someone very muscular like me.

"No," I would correct them. "Big."

"Really tall?"

"No. No, I mean big."

"Ohhhhh. Big down there!"

"No, no, no…BIG," and I would gesture with my hands in front of my belly.

"Oh my god! You mean…like…" At this point they would search for the right euphemism, stammering and wondering if they could say it aloud. "Like… [mustering the courage]…heavy?"

Sometimes people would whisper the euphemism as if they might be overheard. I would smile and nod. My lack of embarrassment would sometimes take them off guard.

"Wow." Then they would usually pause to consider their next move.

That awkward conversation took too long, so I just started saying, "I like fat guys." But then I got, "Ohhh. Wow. Really? Like…over 200 pounds?" (In most A-gay lairs, a man over 200 pounds is fat unless he's very muscular or exceptionally tall.) Finally, to short-circuit this conversation, I now say, "I like enormously obese men." Most people still don't know what that means exactly, but at least the shock value of it keeps them from setting me up with their 200-pound friend who permits himself carbs.

Ultimately, being fat occurs in a context. Being fat is a localized event. We saw in the example with Glenn that he got fat when he was recontextualized as fat in his new school. People who move between different cultures are no strangers to being recontextualized. People from Hawaii or the Middle East are frequently contextualized as Hispanic in Los Angeles. Why? Because in Los Angeles, being Hispanic is the dominant context for people who have certain features and skin tones. A friend of mine from Saudi Arabia once got yelled at in Los Angeles because he refused to speak Spanish. The notion that my friend wasn't Hispanic never occurred to the man yelling at him. For that man, all brown people are Hispanic, and all Hispanics should speak Spanish. That's the context of his world. Culture provides a context for our perceptions, so it shouldn't surprise us that it provides a context for our perceptions of people's bodies.

I had a coworker, Christine, who is Korean-American. Her parents were born in Seoul, but the family immigrated to the United States, where Christine was born. In Los Angeles, Christine is perceived as a pretty, young woman of average size, perhaps even strong or athletic. In Korea, however, it's another story. Somehow, when Christine crosses the Pacific back to Seoul, she gains untold amounts of weight and shows up in that city as "a fat American girl."

"I can feel myself getting fatter as the plane starts to descend," she says. A kinder citizen there might deem her an Amazon. Even worse, she says, is that Koreans see her as an example of what befalls unfortunate children who are fated to be raised in America. Christine says she can't buy clothes in Korea. Actually, she explains, clothes come in only one size there: "free size," which is their version of one-size-fits-all. Even if a store does carry clothes approximating her size, they are not cut for her height or proportions. "I'll never look like them," she says flatly. "I'm just too big for over there." Even in Korea, though, Christine is quite pretty, and her cousins there assure her that "if you lose weight, you'll be beautiful." When the visit is over and Christine returns to Los Angeles, the miracle reverses itself. Christine magically loses all the weight on the 15-hour flight, and once again people react to her as the pretty Korean-American girl next door.

At this point, you might find yourself saying, "Well, what does Christine weigh? Let me see her picture, then I'll tell you whether she's really fat." Do you think your judgment in the matter would be objective? The problem is that reasonable people even from the same country don't agree on where to draw the line on Fat.

TRY THIS AT HOME

Find a picture of some stranger off the internet whom you consider "big" but not "fat."

Email the picture to three friends, and ask them separately, "Do you think this person is fat?" See which friends agree with your assessment. See if you can predict the reaction of the people you send the picture to.

If you've traveled to other countries, you know that Americans stand out in all sorts of ways, not the least of which is our height, our muscularity, and yes, often our obesity. At some bodybuilding gyms in the United States, I'm medium-sized. At other gyms in the U.S., I'm the biggest guy on the floor. In Spain, I'm the Incredible Hulk. If I buy clothes from Target, I wear a medium. If I buy a designer brand in Beverly Hills, I wear extra-large. When I go to Italy, XXL is a tight fit.

But surely there is an objective measure of whether someone is fat. It's body mass index (BMI), right? BMI is the ratio of height to weight, so that's got to be objective, right? Well, even if we take BMI as gospel, BMI does not measure our perception or prejudice of fat. Kids don't use BMI to determine whether to hurl insults at the chubby kid on the playground. Glenn's BMI didn't change when he went from public school to private school. He was, however, considered normal one day and fat the next.

BMI also has various categories—various stops along the scale, including Normal (BMI 18.5–24.9), Overweight (BMI 25–29.9), and Obese (+30). Nowhere in the use of BMI is the term *fat* used to characterize a person. That's because *fat* is neither objective nor scientific. Let's face it, it's not even polite.

We'll talk more about BMI later. But for now, I just want to unlink it from our ideas and perceptions about Fat.

Who You Callin' Fat?

My friend Jonathan is six foot two and 375 pounds. He was invited over to a friend's house, and the friend's little daughter asked quite innocently, "How come you're so fat?" The friend sprang to his feet and whisked the child away, admonishing her under his breath. The friend returned from banishing the child and apologized profusely for the embarrassment, saying, "Hey, I'm really sorry about that." Then he added sheepishly, "You're not fat." Jonathan smiled big and said, "C'mon, get real! I'm almost 400 pounds." The friend was shocked and began to argue that it was impossible that Jonathan weighed that much.

Another example: My friend Perry was complaining to a coworker about how the new chair for Perry's office would take weeks to deliver. Perry hoped the old chair would hold up until then. The coworker asked why on earth it would take weeks to get a simple office chair. "I had to special order one," Perry explained. "I'm too fat for the regular chairs."

The coworker jumped on him. "Don't say that! You're not fat!" Perry gave his friend a withering look of disbelief. Perry is five foot ten and 430 pounds.

According to Jonathan and Perry, the people mentioned above clearly meant what they were saying. They were being sincere, not just kind. They don't think of Jonathan and Perry as fat. In fact, if you ask most fat people, they'll tell you that their friends drastically underestimate their true weight. Even if Jonathan and Perry's friends did think they were fat, they would never say such a thing. But Jonathan and Perry are fat by almost anyone's reckoning; it would be absurd to claim otherwise.

Why the denial? This doesn't happen with tall people. Imagine that someone extremely tall hits his head on the top of a doorframe and makes a joke: "You'd think I'd know how tall I am by now." No one would say, "Don't be silly, you're not tall!" Okay, being tall isn't considered a stigma like obesity is, so then what about being short? Women tell me all the time they don't want to date a short guy, so it must be somewhat stigmatized. Perhaps then imagine a short guy who can't reach something on top of the refrigerator. Casually he says to his taller friend, "I'm too short. Can you get that for me?" I don't think there would be a rejoinder of, "You are not short! Don't you call yourself that!" So pretending people aren't fat isn't just about pretending some people are outside the norm or pretending there isn't a stigma.

Of course, some people might think that Jonathan and Perry's situations were embarrassing. Fair enough, but we don't contradict obvious facts when something is embarrassing. If someone spills wine all over a white tablecloth at a dinner party and apologizes for the mess, no one says, "Nonsense, you didn't spill anything." People lie to this absurd degree about Fat because the word *fat* does not mean fat. For most people, *fat* means disgusting. The friends in these two stories don't see Jonathan and Perry as disgusting, so calling them fat seems unjustified to them, even cruel. For many people, saying "You are not fat" is the same as saying "You are not disgusting." In polite society, fat is not a description like tall or yellow or rectangular. It's a judgment like awful or beautiful or lazy.

Fat: Judgment or Feature?

If you tried the experiment above, how many words did you come up with? Notice that the list might have phrases that are positive or negative. For example, maybe you thought of "fat and lazy," but you also thought of "fat and sassy." In any case, I bet you probably didn't have much trouble making up an ample list of catchy phrases. What about the list for "short and…"? Is that list as long as the list for Fat? Maybe you came up with "short and stout," or even "short and scrappy" if you're particularly witty. Short and lazy? Probably not. Short and productive? Hmm…That doesn't really zing. If this intrigues you, try the same exercise with your friends: Tall and _____. Blond and _____. Disabled and _____. See whether or how these differ from fat and _____.

Even though words like *short* or *disabled* are often thought of as negative, these words don't carry the same baggage and associations that *fat* does. That's because all these other words describe the body, but *fat* goes beyond and describes the person; it's a judgment. That's why *fat* fits so well with other judgments like lazy, jolly, or ugly.

In other cultures, *fat* isn't a judgment. My friend Helena spent quite a bit of time in Korea teaching English. Years later, she went back to visit after having gained quite a bit of weight. When her Korean friends came to pick her up at the airport, they said almost immediately, "Wow, you got fat!" Being fat in Korea is definitely not positive, to say the least, but mentioning it is definitely not taboo either. It's negative, but not disgusting. You can tell someone thinks that *fat* is disgusting when they refuse to use the word—when the word is literally unspeakable. You can tell someone thinks *fat* is obscene if they lower their voice or mumble, even when substituting euphemisms for the word.

Fat as a Feature

Now, some folks argue that using the word *fat* is unkind or disparaging. I argue that it isn't the word that people have a problem with at all—it's the very idea of Fat. Think about it: In every case of a negative slur—a racist epithet, a mean descriptor, a gross metaphor—there exists another word that is not only more polite but also more accurate. There is a word that describes the characteristic without the condemnation. For example, *wop* is a pretty insulting term for one of my Italian relatives. However, the more accurate word, *Italian*, is clear and nonjudgmental. Every racist or derogatory word you can apply to someone—kike, nigger, faggot, chink—has a clearer, more accurate, and nonjudgmental form: Jew, black, gay, Chinese. (In case you're wondering why I didn't say African-American, not all blacks are American.) But this is not the case with *fat*. All of our supposedly more polite terms for fat point away from the characteristic we're trying to describe, almost to the point of absurdity. That's why vaguer terms like *heavy, big,* and *large* seem more acceptable. It is not the word we find offensive; it is actually the characteristic itself. These euphemisms are vague enough to include the idea of fat without actually forcing the listener to picture that grotesque trait.

Consider also that if it were just the word *fat* itself that caused a problem, then surely no one would object to using the medical term *obese* to describe a friend. I mean, if *fat* were crude and insulting, then *obese* should be the accurate and polite word to use: "You know, Julie? The obese gal in Accounting?" But somehow *obese* seems even worse, doesn't it. Why? Because *obese* connotes someone even fatter than *fat*: "He's not just fat, he's obese!" So I don't think people find the word *fat* insulting. I think people find the idea of being fat so disgusting that we've actually banned the word, or even any synonym (*obese, portly, rotund, corpulent*), from polite conversation. So in the end, the only polite way to say that someone is fat is not to say it. The image is just too terrible to imagine.

Ask three or four friends...

TRY THIS AT HOME

"Do you think you are the right weight?"
(Don't explain or change the question to make them more comfortable.)

Now ask another set of friends, "Do you think you have the right level of intelligence?" Notice the similarities and differences between the answers of the two groups.

Getting Over *Overweight*

Now, there is a word for fat that I find highly degrading and judgmental: *overweight*. The term brandishes its condemnation right from its prefix. You might think, "But fat people *are* overweight!" Really? Over what weight? They certainly can't be over the weight they are. Are they over the weight you think they should be? Over their doctor's prescribed weight? Well, what weight is that? As we saw previously, people have all sorts of different ideas of what's too fat. What about BMI? I'm afraid that's not much help either. For example, no person or even medical professional tells me that I need to lose weight or get leaner. However, I am 50 pounds over my medically ideal weight, and my BMI officially classifies me as obese. That's true of all bodybuilders my size.

Not only does bodyweight not consider body composition, but it is also completely inadequate to measure health. If it were, then there would be no need for physical exams; we would simply all get weighed to determine our health, and the doctors would cure diseases by lowering a person's body weight. So clearly *overweight* has no use as a medical term despite its widespread use in that field.

Overweight is a judgment, not a statistic. After all, I am technically very overweight, but the term is never applied to me. By contrast, the term is always applied to fat people, no matter what they weigh.

I think the reason we're so comfortable with *overweight* is that, again, it doesn't refer to the person's fat. It avoids calling to mind any image of rolls, folds, blubber, or jiggling. Fat, the very idea of it, tends to upset people. By contrast, *overweight* refers to normalcy, which is far more comfortable and allows us to justify our prejudice: "I'm not calling him fat. That would be insulting. I'm simply saying that he should weigh less." To me, *overweight* is something far more judgmental and derogatory than saying someone is fat. *Fat* is an accurate description that may make us uncomfortable. However, *overweight* is a condemnation masquerading as objectivity, thereby absolving us of guilt.

Personally, I try to use the word *fat* as often and in as many contexts as possible. I think using it takes the stink out of the word and airs it out. What's more, when I use *fat* to describe whom I'm attracted to, then words and worlds collide. When I say, "I met this really hot fat guy at a party last night," I can see my listener's face freeze as he tries to put *fat* and *hot* together in a meaningful way. The result is amusement sometimes, sometimes confusion or even anger. Funny how other supposedly negative characteristics, such as *short* or *disabled*, are seldom so provocative.

TRY THIS AT HOME

Insert the words below into the sentence.

Then rate how acceptable or unacceptable it would be to say to a friend. Say each out loud (it makes a difference):

"I met this really hot _____ guy/girl last night."

short	Asian	Christian	fat
black	disabled	Mexican	lawyer
stupid	rich	tall	drunk

FAT FUNDAMENTALISM

Sooner or later when I talk about my attraction to fat guys, when the listener truly fathoms that I like guys who would be considered fat by almost anyone's standard of that word, people ask me the big question: "How can you be attracted to something that is fundamentally unhealthy?" It's a valid question. More than valid, it's a question that is deeply personal to us in the Round World—sometimes more personal than we care to admit. Chasers in particular are torn between our desire for Fat and our concern for our partner's health.

In looking at this conflict, we need to examine some of the underlying beliefs about obesity, health, and medicine. Whatever you believe is true about Fat determines what you think of me and my kind. I've been called everything from a hero to a pervert to a predator. Once someone knows that I'm attracted to obese men, I show up inside the context of whatever that person thinks about Fat. And some people have some extremely strong and inflexible ideas about Fat. We're going to look at those ideas in this section.

Let's start by noticing that the question that I posed above is actually a moral one. "How can you be attracted to something that is fundamentally unhealthy?" is a more polite version of the underlying question, "How can you love someone and want to see them die?" This might seem an overdramatic paraphrase, but I assure you that when I have this discussion with some folks, this point can become their central objection. Of course, it's pointless to object to someone's sexuality; that's like objecting to the rain. Nevertheless, many people do, and more often than you might imagine. I call this section "Fat Fundamentalism" because we're dealing with certain ideas assumed to be facts—facts that other people call beliefs or even prejudices.

In using the term *fundamentalist*, I'm not taking aim at Christianity or any other religion. I think you can be a fundamentalist atheist or a fundamentalist capitalist. Anyone from any belief system can be a fundamentalist: someone who believes in a strict and invariable interpretation of basic principles or fundamentals. You might think in reading what follows that I'm trying to sway you to my point of view. However, my purpose here is not to convince you of anything, but simply to point out that what is factual or common sense to some folks is not so for everyone.

Most people are familiar with the fundamentalist argument against homosexuality. It goes like this: "It doesn't matter what *I* think about homosexuality. Homosexuality is a sin, and all the gay pride in the world can't save you from hell. So *I'm* not condemning you to hell. That's just how it is." Now, let's say I try to dissuade the fundamentalist, or even just try to raise a doubt that his interpretation is the only possible one. Even if I cite scripture as the basis for a counterargument, the scripture I point to will not be considered legitimate by the fundamentalist, who will find my evidence irrelevant or misconstrued. For the fundamentalist, the evidence points to one and only one conclusion, and he knows what that one conclusion is. Even though we may be looking at the same set of evidence, any alternate interpretation will be seen as impossible by the fundamentalist. In fact, in my experience of such discussions, the fundamentalist will not only dismiss my argument as meritless, but dismiss me personally as being delusional or self-serving: "Of course you don't think gay people all go to hell. You're not objective because you're gay." No matter what facts I present to the fundamentalist, his ultimate counterargument is my identity.

Those of us who are fat or attracted to fat people hear a similar fundamentalist cant: "It doesn't matter what *I* think of Fat. Obesity is unhealthy, and all the self-esteem in the world can't save fat people from living shorter, unhealthier lives. That's not my opinion, that's just how it is." So for the Fat fundamentalist, it doesn't matter what else might be true about an obese person: Fat = Death. You can test this by offering contradictory studies. No study will be credited if it goes against that fundamentalist position. The parallel between fat and homosexuality, science and religion, might seem improper to some. However, I want to talk about the reasoning and the ethics of condemning the obese and, by extension, people who are attracted to them. In many ways, the scientific and moral arguments used to condemn the obese parallel those used to condemn gay people.

People argue over whether being gay is a choice, whether it is caused by environment or genetics. And even if it is caused by genetics, can't it be suppressed or combated? Similarly, society asks whether being fat is a choice, a predisposition, an addiction, or perhaps a lifestyle. Is it caused by the environment or a person's genetics? And if it is caused by genetics, don't some people seem able to suppress or combat it through diet and exercise?

Facts & Morals

Once upon a time in America, homosexuality was a mental disorder. It was a diagnosis for a serious and stigmatized illness. Medical professionals treated homosexuality with everything from snapping a rubber band on one's wrist to electroshock therapy. Popularly, gay people were perverts and social deviants. But even seen through the supposedly objective eyes of doctors and scientists, homosexuals had an illness that would unquestionably lessen the quality of every area of their lives and could in many cases lead to sexual diseases, depression, or even suicide.

So you can imagine the surprise and controversy in 1973 when the American Psychiatric Association (APA) de-listed homosexuality in the *Diagnostic and Statistical Manual of Mental Disorders* (DSM II), the bible of psychiatric pathology. In that year, homosexuality ceased to be a mental disorder. In 1972, we were sick; in 1973, we were well…almost. The backlash from some psychiatrists in the APA was fierce, and they insisted that the entire membership of the association vote on the issue. (Vote? You get to vote in science?)

The following year, the members voted to uphold the decision to remove the diagnosis of homosexuality from the DSM…almost. Controversy still raged, so another diagnosis was created in 1980: ego-dystonic homosexuality. Finally, in 1986 that was removed.

Now, the DSM is not just a big book; it is the medical authority when it comes to the diagnosis of what is and isn't a mental disorder. It's used as a reference for everything from setting social policy to paying medical insurance claims. So when a bunch of guys in a room vote to list or de-list an item in their bible, so to speak, it doesn't matter whether you agree with them. The decision simply becomes the science of the day. It becomes the way things are.

Perhaps you think that psychology isn't a so-called *hard science* such as physics or chemistry, so claims in psychology are more open to interpretation and prejudice. Well, the same sort of controversy is raging now in the medical field about whether to classify obesity as a disease. This is more than a question of semantics. In science, homosexuality went from being an abomination to a sickness to a diagnosis to an aberration to a variation. Popularly, homosexuality can still be any of these, depending on whom you talk to. The same could be said for obesity. Medical science doesn't know exactly what causes it, how to effectively treat it, or how to classify it. (That may be shocking, but we'll get into details in a moment.)

My point here is that science, and medicine in particular, is not immune to the same moralizing and prejudice found in any other area of society. Some might argue that what happened with the APA was not science; it was politics. Well, if you're gay, and it's 1970, and your family is sending you to electroshock therapy to correct your sexuality, that distinction is not really relevant. Similarly, if you're fat, and your doctor says your only choices are death or a surgery to cripple your digestive system, the line between practice and politics is meaningless.

Science is a noble discipline, but it enters the world through human beings. And if certain human beings say some-

> **B**efore man could act in his capacity as a physicist, he had first to be a social being; there can be no science without a social background.
>
> ...Every social problem is unconsciously approached from this standpoint. It is the origin of analysis. It is this outlook that in its time is applied towards the resolution of the scientific problems that are encountered in the effort to carry forward the work of that society.
>
> —**Christopher Caudwell,** *The Crisis in Physics*

thing is the truth, then it's the truth. Of course, Science never claims to know "The Truth," but that's how physicians and policy makers often interpret scientific conclusions. And when there are a variety of conflicting conclusions, perhaps it's only natural to adopt the ones that agree with our own prejudices. We do this all the time with news and politics. We collect information that supports our view of the world, and we pay less attention to the information that doesn't. In fact, perhaps that's how we judge information to be accurate. We often mistake what is accurate for what agrees with our beliefs and experience.

Using Science to Prove Sin

In my previous example about homosexuality, scientists shared a tacit assumption that homosexuality was bad. In fact, homosexuals who sought treatment were the first to admit that their desires interfered with their lives, disrupted or destroyed their most intimate relationships, and created such inner turmoil that many considered suicide a preferable alternative to living with such a horrible condition. (This parallels what many fat people think about being fat.) So the scientific evidence that homosexuality was a disease seemed not only overwhelming, but also completely obvious. The intractable nature of homosexual behavior, and its persistence despite a person's pleas to God and physicians to be cured, seemed to indicate that homosexuality was itself the problem—a disease in need of cure. And yet today in the West, no credible physician would ever diagnose a patient with homosexuality. In fact, they couldn't—because the diagnosis no longer exists. What changed? A definition.

As with homosexuality in the last century, obesity is sometimes considered a disease. We hear all the time that obesity is an epidemic, so it must be a disease, right? Moreover, it's a disease that seems to have a very simple and scientific explanation: Fat people are fat because they eat too much and exercise too little. It's basic physics—calories in and calories out. I can analogize all I want, but surely there's no way to get around the first law of thermodynamics! All that body fat has to come from somewhere, right?

Contrary to what many people seem to think, the first law of thermodynamics does not prove that fat people are greedy overeaters. In fact, it really doesn't give us any insight into obesity at all. All it says is that you can't get energy from nowhere, and you can't make it disappear. All energy, in this case calories, has to be accounted for in a given system like the human body. This means that if you eat energy in the form of food (calories), that energy has to go somewhere. Most energy is used just to keep the body functioning. The rest is used for exercise or stored as fat. Conversely, you can't get fat from eating nothing. The energy stored as body fat has to come from somewhere, and the only energy source outside the body is food. So if you're fat, that fat came from food you ate.

That's the physics, and nothing I've said about calories is in dispute by anyone. However, nothing I've said explains how or why some people are fat. Not even hints at it.

New York Times science writer Gary Taubes in his book *Why We Get Fat*, gives a brilliant explanation of why the idea of calories-in/calories-out is factual but ultimately empty in providing any answers about obesity. Taubes makes the following analogy: Imagine that the calories going into our body as food or being expended in exercise are like guests entering and leaving a party. All night long, guests arrive and enjoy themselves while other guests leave and say their goodbyes. Now, imagine that at one point during the party, the room becomes full of people. The party becomes quite loud, the temperature rises from all the body heat, and the guests can barely move because the room is so terribly crowded.

You turn to your friend and ask, "Wow, what happened? It's so hot in here, and I can barely hear you. Why is the party suddenly so crowded?"

"Well, it's really quite simple," your friend replies. "More guests are entering the party than are leaving the party."

"I know that," you say. "But why?"

Your friend seems confused. "I just told you: More people are entering than are leaving. The first law of thermodynamics tells us that the body heat of all these people can't just disappear. It heats the air and makes us feel hot."

"But why?" you press. "Why are all these people in here!?"

"I told you!" your friend says in exasperation. "It's because they're not leaving as fast as they're arriving."

Of course your friend is right. But it doesn't explain why the party is crowded in the first place. It doesn't explain *why* people are staying and *why* people are not leaving. Your friend's explanation is true because it's a truism. That's why it's not terribly useful.

In the same way, calories-in/calories-out gives no explanation for why a person eats a particular number of calories, or how those calories get used by one person or another. Some people use calories for extra body heat, but others store them as fat. Some feel energized after a meal, while others feel lethargic after eating the same meal. The explanation for any or all of that is still up for grabs.

TRY THIS AT HOME

Make a list of what you consider the facts about how or why people get fat.

Show your list to three friends and ask them whether they agree.

Now form three statements that are the opposite of what you wrote and Google them. For example, if you wrote, "Fat people eat too much," then Google "Fat people do not eat too much." Note the results.

But surely there are facts about obesity, aren't there? Yes, but as we just saw, these facts don't provide explanations. Furthermore, we don't even agree on the explanations we do have, and yet we live as if the way to get lean were perfectly obvious.

If you're like most people, you know perfectly well what causes people to gain fat and how to lose it. Whether you think of it as common knowledge or a closely guarded secret, you know how to lose weight. Even people who have failed at every diet they've ever tried will tell you that even though they haven't been successful at it, they know how to lose weight. Yes, everyone knows how to lose weight. However, not everyone agrees on what that way is. In fact, not even the doctors and scientists agree.

So we don't agree on *who* is fat. We don't agree on *why* they're fat. And we don't agree on *what to do* about being fat. In light of all that uncertainty, it seems a bit premature to proclaim from the pulpits with zealous fervor that Fat = Death. It seems more like a prejudice than a prognosis to judge the quality of someone's life by their body shape.

Beyond Fundamentalism

A detailed look at the scientific controversy surrounding obesity is beyond the scope of this book, but I'll briefly mention three authorities you might consult if you're looking for something beyond the Fat = Death dogma.

First is Dr. Linda Bacon, who holds advanced degrees in physiology, exercise science, and psychology. Bacon has been at the center of controversy for exposing what she describes as three principal myths about obesity. Her research shows that (1) on average, so-called overweight people outlive people of normal weight, (2) biological factors dictate that people will regain all or some of their fat loss over time, and (3) no study has ever proven that people who lose weight live longer as a result. In her book *Health at Every Size*, Bacon advocates healthy eating and exercise as opposed to working toward a target weight goal. Her book has been widely adopted by health professionals and size activists under the umbrella term HAES, a health-care practice intended to help people achieve a better quality of life regardless of their size or health circumstance.

Peter Attia, MD, is another health professional trying to change the way we think about obesity. Dr. Attia started his medical career as a surgeon and went on to research cancer and immunological diseases. However, his current research efforts focus on questioning our assumptions about obesity and the underlying causes of obesity-related illnesses. In a popular TED Talk video, a fit and muscular Dr. Attia tells how he used to disdain the obese as irresponsible patients who wasted the time and resources of an over-taxed health-care system. That was until Dr. Attia became obese himself and found that the diet and exercise that he had always followed and prescribed to his obese patients didn't seem to work any better on him than it did on them. It was then that he started questioning the established medical paradigm that obesity causes insulin resistance and subsequently ill health. He now posits an opposite view: that obesity is the body's natural response to insulin resistance—natural in the way that a bruise is the body's natural response to banging your shin on a coffee table. He asserts that we shouldn't treat obesity to cure health problems any more than we should treat a bruise to heal a shin fracture. He supports his hypothesis with a surprising statistic:

There is a group of people who seem to be in good health. They are not insulin-resistant and seem to have no greater risk of ill health than anyone else. There is another group of people, however, who have all the signs of increased health risk and they all have insulin resistance. Okay, so there's a healthy group and an unhealthy group. The surprise is this: The first group—the group with no increased health risk—are all obese. And in this country, that group of healthy obese people numbers 30 million. The second group—the at-risk group—are lean, and all 6 million of them live in the same country as the other group. Though Dr. Attia concedes that obesity may not be benign, he theorizes that obesity itself is not the problem we think it is.

The last of these three authorities is *New York Times* science writer Gary Taubes, who has researched the science of diet and weight loss extensively. After graduating with degrees in physics from Harvard and aerospace engineering from Stanford, Taubes turned to journalism to reveal scientific controversies and misinformation. In recent years he has focused almost exclusively on the source of the biggest scientific controversy that affects the most people: obesity and weight loss. His book *Why We Get Fat* is a detailed and readable investigation into the scientific approaches that have been applied to curbing obesity and where the current state of research stands. Among other things, the book tells how nutritional science keeps rediscovering and forgetting explanations for weight gain and weight loss.

So am I arguing that prejudice is the only link between obesity and health? After all, we've seen in the last 50 years that prejudice was the only link between homosexuality and illness. No, I'm saying that obesity doesn't cause a particular illness any more than homosexuality causes AIDS. Many things contribute to health and many things contribute to obesity. But which things? Science does not yet have the full picture. We only have theories, or maybe only ideas. Let's look at how these work.

On the Bus to Fat Camp

No matter how we relate to Fat—as a stigma, a context, a taboo, or even a source of empowerment—we're still left with the question of why some people are fat and others are not. The question may seem to have an obvious and objective answer. However, just like everything else in the Round World, "obvious" and "objective" are hard to come by.

You might think that fat people are just fat by nature. Maybe some people are naturally thin, and others are naturally fat. But then what are we to think about the people who have lost hundreds of pounds of fat? Or the people who get fat later in life or after childbirth? Maybe exercise holds the key. We see news stories and YouTube videos of people who've dieted and exercised their way to slender beauty. Something seems to be working for these people. Of course, we also know fat people who exercise vigorously almost daily and don't seem to be any thinner—think of power lifters, sumo wrestlers, or NFL linebackers. And then, many fat people seem so unhappy about their bodies. Surely self-esteem or even clinical depression might play a role in their obesity, right? But what about the fat people whose outlook on life seems quite positive despite the stigma of their body size? Do we simply dismiss all of those people as being in denial? Our popular diagnoses and conclusions all seem contradictory and confusing.

Rather than answers and explanations about Fat, we have camps, or factions, with distinct points of view. If you have an opinion about why people get fat, then you're already in one of these camps. Any time a fat person starts a regimen to get leaner, he gets on a bus to one of these camps. All fat camps guarantee their results, and all have ex-fat former campers to attest to these results. This is nothing new in science. When experimental data don't point to a single conclusion, it's common for camps or factions to spring up in support of one point of view or another. You might think that how to eat healthfully or lose weight is settled science, but if that were the case, there wouldn't be hundreds of ways to go about losing weight, all claiming success.

Michael Pollan, a journalist and well-known author on diet and food, writes that our knowledge of food and nutrition is in its infancy. He's often quoted as saying that the science of nutrition today is about where surgery was in the late 17th century. It's no wonder we have so many ideas about Fat. And even when the science is settled, some people still won't give up their traditional ideas. Consider that even a hundred years after germ theory, some people still blame their sniffles on changes in the weather or walking home without a jacket, even though we now know that viruses cause colds. We don't have much of a handle on Fat. As we've seen, we don't even agree on who is fat. So the explanation of *why* people are fat is a morass of facts, opinions, and theories, which are further muddied by prejudices and morality. Never fear, however, because there are three fat camps to help anyone who seeks answers to obesity:

Camp Willpower

As soon as you arrive at Camp Willpower, you're greeted with the assurance that fat loss is all about self-discipline and resisting temptation. That's great news, because these are things within our control. The campers have little doubt about how obesity works: At Camp Willpower, they place the onus of obesity squarely on the shoulders of the obese. If the obese had more self-control, they say, they wouldn't eat so much and be so fat. The folks at Camp Willpower have seen over and over again that successful weight loss can be achieved by staying away from treats, sensing when you're full, and regarding "Drive-Thru" as a convenience, not a commandment. Because they see that getting fat is so easily avoidable, the folks at Camp Willpower often look on extreme obesity with utter incomprehension. They assume that a person weighing over a quarter of a ton must somehow lack the basic common sense—or even self-preservation—to just quit eating when he's had enough. The fat campers who come for cure, say things like "I have a terrible sweet tooth" or "Cheesecake is my downfall." In this camp, chronic obesity is a chronic failure of will, and Fat is a character flaw.

Camp Metaphor

Right down the road from Camp Willpower is Camp Metaphor. Here the campers have psychological explanations of why they and others are obese. They see eating as filling an emotional void or needing to erect a barrier of blubber. "Food is love," many of the campers say. "Fat keeps the world at bay" is also a common explanation, as is "He eats his emotions." These common metaphors offer an explanation of fat people that is elegantly symmetrical, making it all the more appealing: Camp counselors point out that obesity often results from an inner lack that manifests as an outward excess. Events and feelings from the fat person's life are fitted into the metaphor to prove its validity. The metaphors can be more complex than those I've cited; in turn, they have a correspondingly complex narrative drawn from the fat person's biography. Introspection is usually the route to discovering the function that obesity serves in the fat person's psyche. Whether the function is simple or complex, this camp always posits a psychological construct as the primary force behind a person's eating and subsequent obesity.

Camp Biology

There's only one other fat camp, and it's probably the largest and most diverse: Camp Biology. The campers here see the phenomenon of obesity as a complex system of hormones, enzymes, vitamins, minerals—or the lack or excess of any of these. The camp cafeteria is incredibly flexible, since approaches to fat loss here often advocate such a wide variety of eating styles: consuming or eschewing certain foods or certain preparations of food, or certain macronutrients (carbohydrates, fats, or proteins), or mandating their consumption at particular times. For example, some people at Camp Biology say that fat people are depressed and listless because carbohydrates trigger a cascade of complex hormones that makes them depressed and listless. Others say that perhaps certain genes or biological predispositions make it harder for them to lose weight. At night around the campfire, the folks at Camp Biology trade stories about leptin-resistance, ghrelin production, reactive hypoglycemia, body-mass set point, insulin sensitivity, cytokine activity, and metabolic syndrome. Some stories have more science behind them than others, but all are quite exciting and keep campers up till the early hours.

I don't mean to belittle any of these camps. After all, I've been a camper at each of them at one time or another in my life. Besides, as I've said, all three camps have their success stories and famous camp alums. Nevertheless, all the basic explanations of obesity have to do with the will, the mind, or the body. Even a successful weight-loss surgery can be explained according to views from each of these camps. After surgery, patients report things like "I don't get those cravings anymore" (Camp Willpower), or "I don't have that empty feeling like I need to get full" (Camp Metaphor), or "The cells that produce ghrelin are at the bottom of the stomach which my body no longer has access to" (Camp Biology). So no matter how fat loss happens, each of the camps can somehow take credit for it by managing the will, revealing the subconscious, or outsmarting the body.

It's even possible to be a member of all three camps at the same time. For example, my friend Diane says she needs to lose about 20 pounds, so she's staying away from dessert and pasta at dinner tonight. (She's on the bus to Camp Willpower.) At dinner, she tells me about what's going on at work and about the problems she's having with her boss. He's over 300 pounds, and Diane says it's no wonder: he's difficult to communicate with and stuffs down his emotions just like he stuffs down his lunch. (So she's recommending a trip to Camp Metaphor?) I chide her, and she laughs. She knows that idea might be too simplistic. After all, she confesses, her sister Ruth is close to 200 pounds and has been chubby since she was a baby. "She's just a big girl, I guess." That's a possibility only at Camp Biology, where being fat is not a sign of a weak will or a psychological issue. At Camp Biology, it's sometimes okay to be fat, but sometimes it's not. It depends on your counselor.

So when one solution fails—willpower, self-awareness, or biology/nutrition—we seek another. When that new solution fails, we try yet another solution, undeterred: another diet, another treatment, another guru, until the treatment works. Together, these three camps expound a lot of advice on how to help the obese. It is curious, however, that obesity seems to be a medical condition for which the patient is always to blame for the treatment's failure—no matter how often the treatment fails or how bad the outcome after treatment. When the treatment fails, it's because there was not enough willpower, or not enough introspection, or not enough control over the biological cause. If the patient takes a turn for the worse after treatment, it's never the fault of the treatment. Blame usually falls on the fat person—once again—for not having sought help sooner, or for just being fat in the first place.

For every person who believes obesity is a question of willpower, there seem to be two other people who believe something else. All three believe their argument is based on rationality and common sense borne out by scientific studies—different studies, no doubt, but scientific studies nonetheless. We keep asking, "Why are people fat and how can they lose weight?" Personally, I think the breakthrough will be found by asking a different question. But for now, I just want to open the door to the idea that whatever you think is the cause or cure of obesity, two other vast camps of people disagree with you—and with each other.

Blinded by Science

We'd like to trust in science to settle questions such as "Why am I sick?" or "How do I get well?" But most of us don't believe health advice just because it's labeled "scientific." We read in a magazine about the latest miracle food—oat bran, broccoli, algae, or fish oils. We have friends or family who swear by it, and they trot out scientific studies that do seem to imply the claimed benefits. Of course, there is no study out there that says broccoli prevents cancer, but many studies suggest that it could help and hope can carry us the rest of the way. So we try to eat more broccoli. Besides, it couldn't hurt, right?

Many of us are quite committed to our views on diet, health, and nutrition. We seem willing to take a stand on what's healthful, even if we can't quote a study to support our opinion. When a friend cites a study that contradicts our view, we're quick to question that study, if not dismiss it outright. For example, where do you stand on the question of eating meat? Healthful or not? What about being vegan? Fruitarian? Do you believe in so-called good carbs and bad carbs? What about good fat and bad fat? Anyone who has paid attention to health news over the years has seen good foods and bad foods come and go—and even change sides. Every one of these diet fads had evidence behind it.

Some are more scientific than others, to be sure, but most of us do not examine primary studies (much less source data) to determine which health claims to believe. Whether we embrace the fad or flout it, most of us do so based on faith, hope, cynicism, or so-called common sense.

In other areas of health, however, the scientific evidence seems more coherent and therefore more compelling. For example, the evidence that points to cigarettes as a cause of cancer is well accepted. In modern societies all over the world, it's simply a fact that cigarettes cause cancer, and to say that you believe otherwise would be heresy. For most people the world is round, cigarettes cause cancer, and fat people eat too much. We tend to see all of these statements as facts and take it for granted that science has worked out the reasons why. Few of us actually delve into specific biological mechanisms or the evidence by which these statements have been proven, and even less do we question the chain of logic that led to them.

Now, don't worry. I'm not arguing for a flat Earth, healthful cigarettes, or anorexic fat people. Nevertheless, there are parts of the Earth that are extremely flat. There are people who smoke for decades without succumbing to cancer. And there are fat people who are hungry and malnourished. So even when science gets it right, we often oversimplify its conclusions to the extent that they become little more than dogma in our everyday lives. When observation or experience contradicts that dogma, we seldom go back to the original science. We are actually more likely to disbelieve our experience than our dogma. Either we say, "That did not happen; it does not really exist," or we concede that it did happen, but dismiss it as a fluke. A fluke doesn't fit our beliefs about the world, but it seems too insignificant to cause us to revise those beliefs.

So in the same way that religious fundamentalists have a simplified and dogmatic view of certain religious texts, fat fundamentalists have a simplified and dogmatic view of the scientific studies behind obesity. Also, in the same way that religious fundamentalists often read texts to fit their own view, fat fundamentalists often select particular studies—or design the studies—based on assumptions about obesity that may not be accurate. To the fundamentalist, context, circumstance, or the person counts for nothing. Their point of view is ideological, categorical, or statistical.

Another pitfall is that sometimes we shift the scope of the evidence to an area of our lives that has nothing to do with the original study or model. A good example is body mass index (BMI). Adolphe Quetelet originally developed BMI in 1832 as a way to compare the population of one country or culture with another's by measuring the weight and stature of their citizens. BMI was never used in connection with obesity until the 1970s, and its widespread use as an *individual* metric of health happened only in recent years. The problem is that BMI doesn't even measure obesity, much less health. There are tens of thousands of people all over the world whose BMI classifies them as overweight, obese, or morbidly obese even though they have less than 15% body fat. As I pointed out earlier, I'm one of these people, and so are many other bodybuilders. In fact, professional and amateur bodybuilders sometimes face discrimination in getting health insurance because their BMI ranks them as morbidly obese.

Scientific Prejudice

I often ask participants in my seminars, "Is it possible to be fat and healthy? Is every obese person condemned to die before his time?" Answers vary, but my point is to get folks thinking about what they believe. When fat fundamentalism masquerades as science, there are only two possible answers to that question. The first answer is that there are no healthy fat people because obesity itself is unhealthy. This is a fundamentalist tautology: obese people cannot be healthy because obesity is not healthy. The argument is unassailable because it is circular.

The other possible answer often given by fat fundamentalists is that a fat person who seems to be healthy by all other standards is only temporarily healthy. I call this the "wages of sin" argument. Just as God will sooner or later punish the guilty, nature will eventually punish the obese. In contradiction of this view, recall Dr. Attia's statistic: Thirty million obese people in America have none of the metabolic conditions associated with obesity. What are we to do with these 30 million people? If we are dedicated to the dogma that Fat = Death, we have only two choices: We can discard the statistic as irrelevant because obesity is by definition unhealthy and requires no other statistical marker of morbidity. Or we can admit these 30 million fat people into the ranks of the healthy, but only on a temporary basis because dogma requires that they must eventually sicken and die as a result of their unrepentant obesity.

Let's put this in practical terms: My friend Roland is six foot two and almost 500 pounds. It may shock you to learn that he has normal blood pressure, normal cholesterol, and normal glucose and insulin levels. In fact, his doctor had the tests done twice because fat fundamentalism excludes the possibility that obese patients can have normal test results. Roland said the doctor seemed almost irritated with him in that regard. He's had these unrelentingly normal readings his whole life, in fact, much to the suspicion of his physicians. His body is stubbornly unconvinced that it should be breaking down.

His latest doctor, however, has responded to Roland's normality by prescribing pills for high blood pressure and water retention, and scheduling an appointment to have an urgent conversation about surgically removing part of his stomach. "But I thought you said all my tests were normal," Roland protested.

"They are," said his doctor, adding ominously, "for now."

Despite all empirical evidence to the contrary, the doctor concluded that Roland cannot be healthy because of the fundamentalist tenet that Fat = Death. To his doctor, Roland is a ticking time bomb who only appears healthy for the present. Therefore the prudent physician must head off the inevitable illness and not be hoodwinked by the patient's current indicators of health.

Although this reasoning seems irrational, it is more common than you might think. If we can't count on physicians to treat obesity objectively, we can hardly be surprised when the general public lets loose with their prejudices. Most people would look at Roland and assume from his size that he's got one foot in the grave. Even if he produced his blood test results on the spot, I think most people would be unconvinced by them and still implore him to lose weight before it's too late. Their advice is based on an ideology, not on the facts of a blood test. Roland's doctor wasn't treating his patient. He was treating a statistical probability. Even if it's statistically true that fat people die younger than thin people, which is far from proven, it's wrong to treat any person as a statistical class.

You may think I've run off the rails at this point. After all, science is the opposite of religion, right? Religion is based on faith; science is based on testable, reproducible results. Perhaps that's the ideal, but the *practice* of science is often quite different. A good friend of mine was going to do his doctoral dissertation at Yale on a controversial theory, and he proposed to conduct experiments to test it. However, his advisor rejected the dissertation topic flat out.

"Why?" my friend asked.

"Because the theory can't be right," his adviser told him. My friend stared in disbelief. "Look," his adviser patiently continued, "it's a waste of time. If your results are negative, then you've proven the theory is wrong, which is already obvious. If your results are positive, then it'll just show that there was something wrong with your data."

The adviser had already rejected the theory as nonsense, so an experiment was unnecessary. No proof could exist that would substantiate a theory that seemed to have no basis in orthodox science. The theory was heresy.

By the way, my friend ended up leaving the PhD program and even that field of study. He did, however, conduct his research, and his conclusions were published in a prestigious scientific journal. As it turned out, his results supported the validity of the controversial theory. He sent a copy of the article to his former adviser.

You might say that my friend just had a bad adviser. You might say that Roland just had a bad doctor. However, the dogma that persists in science and medicine is so common that many fat people ask their fat friends for referrals to physicians who will treat them as patients, rather than as diseases waiting to happen. I've talked to physicians who have told me that it would be irresponsible to treat an obese person for a sinus infection without also discussing weight-loss options.

The anecdote about my friend's dissertation was not about Fat, but what if it had been? What would you say about a study that showed that people with more body fat lived longer? What if I showed you a study that said that high cholesterol is not an accurate predictor of heart disease? These studies exist. Are they right? Are they reproducible? There's not much interest in finding out. Just like my friend's dissertation, studies that investigate or seek to corroborate heretical ideas usually don't get authorized or funded. It's not incompetency or a conspiracy. It's just human nature: Fund a study to determine the efficacy of a new medication to lower cholesterol, or fund a study to question the fundamental link between cholesterol and heart disease? Common sense would seem to dictate the former as more worthwhile, but the next breakthrough in medicine may well come from the latter.

Scientific Progress

As it turns out, science has a long—though little-known—history of rejecting evidence that doesn't fit the thinking of the day. Likewise, scientists have a curious amnesia, forgetting that accepted fact today was fantasy or even heresy just a few decades ago. It's beyond the scope of this book to delve into the complex story of Western scientific advancement, but if you're interested, you might pick up a copy of *The Structure of Scientific Revolutions*. In this book, science historian Thomas Kuhn meticulously describes how paradigm shifts in science occur. They do not occur objectively or rationally, as you might expect. In fact, often they don't even occur civilly.

For our purposes, however, just think back a few decades. You may be old enough to remember how, in the 1980s, eggs were vilified as little bombs packed with cholesterol and saturated fat. Through a triumph of modern science back then, eggs were revealed to be hidden killers, and anyone who took their health seriously tried to avoid eggs assiduously. No more than two or three per week was the recommendation. Egg substitutes then filled supermarket shelves. I remember friends raising their eyebrows if I ordered eggs in a restaurant. Eating an egg was tantamount to flouting death. This seems overly dramatic, but if you think back to those times, you might remember how virulent the campaign was. It seemed to matter not one whit that eggs had been a staple of the human diet for tens of centuries in every culture all over the planet. Now science knew better: Eggs were dangerous.

But then science triumphed again! In the 1990s, science proved that eggs had many nutritional benefits far outweighing any negative aspects that some misguided nutritionists had claimed. Science showed that

2: You Don't Know Fat

eggs were wholesome and healthy. After all, they had been a staple of the human diet for tens of centuries in every culture all over the planet.

I mention the story of eggs as one example that I think you might remember. However, nutritional science often reverses its edicts, and recommendations change from decade to decade. Remember the Food Pyramid? It's changed a lot since the 1950s. Changed for the better? Some have pointed to the ironic coincidence that as the government and nutrition advocates have changed the American diet to favor carbohydrates over meat, Americans have grown more obese. In 1950, eating a steak was healthful. In 1990, it was deadly. Today, it's merely controversial. But let's look at a bigger story. It's not about Fat, but it shows the influence that science can have over a culture and our most intimate relationships.

Imagine that you're a mother. It's naptime for Junior and you just put him down, but he's fussy and squirmy. As you leave the room, Junior begins to cry. As you shut the door, he starts to scream. You hear him bawling as you walk down the stairs to the living room. But you're a good mother, and you know that picking the child up and comforting him is the worst thing you could do right now. Your motherly instincts notwithstanding, you hold firmly to your pediatrician's advice to handle the child as little as possible. Kissing him and touching him affectionately, particularly when he's crying, will only weaken him later in life. The advice seems strange, but all the experts agree: *Parents* magazine, *Atlantic Monthly*, even your own doctor. He has given you pamphlets from the government. One warns harshly, "Never kiss a baby. Especially on the mouth. Don't rock or play with children."

This isn't some dystopian novel of the future. It's America in 1930, as brought to light by Deborah Bloom, a Pulitzer Prize-winning journalist and science writer. Blum explains how child-rearing books in the early 20th century advocated social conditioning and discipline as the proper way to raise children. The theory was substantiated by medical data gathered from orphanages over the previous decade: It seemed that the more often children were picked up and held, the more likely they were to get sick and even die. In hindsight, we can see that a nurse going through a ward, holding and kissing each crying infant, would have been a vector for spreading all sorts of illnesses, including deadly ones. In the

1920s, however, medical professionals saw the same data as evidence that holding children weakened them. They concluded that children needed to be toughened in their early years to withstand such illnesses.

Psychologists of that day knew of all sorts of external stimuli that could influence human beings, especially babies. Love, however, was apparently not one of these stimuli: "Love was unmeasurable and unscientific," says Blum in summarizing the scientists' thinking of that time. Therefore, love was unnecessary to the proper social conditioning of a child. One prominent psychologist even boasted of the day when mothers might be completely eliminated from the child-rearing process.

This was not the ramblings of one odd scientist. Indeed, a dominant idea of that age was that science would one day free humanity from being human. However, the fear that science would succeed was also a cornerstone of the age. Aldous Huxley's 1932 novel *Brave New World* is set in a future when children are communally conditioned in nurseries, and the idea of natural childbirth and parenting is a repugnant obscenity. This is a dystopian exaggeration of the fears of an age, to be sure. However, as our governments today bring science to bear in prescribing the proper way to raise children who won't get fat, I am reminded of the 1930s, when medical science and the government brought forth the proper way to raise children who wouldn't turn out to be delinquent.

In the 30s, there was an overriding orthodoxy: Children could not be left to the unhygienic, unscientific care of their mothers. In our time, we often hear of obese children who have been rescued from the ignorance and denial of their overindulgent mothers. Several state and local governments around the United States are considering passing laws that would take obese children away from their mothers and fathers, on the grounds that an obese child is being overfed and therefore abused.

As for the scientific stance on love, Blum asserts that it wasn't until 1946 that Dr. Benjamin Spock would deem mothering to be nonlethal. His book *Baby and Child Care* revolutionized the field. He suggested to mothers, "You know more than you think you do." The book was very successful, perhaps because parents had been aching to hold their children without being looked upon as immoral or irresponsible. Later researchers like Harry Harlow would go on to establish a scientific basis for love and the need for mother-child bonding. But in 1930, motherly love was more than just irrelevant; it was dangerously counter to scientific evidence, especially when you considered that the life of a child was at stake. Kissing your child too often or hugging him too freely constituted a kind of heresy from the scientific thinking of the day.

Science does make advances, of course, and these advances often benefit us and even save our lives. But what about the children who were never held and kissed because they had such well-informed parents? Yes, science marches on, but it makes mistakes. In fact, science is *supposed* to make mistakes; it's necessary and integral to the scientific process. But science has such a poor memory. It so often forgets the theories and hypotheses that were wrong and teaches only the ones that have proven to be correct so far. What about the people who had the misfortune to be around when science got it wrong? It's bound to happen, isn't it? If the scientific method inherently involves blind alleys, wrong assumptions, and premature conclusions, then surely no age—including our own—is immune.

Science marches on. So in 100 years, what scientific pronouncement will people look back at and laugh—or gasp? I can well imagine a day when advising fat people to count calories seems as superstitious as telling asthmatics to balance their phlegm with their other three humors. A day when bariatric surgery is looked at the way we look today at prefrontal lobotomy. Science marches on, but the scientists who got it wrong are usually never around to say I'm sorry.

Evidence and Belief

We'll never know how many mothers successfully stifled their urge to shower their children with affection. The scientists of the day were sure of their conclusions and effective in promulgating their advice, but to what extent were mothers of that time persuaded? I suspect the answer then was the same as the answer today: Much of what we consider true is largely a matter of what evidence we deem credible, and what we deem most credible is evidence that most strongly supports our personal experiences and beliefs. Whether we're repulsed by Fat or attracted to it—whether we blame society or fat people themselves for their rough road in life—we can find ample evidence to support our existing beliefs.

Perhaps then it isn't the scientific evidence about health and obesity that informs our opinions about Fat. Perhaps it's the reverse: Perhaps our opinions about health and obesity inform our evidence.

I've talked with many people who regard their revulsion to obesity as logical, even natural. They reason that humans are naturally revolted by anything associated with morbidity: rotting food, infections, tumors, and so forth. We don't have to know the scientific theory of bacteria and infection to know that a festering wound is a bad thing and to avoid it. It's not only an instinctual response, but also a correct one, as modern science has corroborated. The problem with that argument, however, is that there are many other rotting or infected things that we quite like and even admire: yeasty bread, fermented wine, sour cream, and stinky cheese. In the sexual realm, many people are turned on by body odor and other strong scents, which are squarely at odds with proper hygiene. Let's face it, these things are alluring *because of* (not in spite of) some degree of rot or decay. Saying it is natural to hate fat because it's unhealthy is like saying it's natural to hate cheese because it's rotted milk. Of course many people do hate cheese, but it would be silly to justify a revulsion to cheese on scientific grounds. How we see the evidence has a great deal to do with how we see the world.

For example, what do you conclude from the evidence in this account of the death of an obese man? He weighed 240 pounds and smoked two packs a day. He was only 35, but his doctors warned that if he did not change his life, it was just a matter of time before his unhealthy lifestyle caught up with him. Well, you can guess what happened. The doctors were right, and the man died of a massive heart attack due to arteriosclerosis, a condition that was determined upon autopsy to have clogged up to 90% of some of his coronary arteries. What killed this man? Why did he die?

Now, I did leave out part of the story. Shortly after his doctor's visit, the man lost 60 pounds over the next ten years, quit smoking, and started running. In fact, almost singlehandedly, he started the running craze in this country that continues to this day. The man's name was Jim Fixx, and his book, *The Complete Book of Running*, became a national best seller. Fixx promoted the book across the country and on television, all the while extolling the virtues of physical exercise, and how it improved health, vitality, and life expectancy. Fixx actually dropped dead shortly after a 15-mile run at the age of 52. The cause of Fixx's anomalous death has generated a lot of speculation. One theory attributes his collapse to his high-stress personality; another, to the fact that he smoked and was obese for many years. However, the second theory seems particularly unconvincing since during the last 20 years of his life he was a lean, avidly exercising non-smoker. Science, however, tends to credit what it can measure. It's easier to measure 60 pounds and 40 cigarettes a day than it is to measure "a high-stress personality."

My point is that if you're fat and you die, you are simply the fulfillment of the "wages of sin" dogma—no matter when you die. No one asks about your personality type. No one talks about your stress levels. If a thin man drops dead of a heart attack, he dies of myocardial infarction. If a fat man drops dead of a heart attack, he dies of an "obesity-related illness." If a thin man gets hit by a bus, the poor guy never had a chance. If a fat man gets hit by a bus, it's a pity he was too fat to get out of the way in time. My good friend Mike, who is almost 500 pounds, says that perfect strangers as well as close family have come up to him and said, without a word of introduction, "You're gonna die, ya know." Mike's response is to feign amazement and say, "You mean if I lose weight, I won't die?"

On the other end of the scale is my friend Rich. He's quite tall, muscular, and pushing 280 pounds. His doctor confessed to him one day, "You're a tough case, Rich. I have nothing to threaten you with." When Rich asked for an explanation, the doctor added, "Most of my overweight patients have wives or husbands or children that I can threaten them with. I tell the patient they're gonna die of a heart attack or cancer and leave their family all alone—widowed and fatherless. But you're a young, single guy with no wife or kids. I can't use that to motivate you." Actually, I find it almost refreshing to hear of this doctor's blunt admission of manipulation. Usually it's much more covert or even unconscious. Shortly thereafter, Rich found a new doctor.

Although the images of grieving widows and bereft orphans can be a compelling inducement for some to get lean, I think most people would laugh at the idea that without obesity we would have no widows and orphans. Treating obesity is not the same as treating mortality. Every fat person alive today will be dead within a matter of years. So will every thin person. We're quibbling about the number of years. Death is the inevitable result of living. No matter what condition our body is in or how scrupulously we attend to our health, no one gets out of life alive. I think we forget that sometimes. There are certainly many fat people who believe in Fat = Death. But many have decided to spend their years in pursuit of what makes them happy, rather than be granted additional years of failure and frustration in pursuit of leanness. It is a quality-of-life issue. Even if you believe that Fat = Death, living longer is not necessarily living better.

In contrast, it might surprise you to learn that there are cases in which being massively obese has saved a person's life. My friend Paul was in a serious car accident. He was driving down the road when a car coming in the opposite direction swerved out of its lane and came straight at him. Paul didn't have time or room to maneuver, so he caught most of the impact. It drove the steering wheel into his torso. When the paramedics arrived, they told Paul how lucky he was to be alive. Actually, they told him how lucky he was to be fat. Apparently the several hundred pounds of fat Paul carried in front of him was enough to dissipate the shock of the impact and cushion his internal organs. They said if he hadn't been so fat, he never could have survived the crash. Maybe his obesity would have killed him 20 or 30 years down the line, but at that moment, being thin would have definitely been fatal. Is that a statistical rarity? An exception? An anomaly? Maybe, but not for Paul. When we talk about obesity causing death, we're talking about statistics and correlations—not about the actual lives of people.

Justifying Fat Prejudice

Let's grant for the moment the fundamentalist view that being fat always leads to an early grave. Even so, that hardly explains the disdain with which obese people are treated. If our objection to obesity rests solely on our objection to ill health, why don't we roll our eyes when we see someone taking medication? Why don't we make fun of the co-worker whose cold is too severe to allow him to attend the big meeting? Why don't children taunt a classmate who has just received a cancer diagnosis?

As children, we don't hear about a scientific study linking heart disease and obesity, and then decide not to be friends with the fat kid. Actually, I was that fat kid. I remember distinctly being teased by a pretty, thin girl who told me, "You're gonna die, ya know, because fat people always die young." We were seven years old. I don't think she decided to make fun of me because of any medical insight. I don't think she'd been calling me names all year but saving her indicting medical prognosis for that specific moment. No, like most children—like most people—she had a visceral reaction to obesity; the medical reference was simply her way of justifying her prejudice and emphasizing her disgust.

But let's look at the opposite: Few things elicit more congratulations and backslapping than a fat person who has lost a lot of weight. "That's fantastic!" and "I'm so proud of you!" are common rejoinders. People who lose hundreds of pounds are regarded as heroes and role models. In fact, few things rise to this level of exaltation. We televise people's fat loss; we celebrate that sole achievement in every media. TV producers go to significant expense to document (or manufacture) the story of a victim of obesity who became the hero of health. Even a person who recovers from cancer seldom gets that kind of media attention unless they're already a celebrity. By contrast, losing a quarter ton of fat is a news event all by itself.

Might the person become healthier by losing weight? Perhaps, but I don't think that's what we're cheering. If a thin person announces that he's given up junk food or taken up tennis to get fit, people are encouraging, but no one stands up and cheers. The spectacle of extreme weight loss in the media isn't a celebration of regained health. After all, the media accounts seldom mention the person's new and improved metabolic statistics. On the contrary, any media story about extreme weight loss depends on pictures of the person's transformation. The narrative tells us of a heroic transfiguration, using the *before* and *after* pictures to create the story of tragedy turned into triumph. If the story were really about health, an *after* picture of the newly healthy thin person would suffice. Any mention of health is included only to assure us that we care about the obese person's well-being, and that we're not merely gawkers at a sideshow, gaping at a freak made human.

Lastly, if celebrating weight loss is really cheering a person's good health, then what are we jeering when we make fun of weight gain? If it's merely the good health of half-clothed fitness models that we admire, what is it we deplore when we see fat people in clothes that suggest any part of their form? I don't think we're decrying their ill health. We do not condemn the unhealthy. We condemn people who offend us and we laud people who inspire us, but we condemn or laud them to the degree that we think they are responsible. Intent and responsibility matter to us in whether we praise or condemn. So what are the things that offend us? What do we blame people for? Why are some people actually outraged when they see someone fat?

The obese are usually assumed to be gluttons. The obese are the literal embodiment of one of the deadly sins. So if I am attracted to a fat person, some people reason I must be attracted to the weakness of their sin. Now, I don't think you can spot a greedy person just by watching them walk down the street. And it's almost impossible to spot a lazy person in a park or on a beach full of sunbathers. But the glutton seems to be readily identifiable,

Laziness   Anger   Envy

Greed   Pride   Vanity

Gluttony

Is Obesity a Sin?

FIGURE 3: The Seven Deadly Sins

even in the most fleeting glimpse, because we assume that being fat is the same as being gluttonous. I wonder how many skinny people have ever been condemned for gluttony no matter how much they ate. No one witnesses the lanky teenage boy inhaling burgers and accuses him of gluttony. However, the fat woman at the food court toying with her remaining French fries might as well be wearing a scarlet G clear enough to see from 50 feet away. Of course not everyone believes in the Seven Deadly Sins. Maybe you don't believe in sin at all—deadly or otherwise. But I think most people have at least the underpinnings of an ethical framework that holds these seven qualities as shameful and bad.

Whether we call it religion, spirituality, aesthetics, or just common sense, we seem to make the equation that truth = beauty = goodness. We apply it to every human concern, including diet and exercise. We talk about good foods and bad foods, good cholesterol and bad cholesterol, good carbs and bad carbs, good fats and bad fats, gaining good weight or bad weight. So if a person "looks beautiful," we assume they "eat good food" and that their diet must be the right or "true" one for optimal health. Some people attempt to escape the morality of the terms *good* and *bad* by replacing them with *clean* and *dirty*, or *healthy* and *unhealthy*, but the meaning and consequence are the same.

For example, if I tell you that my friend Sue is healthy, what do you imagine about Sue? What does she look like? Most people don't imagine she's fat. (Many would argue that she can't be healthy if she's fat.) If I tell you that Sue eats a "healthy" diet, what do you imagine that Sue eats? What doesn't she eat? The answer depends entirely on the network of assumptions we have about what is healthy and unhealthy—good and bad. We've turned our health, our food, and even our bodies into a moral quandary. We describe our choices of food, diet, and exercise the same way we describe our moral choices. These things must be moral issues or we wouldn't be able to have a "cheat day" on our diet, or buy "guilt-free" potato chips, or refuse dessert by explaining that we're "being good." The morality rings clear in the vocabulary we use. We take it for granted that health and beauty are manifestations of goodness. We must, or we wouldn't take it for granted that "eating right" leads to "looking good" and "being healthy."

I often encounter this sort of morality because of my body. Strangers occasionally compliment my health and mental resolve, based on my muscular appearance. Because of the aesthetics of my body, they congratulate me on my dedication to good health. Of course, they have no way of knowing my blood pressure, cholesterol, blood sugar levels, or any of my metabolic stats. However, since I look like their picture of beauty and vitality, I must therefore be healthy. Their assumption of good health also extends to my diet and exercise. If they believe good health comes from vigorous exercise, they ask where I find the time to spend hours every day in the gym. If they believe good health comes from eating certain foods, they believe I live on those same foods. For example, people who believe in low-carb diets say, "I bet you eat low-carb, right?" People who believe in low-fat diets ask, "So you eat...what? Chicken with lots of brown rice and oatmeal?" One man, who put great stock in the life-giving benefits of a strictly vegetarian diet, assumed that my hyper-muscular form must be the result of rice, beans, and tofu. Fat people are greeted by a set of opposite assumptions: However health is measured or achieved, the fat person is assumed not to have it or not to be doing it.

These assumptions all contain an element of morality. I've had strangers come up to me and say, with a withering sigh, "God, you remind me I have to get back to the gym." One guy sized me up in the aisle of a supermarket and actually said, "You make me feel awful about myself." I understand that it's not personal—I'm just an object in their world. Nonetheless, I am an object that exemplifies part of their moral code of health, beauty, diet, and exercise. They pass judgment on themselves based on judgments they have about me. In that way, they use me like a fun-house mirror to look at themselves.

TRY THIS AT HOME

Choose a friend, relative, co-worker, or perfect stranger.

Tell this person that you have a friend who is trying to eat a more healthful diet. Ask the person what he/she thinks your friend should be eating. Repeat this with two or three other people and note the variations. You might follow up by asking whether there are any foods that your friend definitely should or should not eat, or any practices that must be included or avoided.

If the virtues of good diet and exercise lead to good health, then what about the opposite? What about disease? We're often at a loss to explain how supposedly healthy people fall victim to degenerative diseases such as cancer, multiple sclerosis, or arthritis. We find it more reasonable when disease comes from vice: cancer from smoking, or diabetes from obesity. We find it far more disconcerting when disease strikes where there is virtue. We seem to be at a loss to reconcile diabetes in an athlete or cancer in a child. I think we're more inclined to use words like *tragic* or *heartbreaking* when disease befalls people we have enshrined as healthy.

It's the same loss we feel when reconciling why bad things happen to good people. It challenges our notions of justice, ethics, or fairness.

Health As a Higher Authority

We all tend to moralize our diet, health, and fitness. However, when these concerns rise to become part of our identity, the stakes rise correspondingly. For example, it's one thing to tell people you don't eat meat. That's a practice, something you do or don't do. However, it's another matter to say that you *are* vegetarian. That's an identity, something central to how we define ourselves and the world. For example, one might be a strict vegetarian as one might be a strict Catholic. Another person might feel the same sort of moral conviction about being a vegan as someone might feel about being a Muslim. Just as with a religious identity, an identity based on diet or health is expressed through practices and prohibitions. Indeed, I don't think it's a coincidence that some religions proscribe or encourage the eating of certain foods at certain times. Eating food is one of our most basic and intimate interactions with the world. Both the morality of health and the orthodoxy of religion go far beyond being a mere list of dos and don'ts. The true believer intends the sacraments, rituals, and practices of his belief system for the same purpose: to keep himself in harmony with all that is good and right.

I think human beings seek to be part of a bigger picture; we seek access to a realm that is beyond our personalities or identities. We yearn for a realm that connects us all. Some find it in science; some in religion. We will seek it through whatever calls to us: physics, mathematics, politics, religion, art, and, yes, even health, diet, and fitness. We seek a system that will tell us what's good and true about the world, and to this extent we can elevate diet and fitness to a moral code.

The logical extension of creating a higher moral authority—a morality more universal and far-reaching than mere personal opinion—is that we construct rituals around this moral authority to support its mystery, to keep it aloof and inaccessible, to keep it from devolving into something merely human and personal. In the realm of health, these rituals often take the form of diet and exercise. It's not just the food, but also the way the food must be prepared. It's not just exercise, but also the euphoria and community that comes with exercise. Such devotion can even become evangelistic. Perhaps you or someone you know seeks to convert people to vegetarianism, or extols the superior benefits of yoga, or entreats their friends to eschew the consumption of living things in favor of a more enlightened form of sustenance. Of course, we're all interested in dying later rather than sooner, but most of us know someone who maintains a complicated or restrictive diet, or an exacting exercise regimen, or a library of esoteric alternative medical knowledge. These are the practices and codes that emerge when health becomes the ultimate morality, when maintaining one's health becomes like a religious practice.

Prejudice & Common Sense

But even if we take religion and health out of our discussion, would you hire a fat kid to work at your ice cream parlor? Would you hire a fat woman to be your receptionist? Would you put yourself in the care of a fat physician? What about a fat psychotherapist? As I said earlier, whatever system we use to assess people—religion, spirituality, aesthetics, or even so-called common sense—the ranking and appraisal of people based solely on such abstractions goes by the name of prejudice.

For some people, a tacit logic runs through their head like this: Anyone who can't control their appetite, who can't help that their body is hundreds of pounds overweight, probably has other psychological problems that might affect their job performance. If they can't manage their weight, maybe they can't manage their time—maybe they can't manage their personal lives, their money, or the company's money. And what about the children? What bad examples are they setting for their children? What sort of example are we setting for our clients if we let a fat person represent us? If someone is grossly obese, they must be grossly out of control. A man at a supermarket approached my friend Eric, who is fat. The stranger handed him a card and said, "My son is a personal trainer. I think he could really help you get your life back on track." The stranger reasoned that someone whose body is so out of sorts must also have a life that's out of sorts. Again, this sounds like a logical deduction, but it's actually a moral judgment.

Anyone can be incompetent, obviously, whether they're fat or thin. Nonetheless, I've never heard anyone make this kind of argument: "Wow, did you interview Jerry, that really fat guy? Geez, he is as big as a house! He must eat and eat until he's way past full. Ya know, I'll bet he'll work and work way past when other employees have had enough. He'll be twice as productive as any of our other employees because clearly he doesn't know when to quit! Let's get his fat ass signed before someone else makes him a higher offer!"

I don't think it's our thorough study of metabolic syndrome or endocrinology that has led so many people to conclude that fat people are lazy. (Laziness, by the way, gives the obese a doubleheader on the top seven sins.) Moreover, in many cases, employers assume that hiring an obese person will lead to greater health costs for the company in the long term. We feel justified in discriminating against Jerry to the extent that we believe Jerry's obesity to be within his control, to the extent that he is to blame. This same argument has been applied throughout history to groups of people who have been considered undesirable: Many religious people say they don't condemn homosexuals for thoughts they can't control; they condemn only the immoral behavior of acting on those thoughts or talking about them in public. The Spanish government in 1492 expressed no animosity toward the Jews; it just had no tolerance for people who practiced any religion other than Roman Catholicism. Similarly, many people today think that fat people are every bit as good as thin people, except to the degree that they're fat. It's not that these people think Fat is bad; it's just that they believe Fat leads only to disease and loneliness. These are all corollaries of fat fundamentalism. They are variations on the age-old idea "Hate the sin, not the sinner."

As a chubby chaser, I've heard all these well-reasoned conclusions applied to me as well. In referring to the size of the man I was dating, one of my relatives asked me sheepishly, "Do you have to go so far with the Fat thing?" Another relative diagnosed my attraction to fat men, saying, "You've definitely got mommy issues." Some strangers, however, have been far less kind. One guy at a bar asked me what my type was, so I showed him a picture on my phone of a guy I thought was attractive. "That's sick," he said, before turning away and shunning me. But Fat is a big deal for some people. I suppose it's a big deal for me, too, but in a different way.

The Why and the Which Hunt

The question at the center of everything I've been discussing in this section is this: Where do we locate the source of obesity? Science seeks the cause; ethics seeks the blame. In talking about the cause and cure of obesity, it might be helpful to place Fat in the context of other poorly understood stigmas and maladies. The American intellectual Susan Sontag wrote a book titled *Illness as Metaphor,* which *Newsweek* called "one of the most liberating books of its time." One of the points Sontag makes is that the less we know about an illness, the more we blame the victim. Think about the bubonic plague of Europe in the Middle Ages. Plague victims were seen as sinners who had somehow incurred God's wrath, and disease and death were their punishment. Today, however, we find it ridiculous to blame the plague victims for something that is clearly caused by bacteria and spread through innocent contact.

We sometimes think that people of the past believed foolish things because they were ignorant, superstitious, or just not as smart as we modern folk. But as far as I can tell, people of every age are pretty smart. We differ from our ancestors only in how we model the world. God's wrath sounds like a perfectly reasonable explanation for the death of a third of Europe if you believe in a certain model of the way the world works. If your model includes germ theory, however, another explanation is possible, and the explanation of "God's wrath" might seem like ignorant superstition.

Another example that Sontag and others have cited is AIDS. In the early 1980s when the disease broke out in San Francisco and New York, it was referred to as the Gay Plague. Indeed, in some circles AIDS was seen as God's punishment for homosexuality. Even when a medical model was developed that helped explain the illness, gay people were still singled out as the cause and the target of the disease.

Obesity is perhaps the most current example. What do you believe causes obesity? Science doesn't know for certain, so the answer is up for grabs. We're pretty sure we can't catch obesity. Can a bad diet cause obesity? Maybe, but then how can so many thin people eat bad diets and not get fat? Maybe it's genetic? Environmental? Some say obesity is linked with poverty, but isn't eating all that food expensive? What about constant negative thinking? Can that make you fat? How about an unresolved issue from a past life? Our feelings about people, our reaction to circumstances, depend on how we think the world operates. For the obese and those of us attracted to the obese, any degree of suffering comes from our view of the morality of Fat—the blame, pity, virtue, or vice of having or desiring a particular stigmatized body type. The good news is that suffering is not inherent in obesity. It is, however, inherent in blame, pity, virtue, and vice. As one fat woman once told me, "I don't have a weight problem because I don't have a problem with my weight. But a lot of other people sure do!"

WHERE DO YOU STAND?

Whatever you think about fat people directly correlates with what you think about people like me who are attracted to fat people. When it comes to obesity, people's beliefs and judgments run the gamut, and they run deep. I certainly have mine. What's more, the passion with which people believe whatever they believe about obesity can be quite surprising.

In this section, we'll create a map of the vast terrain of judgments and affinities about Fat. Since all of these points of view are also held by people in the Round World, I suppose you could say we're going to create a map of the Round World. You'll have the opportunity to put yourself on this map and see where you stand in relation to other people. I've found that we can actually diagram what we think about Fat in a way that reveals our deeply rooted feelings on the topic and the extent to which those feelings affect our experience of people.

For some people, their views about obesity scream in their ears on a daily basis. For example, many fat people hate being fat and are acutely aware of that opinion almost every moment of the day. The chair they're sitting in, the dressing on their salad, and the shop window that reflects their image are all reminders of how wrong their bodies are, compared with what they would like them to be. But you don't have to be fat to suffer from fat hatred. Some thin people become enraged at the sight of a fat person eating. They feel contempt for fat people in general, and most particularly when they see a fat person in an environment where there is food. As I'll talk about later, they might even feel it's their moral duty to say something to the obese person. These are the extremes, to be sure, but well-meaning strangers often make comments to fat people—comments that the strangers believe to be important, helpful, and urgently needed.

Then there are the people who would never talk to complete strangers. Instead, they content themselves with thinking loud thoughts. Maybe you're one of these people? Imagine you see a woman handing her fat daughter a bag of fries at a food court. Do you have an opinion about the mother? About the daughter? Are French fries okay for some people to eat, but not for others? More importantly, are you aware that your feelings are actually a judgment of another person, or do your feelings simply occur to you as an appropriate response to a problem in the world? At what point might your opinion about this situation turn into action?

On the other hand, perhaps obesity is more like wallpaper for you, something inconspicuous and innocuous unless someone points it out. Many fat people, for example, go through life without much concern for their size. They wouldn't choose to be fat, but their obesity poses no grave problems for them medically or socially. This may be true even if the persons weighs hundreds of pounds. (I know some people may find that difficult if not impossible to believe.) Likewise, some thin folk don't have much of an opinion about their fat fellows. They don't think obesity is a benefit, but to them it's also not damnable. They recognize that people come in various sizes and shapes, and some sizes and shapes may even be extreme.

I propose that there are two basic attitudes that determine our reactions toward Fat. The intensity with which we experience these basic attitudes varies from person to person. But I believe they are at the heart of our experience of Fat, and they can be used to draw valuable insights about ourselves and about how we relate to others. Whether your feelings about Fat are mild or extreme, this section will be a useful way to tease out more specifically how you see those of us who live in the Round World.

Affinity: Repulsion ←→ Attraction

Repulsion

The first and most obvious way to feel about Fat is to either like it or dislike it. In my experience, it's safe to say that most people dislike obesity, by which I mean they consider it to be an undesirable trait. They don't want to be fat, they don't want a partner who is fat, and they would never wish their children to be fat. I'm not talking about health or other rationales. I'm just talking about your gut reaction when you see someone fat walking down the street or eating at a restaurant. The fat person in question might be a perfect stranger, someone you know, or even you. Of course, the intensity of your reaction probably depends on how fat the person is.

Most people have a range of body size that they consider acceptable, normative, or unremarkable. The further a person falls outside that range, the more he or she is likely to elicit a corresponding degree of like or dislike. For example, if you have a negative reaction to someone fat, you'll probably have a more negative reaction to someone very fat. Certainly other factors are involved here as well. Fashion, hygiene, even hairstyle also play a part, but they are not at the heart of the matter; they'll never turn a negative perception of Fat into a positive one. There's no suit dapper enough, no dress sexy enough, no accessory elegant enough to make someone change their negative opinion of Fat into a positive one. If Fat's just not your thing, no degree of fashion or grooming can ever reverse that negative opinion; it can only mitigate it. If you think Fat is gross, then a fat person in a great suit looks less gross. Perhaps they look great, but you know…great for a fat person.

Attraction

If you're attracted to Fat, then the same holds true in the opposite direction. When I see an attractive guy who falls above what I consider the normal weight range, I have a positive reaction to his obesity. For people like me, fashion and grooming never make us re-think the attractiveness of Fat, but they can serve to augment or diminish our attraction to a particular person. If you see someone with a great body, their fashion or hygiene may make you more or less attracted. However, those things never fundamentally change the fact that, for you, that person has a great body—however you define a great body. It's complete nonsense that chubby chasers find all fat people attractive, or that if a person is fat, a chubby chaser doesn't care about anything else. (This is a frequent misconception among fat people in my seminars.)

It's no different than if you're heterosexual. If you're a straight man, then you find women attractive, but you don't find *every* woman attractive, nor do you find a person attractive simply because she's a woman. However, a person does have to be female for you to consider dating them. It's very much the same for most chasers, except that the characteristic in question is fat rather than gender (though gender may be an equally important factor as well).

Not all attraction leads to sex, so when I say *attraction*, I'm talking about a visceral, physical response—ranging from mild to overwhelming—that makes you want to engage with another person. An extreme attraction can feel very sexual. However, I've seen some extraordinarily beautiful fat women, but I wouldn't call my reaction to them a sexual attraction. Instead, it's an affinity based only on what the person looks like, sometimes described as a non-sexual crush. Sometimes children have a passionate affinity for a particular person or type of person, yet a child is too immature for these feelings to be properly called sexual. When gay people say, "I've known I was gay since I was six years old," this is usually what they mean. (Chasers often describe their attraction to fat men or women this way, too, as a profound fascination dating back to early childhood.)

In cases of sexual attraction, we run into the normative view that Fat is the opposite of Sex. An image of a fat person having sex or just being sexy elicits a guaranteed laugh (or stomach cramp) from most people. For me, though, fat guys are naturally sexy; if a fat guy isn't sexy, it's because he's undermining himself with bad hair, poor hygiene, or a low opinion of himself.

Okay, so some people really like Fat. That's not so hard to fathom, right? Some people think "a little extra meat on the bones" is attractive. They don't mean muscle; they mean the padding of added fat—a curvy woman or a chunky man. But how fat are we talking? Even for the folks who like meat on the bone, there is a point at which someone is too fat to be attractive. However, for others, that upper limit is virtually non-existent. There may be practical, ethical, or health concerns related to someone who is massively obese, but for many of us that doesn't change our basic attraction. This can be confusing, because sometimes shame or guilt can then temper or even mask our attraction. We'll talk more about these concerns and complications later. For now, I simply want to make the point that just as some people dislike and even loathe fat people, other people like and even idolize fat people. It's a spectrum of affinity.

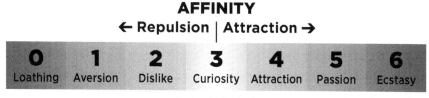

AFFINITY
← Repulsion | Attraction →

0	1	2	3	4	5	6
Loathing	Aversion	Dislike	Curiosity	Attraction	Passion	Ecstasy

FIGURE 4: Scale of Affinity for obesity

A scale of fat affinity ranging from positive to negative isn't really useful, so I've devised a scale that goes from zero to six (similar to the Kinsey scale) to talk about this spectrum. Of course, this isn't very scientific. The numbers represent subjective stages along a range of a particular feeling. The descriptive words in the chart suggest what a person might say if he were at a certain point on the spectrum. For example, "Last summer I saw a really fat person in a swimsuit on a beach, and I felt _____."

Again, many other characteristics such as gender, fashion, or behavior might diminish or augment a person's reaction. This is less likely to be true at the extremes of the spectrum. Most chasers are not attracted to every fat person they see, but others have some degree of affinity no matter what. Similarly, someone who loathes fat people has some degree of distaste for them no matter what the circumstance.

However, extreme reactions to obesity are rare. I think most people come out somewhere closer to the middle; they feel something only slightly negative, such as *dislike*. Or maybe *dislike* seems a bit strong; your reaction to obesity is more of a 2.5, falling somewhere between *dislike* and *curiosity*. The spectrum is pretty broad, with lots of room for people between numbers. Let's take a deeper look at the labels I've chosen.

Ecstasy

You're awed by the presence of something so beautiful and erotic that time stands still. "She was absolutely gorgeous and just immense, so incredibly perfectly fat. I stood there speechless. She was so beautiful that I almost couldn't breathe. Then, the next thing I knew, there was yelling. My friend elbowed me, and I heard him apologize for me."

Passion

You're captivated by the sight of someone so beautiful and sensual that it is difficult to think clearly. "Most big guys are clueless about how hot they are. I mean, they have no idea what they do to guys like me."

Attraction

You're stimulated to get a closer look and discover more. "There was something about her, about her size, that was kinda cool. She was really big, but…I dunno, I guess I liked it."

Curiosity

You're interested in something unfamiliar that warrants exploration. Your reaction is based on difference, that Fat is clearly something different in the world, but it neither attracts nor repulses you. "Did you see that boy, Mommy? He was really fat."

Dislike

You're disinclined to look or engage. Your response might be compared to cringing at a social blunder or wincing at the taste of something you wish you hadn't eaten. "When you're a certain size, you just shouldn't wear certain things. And you're just setting yourself up for ridicule if you wear clothes that accentuate parts of your body that nobody wants to see."

Aversion

You're repelled by the sight of something so ugly that it's difficult to look at. Your response is analogous to feeling shocked by bad behavior or spitting out something that tastes too bad to swallow. "This really fat guy at the food court was eating a burger with fries...like just inhaling grease. It was so gross what he was doing to himself. He probably has mayonnaise flowing through his veins."

Loathing

You're disgusted at the sight of something so sickening that you think it should be banned or expunged. Your feeling is often accompanied by physical sensations of illness and sometimes a strong impulse to take action. "She was so fucking fat! I wanted to put my eyes out. No one should have to look at something so fucking nauseating, especially not on a public beach. Someone should just harpoon that fucking whale."

The spectrum above is quite wide, and its extremes fall into chasms of raw emotion. If your opinions about Fat aren't that strong, some of these examples may shock you. You may have never noticed a fat person being called names from a passing car, or being admonished for having ice cream in her grocery cart. Maybe you've never read online postings like, "Fat people don't deserve to live," "Fat people should be killed," or "Fat people should be locked up and starved." Imagine what it would take for someone like me—someone who finds Fat beautiful—to express his opinion in an environment like that. I'm not trying to say that chubby chasers have it worse than fat people—not at all. I'm just saying that to someone who thinks fat people are filthy and disgusting, chubby chasers occur as perverts feeding off filth.

On the other hand, maybe you're all too familiar with that sort of reaction toward Fat. Maybe it's such a common part of your world that you can't imagine the opposite: people not caring one way or the other about Fat. These people are near the center of the spectrum. I remember talking to a woman at a cocktail party while I was writing this book. She was a woman in her 50s and quite slender, the sort of woman to whom dieting and weight loss might seem theoretical concepts. As I described the fact that I like fat guys and that I was writing a book about it, she seemed genuinely unperturbed by what I had always found to be a taboo for most people. Hearing that I was sexually attracted to obese men didn't seem to make any impression on her at all.

As I elaborated, she looked at me a bit blankly as if I were explaining how I might teach pandas to play chess—how odd, but how interesting. She put her hand on her husband's arm to pull him out of a neighboring conversation. "Did you hear what this guy is writing about?" she said. "I've never even thought about that." She explained that it never occurred to her that fat people would have different sorts of issues in dating and relationships and that some people might even prefer romantic partners who were fat. It made sense to her now that I had mentioned it, but being fat was just something she'd never thought much about. It wasn't important to the way she looked at the world. Again, I doubt she thought of being fat as something positive, but if she had a negative impression, it was so imperceptible that I found it almost shocking.

Now, the other extreme—the love of Fat—is what I'm going to be talking about for the rest of this book. As extreme as some people react against fat, that's how much some people react in favor of it. In fact, that symmetry is worth noting here. The two extremes seem to balance each other. Perhaps for every person who thinks fat people should be put in weight-loss concentration camps, there is another person who thinks that fat people are proof of the divine. I'm not exaggerating when I describe these two points of view. A brief search on the internet will easily bring examples of either of these two polarities into focus.

TRY THIS AT HOME

Surf the internet by searching

...the phrase *fat hate*.

Now try searching the words *fat love*. Adjust the words or parameters to see how extreme passions run on either side.

2: You Don't Know Fat

Whether we think fat is repulsive or attractive, we have plenty of scientific evidence and common sense to support our opinion. Whether we draw our support from studies linking obesity with heart disease, or from anthropological evidence of tribes in which the most obese woman is the chosen of the king, we all come to the table fully armed to defend our attraction to or repulsion for Fat. However, the point I want to make here is that your feeling toward the obese, your affinity, comes first. Explanations and rationalizations come afterward. You may think you're being disgusted by a fat person's supposed ill-health, but as we saw earlier, that is merely the justification for one's disgust. The feeling is not the same as the reason for the feeling. For example, when we see great art or hear great music, we are in awe. Only upon reflection do we have reasons for why the work moves us. When I see a beautiful fat man, the reasons for his beauty do not dance before my eyes. After repeated exposures, the reasons may come to stand for the reaction itself, but they are actually distinct.

Have you found a niche for yourself in the affinity spectrum? You might answer, "Well, it depends." Quite true. You may notice that the fatter someone is, the farther to the extreme you'll be pushed. You might find that a chubby guy is hot, but he'd be a lot hotter with another 100 pounds on him. Conversely, you might think a chubby guy is kind of cute, but if he gained another 100 pounds, he'd be gross. If you like someone who's 300 pounds, you don't necessarily like someone 600 pounds twice as much. Similarly, if you're grossed out by someone 300 pounds, it doesn't mean that you turn into a rabid hate-monger if you see someone 600 pounds. (Yes, 600-pound people walk among us. They just walk more slowly.) People have ranges of what they like, whether it's Fat or anything else. Each of us tends to inhabit a range on the affinity scale, and various factors can push us a bit one way or another.

Take another look at the affinity spectrum.

Where would you locate your own reaction when you see a fat person? Think of a particular fat person you've encountered in the past. Try framing it like this: "The person had to have been at least 300 pounds. When I looked at them, I felt _____." Use a word from the affinity spectrum that seems to capture what you felt. Be honest.

In looking at the affinity spectrum, we notice something interesting. At the ends of the spectrum, the fat person disappears and is replaced by the feelings of the observer. Whether we are moved to ecstasy or wracked with loathing, our focus is on ourselves, not on the fat person before us. Their identity is erased, and they become for us a god or a monster. But what if we are the fat person? Well, then the feelings of ecstasy or loathing are projected onto our observer. For example, many people who find their own obesity monstrous are convinced that the facial expressions and glances directed their way are simply more evidence of how much they are loathed and hated. Similarly, I know men and women who are immensely proud of their obesity. They see such furtive signs from strangers as evidence of just how truly immense and beautiful they have become. At either extreme, the observer is no longer a person or even just a bystander. He becomes an acolyte or an attacker, a fan or a firing squad.

When we can get beyond our own likes and dislikes, we have room to appreciate the person standing before us. Our ecstasy or loathing still exists, but by noticing it we gain the power to set the intense feeling aside for something greater and more rewarding: Meeting another human being. This is the difference between intimacy and objectification, which I'll be talking more about later on.

Judgment: Blame ←→ Pity

So we've just looked at how you might feel about Fat—how it attracts or repels you on a very visceral, almost instinctual, level. I'd like to look at another dimension now that's less about feeling and more about intellect.

Many people are ambivalent when it comes to Fat and fat people in particular: Should we pity the obese for their limitations and suffering, or blame them for trying to milk sympathy for a problem that is of their own making? The difficulty in answering this question, indeed the question itself, stems from a central premise: Fat is a problem requiring blame or absolution. If we only knew whom to blame for fat people, it might ease our conscience or tell us how to feel. For example, if we could be satisfied that genetics, hormones, or physiology were to blame, then we could allow our compassion to pour forth upon the unfortunates. If we could see obesity as a food addiction, we could blame bad parenting, societal forces, or genetic predisposition. We could have compassion for the caloric sinner who seeks recovery, but take a hard line against the grossly unrepentant. If we could be persuaded that being fat were simply a matter of self-control and moderation, we could feel vindicated in our contempt and ridicule of the irresponsible glutton who insists on killing himself at society's expense.

Judgment is a validation or denial of our feelings; it is not what we feel. We can like something, but judge that it is bad. ("I really love smoking, but I know it's bad for me.") Conversely, we can dislike something, but judge that is good. ("I really hate exercise, but I know it is good for me.") In these examples, *I know* comes not from ourselves, but from some higher authority that stands in for our self. Commonly, these sources are God, science, or society.

No matter where we fall on the affinity scale—whether we love Fat or hate Fat—blame and pity are part of our reasoned response to it. Blame and pity may not be our only thoughts about Fat, true, but it may surprise you to see how much of our opinion of Fat is bound up in these two judgments. Unlike the affinity scale, which seems to have a negative side and a positive side (Loathing ←→ Ecstasy), blame and pity are both seen as inherently negative. So why have I picked a scale that is just about negativity?

Well, whether or not we like Fat, it is undeniable that the world in general sees fat negatively. Yes, there are tribes in remote corners of the world that prize fat brides. There were bygone eras when rosy roundness brought adoration. But that's not much different from what we talked about back in "Too Fat for the Room." Fat is relative. So even in fat-positive cultures, you can still be too fat. It's just that these cultures may draw the line at 300 pounds instead of 200 pounds. But no matter where you go or when you go, there's a point at which people say, "That's too damn fat!"

Whether you love Fat, loathe Fat, or are largely indifferent to Fat, we live in a world that considers Fat to be a problem. Each of us has our own tastes and values regarding Fat, but society, science, and even religion have something to say on the subject as well. The accommodation between what the world values and what we personally value is an intellectual exercise that I'm going to call *judgment*. Our intellectual assessment—or *judgment*—of a fat person operates independently of our emotional reaction. I also suggest that it is judgment, not affinity, that leads people to make decisions and sometimes to act.

Consider then that there's a spectrum of judgment, separate from our affinity, along which each of us falls in our assessment of Fat. Even if we are attracted to fat people, or even if we ourselves are fat, we cannot escape the stigma of Fat in our culture. That means that we make our judgments in consideration of that stigma. The poles, or extremes, of this judgment are *pity* and *blame*.

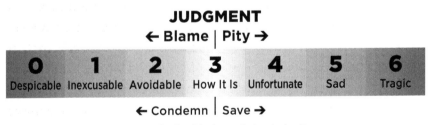

FIGURE 5: Scale of Judgment about obesity

Blame

To what extent do you believe that fat people are responsible for being fat? No matter how much you like or dislike Fat, I think you'll concede that fat people face certain obstacles that thin people do not. The degree to which we feel people are responsible for their obesity correlates with how much we blame the fat person for creating these obstacles. Let's take a closer look at this.

The blame may be slight: "Look, I know I'm fat because of all the fast food I eat, but I'm a busy guy. I get home at two in the morning sometimes, and I just don't have the time or energy to cook. After work, I usually hit the drive-thru, eat it in the car on the way home, and then hit the sack as soon as I'm through the door." In this statement there's not a lot of recrimination for being fat, but there is an obvious, albeit unapologetic, admission that the cause lies with the person himself. The situation seems *avoidable*.

But as the stakes rise, so does the blame: "Joe is a good guy, but he eats too much. He shouldn't lose out on the promotion, but he shouldn't be surprised that the company chose a different salesperson to send to the trade show. They shouldn't have to pay for two seats for him to fly out there." The point is not whether the company is right or wrong. If we believe that Joe is somewhat to blame for his obesity, then we'll conclude that Joe is somewhat to blame when things don't go his way. The speaker doesn't believe he is passing judgment; he thinks he's being reasonable.

But what if the blame rises to the level of indictment? "Have you seen what Joe eats? No company should have to bear the extra costs of an employee who eats like a pig at a fast food trough. A special chair for his desk, two seats on flights, and he'll probably have a heart attack before he's 40. I don't blame the boss for passing him over for promotion and investing in someone else." Here the level of blame borders on contempt and the indictment is clear: "Fat people have no self-control." Another variant is, "It's irresponsible to get that fat." At this level of blame, there is no room for mitigation, extenuating circumstances, or benefit of the doubt. No matter what the fat person's environment, he is fat because he is flawed—a flaw so grave that no circumstance of biology or biography can excuse it.

Pity

Of course, not everyone is so unsympathetic. In fact, many people consider fat people to be victims of obesity rather than its perpetrators. They tend to lay the blame for obesity at the feet of government, big business, bad science, or even urban planners, more than on the unsuspecting fat person. In a country where portions are supersized and neighborhoods are meant for driving, surely a fat person could be forgiven for eating too much and moving too little. In fact, perhaps fat people are merely the victims of an agribusiness conspiracy designed to get us to buy and consume more and more, even at the expense of our health.

If more and more people are becoming obese, surely it can't all be the fault of a weak-minded few. On this side of the coin, the fat person is not to blame; rather, he is to be pitied. Instead of being a weak-willed slob, he is the unsuspecting victim of forces too vast and powerful for him to control, perhaps even including his own biology. As with the previous spectrum of affinity, the fervor of people arising at one extreme seems to balance the fervor of people on the other. The more cruelly that some people blame and punish fat people, the more passionately others pity them and sympathize with their plight. Of course, most of us in the Round World never asked to be either blamed or pitied. Nevertheless, that's what's out there.

As I suggested earlier, judgment—more than affinity—governs how we act in the world: The more you blame someone, the stronger your need to outwardly condemn them for what you blame them for. The more you pity them, the more it tugs at your heartstrings and compels you to try to save them from their plight. Most of us don't live at these extremes. The words I'm using for this spectrum are adjectives meant to characterize a person's appraisal of a situation. For example, imagine that you see a really fat person. You experience a visceral response that falls somewhere on the affinity scale. Then you turn to your friend and say, "Wow, look at that person over there. That's really a _____ situation." This reasoned response or appraisal is different from how you feel on a visceral level about the person. Usually, it's also the justification for your visceral response.

When I present this idea in my seminars, I sometimes get a bit of pushback from people. "I don't blame or pity fat people," participants say. They often resent being forced to chose between two negatives. Well, *blame* and *pity* are pretty strong words. How about "feel sorry for" and "have a problem with"? That might feel more accurate. Remember, we're dealing with a spectrum here, a matter of degree. And of course there's the safe middle ground of "just how it is," but I don't think that's how most people honestly feel about Fat.

I think people resist the labels *blame* and *pity* because they think, "I'm a good person, and good people aren't judgmental." Hmm…Really? What if you see a wounded puppy. The driver hit him squarely and barely even slowed down. You have no judgment about this? I think if your friend standing next to you didn't pity the dog and blame the driver, you'd think he was heartless. What if you see a crying child being spanked hard by an angry mother in a grocery store? Have you ever fought back the urge to intervene and rescue the child? Or chastise the mother? Or maybe you'd like to congratulate the mother for daring to discipline her child in a culture that has become all too permissive and tolerant.

We blame and pity people and situations all the time, and we often feel it is our nature, our right, or even our duty to do so. Perhaps we feel a pang of discomfort when we blame or pity whole classes of people, but the discomfort passes when we justify ourselves. For example, do you feel sorry for black people? For gays? Do you have a problem with rich white men? What about people in America who don't speak English? Blame or pity? When applied to a class or category of people, these feelings are called prejudices.

What's more, these labels for various degrees of blame and pity don't always correspond to a person's weight. For example, on the judgment spectrum, you might find it *sad* that a 700-pound man can't leave his home. But your neighbor might find it *sad* that her 200-pound daughter will never find a husband, even though she has "such a pretty face." Whether you feel justified or guilty for having these feelings, having them is simply part of being human. So let's have a look at the pity and blame about Fat.

Tragic

At the extreme end of the judgment scale, you perceive that an enormously obese person represents a crisis and an opportunity for rescue. Tragic is meant in the sense of classical tragedy, with high stakes, lots of drama, and acts of heroism. The situation represents an opportunity to rescue a fat person who appears helpless or resigned about their obesity. You feel a strong desire to evangelize or save the fat person: "I marched right up to him and told him he was killing himself with food." A tragic situation is one in which a wrong must be righted: "I started taking the junk food out of her shopping cart and told her to do something about her weight before her children were left orphans." In short, tragic labels a response to an obese person as a life-and-death emergency.

Sad

You feel regret for the situation at hand and empathy for the fat person. Sad refers to your appraisal of the situation, not anything the fat person is feeling, though you might project sadness onto him. The situation of someone being very fat seems very negative—maybe even life-or-death—but it doesn't seem to be the emergency that tragic represents. The obese person's health and happiness seem to be at stake, yet no specific, incisive action seems warranted or practical in the moment. This may be because the obese person symbolizes a generalized intractable societal problem: "He can't have much of a life at his size. It's so sad that some people live like that." You long for someone to do something, but you also feel a conflicted resignation as to what exactly should be done.

In other cases, however, the tug on your heartstrings is more personal and particular: "I just worry about him, about his health or finding a relationship. Sometimes I say something, but most times I don't. I know he can't be happy being that big. It must be awful for him." Whether personalized or generalized, you see the situation as *sad* and want to help the victim of obesity. But you refrain from taking overt action because of resignation or indecision about the right action: "I want to help, but I think it would just make the problem worse if I said anything."

Unfortunate

You acknowledge that the situation is clearly not optimal, but there is neither urgency nor gravity about it as with *sad* or *tragic.* You do recognize, however, that being fat presents special difficulties that only fat people have. "Yeah, he's a pretty big guy. We had to take the stairs once when the elevator was out, and he got pretty winded." "She doesn't date much. I suppose it's hard to put yourself out there when you're that size."

How It Is

The situation is how it is. Being fat might be a problem, but the world is full of problems—some big, some small. Everyone's got theirs. The situation is framed as a problem of being different, rather than of being fat specifically. "Fat people might get made fun of a lot, but so do lots of people. Everybody's got their own row to hoe. If a fat guy can't fit in a chair, he should just get a bigger chair."

Avoidable

You're frustrated because the situation of being obese could be easily avoided. You find it difficult to have sympathy because you believe that fat people suffer from problems they create themselves. Losing weight might be hard, but people do it every day. "If you're too fat, just lose the weight. What's the big deal? It's stupid to complain about it and useless to put the blame somewhere else."

Inexcusable

You resent the unfairness of the situation. Fat people deserve the problems that go along with being fat because they created them. They don't deserve special accommodations and advantages. "It drives me crazy when I see a fat guy getting out of a car with a handicapped placard. There's no excuse for being that size. Stuffing your face and being lazy is not a handicap." Unlike *avoidable, inexcusable* reaches beyond the particular fat person and his situation. There's a sense of unfairness, indignation, or incursion into the realm of "normal" people.

Despicable

You feel angry and see no reason to tolerate fat people and the problems they create. Not only is it intolerable that the fat person is perpetrating his obesity in his own life, but he is also actively foisting it on the world in general, making people like you the victims of his obesity as well. As with *inexcusable,* the problem is greater than the obese person himself. However, *despicable* rises to the level of immorality or criminality. For example, it may be inexcusable that Jane had to sit next to that sweaty fat man for five hours on the flight from New York. But it's despicable that thin folks have to cater to fat people because fat people think it's their right to inconvenience and disgust everyone else in the world.

Moreover, someone who sees obesity as *tragic* seeks to save the fat person from himself. Someone who sees obesity as *despicable* seeks to save society from the fat person: "If I weighed 700 pounds, I would shoot myself. It'd be a faster form of suicide and less of a burden on my family. Don't even get me started on the health care costs those people eat up!"

TRY THIS AT HOME

Take a look at the judgment spectrum.

Where do you fall? Try framing it this way: "I saw this really fat guy struggling to make it up the stairs. It's really _____ to see something like that." Be honest and see which of the judgment adjectives you'd use to finish the phrase.

When we looked at the extremes of affinity, we found that the farther away we got from center, the more the focus was on ourselves instead of the person standing before us. Now with judgment, we see that the extremes of *tragic* and *despicable* again show a shift away from the person before us and toward a moral imperative. To encounter the tragic is to wrest good from the clutches of evil. To encounter the despicable is to save society from the monster. Similarly, if we ourselves are fat and

2: You Don't Know Fat

operate at these extremes, we cast the bystander in the role of savior or oppressor, regardless of his true intent. This is, incidentally, how many fat people end up in bad relationships or no relationship. I've seen chubs come to a social event and be swept away by the first guy who paid them a compliment. I've seen it happen to BBWs at straight events and BHMs online. Suddenly the chaser has become their savior instead of just a nice person capable of an intimate encounter. Conversely, I've seen chubs or BBWs disparage the innocent compliment of a nice guy. They cast him in the role of an oppressor because an attraction to fat renders him despicable.

We may have strong feelings and judgments about obesity, however in the end they are only strongly held opinions. They are not facts. Our opinions are no more true about people—even about ourselves—than our opinion about broccoli is true of broccoli. If we distinguish these views about ourselves or others as simply opinions that we happen to have, then we needn't let them interfere with our relationships and our love for people.

Crossing the Streams

Let's look at combining these two spectrums, affinity and judgment, one over the other in a graph, and call it our Fat Map, a description of the terrain of the Round World. As I said, I could have chosen other dimensions, but these two axes allow us to see where we stand across a broad range of opinions and feelings. In particular, the Fat Map is an excellent way to see the inner conflict that so many of us have about Fat, whether we live in the Round World or not.

As you read the statements in the Fat Map, you'll probably see some things you've never heard—and can't imagine hearing. Trust me, people really do say these things. They just have the good taste not to say them around you. Some people even believe one or more of these things about themselves.

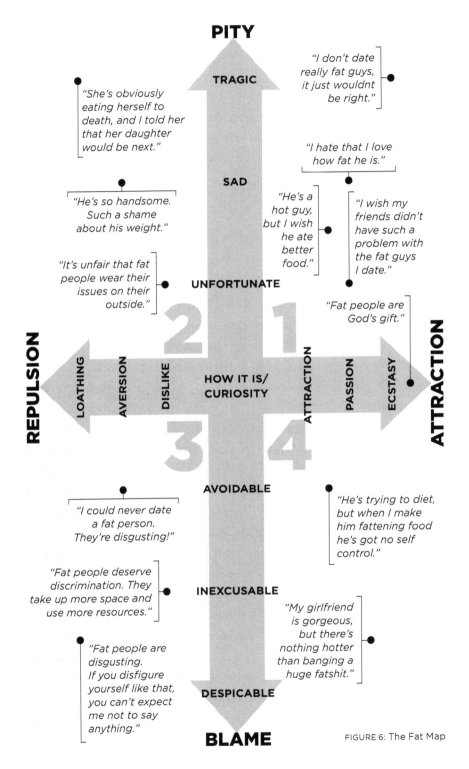

"She's obviously eating herself to death, and I told her that her daughter would be next."

"I don't date really fat guys, it just wouldnt be right."

"He's so handsome. Such a shame about his weight."

"I hate that I love how fat he is."

"He's a hot guy, but I wish he ate better food."

"I wish my friends didn't have such a problem with the fat guys I date."

"It's unfair that fat people wear their issues on their outside."

"Fat people are God's gift."

PITY

TRAGIC

SAD

UNFORTUNATE

2   1

REPULSION   **ATTRACTION**

LOATHING   AVERSION   DISLIKE   HOW IT IS/ CURIOSITY   ATTRACTION   PASSION   ECSTASY

3   4

AVOIDABLE

INEXCUSABLE

DESPICABLE

BLAME

"I could never date a fat person. They're disgusting!"

"He's trying to diet, but when I make him fattening food he's got no self control."

"Fat people deserve discrimination. They take up more space and use more resources."

"My girlfriend is gorgeous, but there's nothing hotter than banging a huge fatshit."

"Fat people are disgusting. If you disfigure yourself like that, you can't expect me not to say anything."

FIGURE 6: The Fat Map

The quotes on the graph are all statements I've heard people make. However, what's more important are the values that generate these statements. It's also important to note that the axes operate independently. We can see this in a story told by my friend Phil.

Phil had just finished eating at Taco Bell and was getting into his car to leave when a man started running toward him. The stranger was waving a paper and yelling, "Please read this! Please!" He managed to shove the paper through the car window, even as Phil tried to close it and drive out of the parking lot. Once he had gotten a safe distance, Phil read the note. It turned out that the man had written what Phil described as an essay in pencil on the back of a paper place mat. He wrote that he cared about Phil and that no one around Phil would have the courage to tell him the truth. The good Samaritan went on to explain how tragic it was to see Phil in his obese condition, and how Phil was going to eat himself to death unless he changed his ways.

This is a useful example because the man clearly has no malicious intent. He genuinely feels that he is doing good in the world by helping Phil wake up and do something about his obesity. He is moved to action for Phil's betterment. The more subtle aspect of this example is that while it's very clear that the man has a high degree of pity for Phil, we have no way of knowing what his affinity is for Phil's obesity. He might think obesity is the most disgusting thing on the planet. On the other hand, he might think Phil is beautiful, but feel wracked with guilt over his intense pleasure at seeing someone so obese. Perhaps his aggressively delivered note was a sort of personal atonement for the guilt he feels for his attraction. The point is that these two scales operate independently of each other, which is why they're so useful.

Pushed to the Extremes

If we follow a diagonal line out from the crosshairs of the graph into each of the four quadrants, the graph starts to describe some very interesting feelings and even behaviors. It's important to remember that I'm talking about turning up the dials, so to speak, on each of the two axes. Many people's thoughts and feelings about obesity are not extreme. Nevertheless, many of us suffer from these extremes, whether they are inflicted on us by others or we inflict them upon ourselves.

Quadrant 1: Tragic Ecstasy

At the extreme diagonal of Quadrant 1, you can find the tortured fat admirer who makes it his business to help the obese. An illustration of this would be a social worker I know. He loves huge fat men, but that conflicts with his identity as a social worker, which dictates that he should help people better themselves and get lean. He experiences a deep conflict over these two aspects of himself: his sex drive and his identity. He's tried to adjust his libido to favor guys who are less obese. It works intellectually, but it doesn't stop him from seeking out the very obese for sex. Inevitably, however, he ends up cajoling them into losing weight. You might say, "Well, maybe he just likes medium-sized fat guys. Maybe that's his taste and he's not conflicted at all." But if that were the case, why date a huge fat guy in the first place? Why does the need to save the fat man seem to go hand in hand with falling in love with him?

In addition, I've talked to many fat guys who have spent an amazing night of sex, every pound and drooping fold worshipped by a hot chaser. Then in the morning at the breakfast table over pancakes, bacon, and eggs, the chub hears, "You know, you really shouldn't eat that." That may seem a kindness, but from the perspective of many chubs, it's an ambush. He just spent a night being wooed with compliments by a man who reveled in his obesity. But in the morning the same guy implies that the chub's too fat and gives him diet tips. As we'll see later, this confusing or even hurtful behavior often comes from chasers feeling guilt or shame about their desires. The conflict can be quite debilitating for some.

Quadrant 2: Tragic Loathing

I suspect most people find themselves somewhere in this second quadrant, though perhaps not at its extreme. It is common to have some degree of compassion for the obese yet also a feeling that obesity is undesirable. This attitude is rarely challenged or distinguished as prejudice. When people feel the two polarities more strongly, they sometimes pursue careers as dietitians, personal trainers, or bariatric physicians. However, as we push further out to the extremes, we find citizen crusaders who are out to save the obese at any cost. Diet evangelists (and perhaps Phil's ardent Taco Bell savior) would be good examples of this quadrant in its extreme: Save the poor monster.

Quadrant 3: Despicable Loathing

In this quadrant live the people who are disgusted by Fat and who place the blame for obesity squarely on the shoulders of the obese. At low levels, this usually comes across as annoyance or even antipathy toward fat people as a category. However, when blame and repulsion escalate, things can get ugly. Pushed to the extreme, this combination can lead to a great deal of emotional pain and even physical violence. We see this drama played out in both real life and movies. Think of the teacher who says, "Hey, Jellybelly! Stop squirming in line." A flippant remark then becomes an authorized insult for any child in the class looking to inflict a little cruelty. Think of Piggy in *Lord of the Flies,* who is so dehumanized by his peers that he dies without anyone knowing his real name. He's the only character in the book without a name—just Piggy.

Quadrant 4: Despicable Ecstasy

Now we're back on the attraction side of the graph, where we see another pitfall for the chubby chaser who operates at the extremes. As we move further out on the diagonal of this quadrant, we find chasers who are blinded by their attraction yet resentful of it too. In these instances, chasers feel ashamed of their attraction to Fat and sometimes experience a good deal of self-loathing because of it. The chaser simultaneously blames the fat person for being attractive and him or herself for finding the fat person attractive. That blame turned inward is experienced as guilt.

In my seminars, many fat people find it surprising that chubby chasers experience guilt or shame; after all, these are the people whom society supposedly finds desirable. However, as we see over and over again in the Round World, the stigma of Fat affects both fat people and their admirers, though in different ways. In many cases, feelings of guilt and shame may be compounded if the chaser has another characteristic that he believes to be a handicap, such as being short, nonwhite, disabled, or gay. One gay chubby chaser summed up this feeling of being double-whammied quite well when he said, "I feel like, 'God, if you had to make me a faggot, why did you have to make me a faggot who loves fat guys?'"

I think the insensitivity, or even contempt, of these chasers toward chubs or BBWs stems from two sources: First, when a chaser sees obesity as a problem in need of blame, then they see everyone in the Round World as flawed and sharing the blame—including themselves. As one chaser said to me, "Look, fat guys are a really hot fuck. If they don't like it, they can just lose weight." In this example, it's easy to hear the victim being blamed for being fat; what's harder to hear is the chaser's admission of thoughtlessness and the blame he puts on himself for wanting someone fat. In talking further to this chaser, I found that "they can just lose weight" really meant, "A fat guy has a choice about his body, but I don't have a choice about my attraction to it." A chaser who lives deep in this quadrant adopts the strategy of distancing himself from his own feelings as well as from his partner's. Unfortunately this often leads the chaser at the extreme of Quadrant 4 to use fat partners for sexual gratification, avoiding any intimacy that might force him to confront his true nature. This chaser often feels like a victim of the stigma of obesity who dates only other victims.

Square Dance:
Meeting Folks from Other Quadrants

Another way to use the quadrants is to see how groups of people see themselves and each other. Certain antipathies and resentments result from crossing over from blame into pity or from repulsion into attraction. For example, if you're having trouble finding yourself in one of these quadrants, you might look at the quadrant that you most despise.

You're probably diagonally across the Fat Map from those people. Let's take a closer look at this.

Diametrically Opposed

If you land in Quadrant 1 (Pity and Attraction), then the person you'll least enjoy in a conversation about Fat is a person from Quadrant 3 (Repulsion and Blame). The Q1 person will probably find the Q3 person to be a heartless bigot. My friend Sally told her chaser boyfriend about a boy in grade school who would tease her about being fat and call her names. Sally was long over it, but her boyfriend was very Q1, and the story about a guy from Q3 made his blood boil. Sally said he was upset the rest of the day. Reversing the line, Q3 thinks Q1 is a sick sexual deviant. Again, this will be more or less true, depending on how far out on the diagonals the two find each other.

Across the other diagonal, two people will have a different antipathy. A Q2 (Pity and Repulsion) might think that Q4 (Attraction and Blame) is manipulative and mercenary. A Q2 might see a Q4 more of a hindrance than a help to the poor chub who deserves to be helped or even saved. For example, a guy once told me, "Chasers are just bad news. They give fat people false hope and keep them from losing weight just to satisfy their own sick fetish." On the other hand, Q4 generally thinks that Q2 is a bleeding heart who should mind his own business and stop trying to save people who don't need saving.

From Above & Below

People on the top of the Fat Map (Pity) often think the people directly under them on the map give them a bad name. The guilt-ridden Q1s (Pity and Attraction) find themselves apologizing for the insensitivity of their Q4

(Blame and Attraction) brethren and rue being mistaken for them. In a similar way, the Q2s (Pity and Repulsion) abhor the bigotry and downright meanness of Q3 (Blame and Repulsion). Q3s smear Q2's good intentions, casting doubt and suspicion on their sincere desire to help. For this reason, Q2s often take extra pains not to be perceived as diet thugs or bullies. An example of this is the mom who doesn't want to broach the subject of weight loss to her daughter for fear that the mom will seem like a Q3. The mother believes her daughter's obesity is a negative and worrisome trait. However, she's hesitant to bring it up, fearing it would alienate the daughter and lower her self-esteem. She doesn't want to be seen as a Q3, as a shrew who constantly nags her daughter about her weight and makes her feel inadequate.

But there are two sides to every story. The people from the blame side of the Fat Map have a bone to pick with the sanctimonious folks on top. I've talked to many Q3s who don't understand why there's all this coddling of the obese by Q2s. Overeating is a simple problem, they say. It doesn't require a complex solution. On the right side of the Fat Map, Q4 doesn't see why Q1s are so knotted up with guilt. They may seem insensitive about the stigma of obesity: "If a fat guy can't enjoy a good fuck with a hot girl because of his size, he's just missing out." Here's another version: "A fat girl who can't enjoy her size is just a downer. Who wants to get with that?"

Of course, these are huge generalizations, but that's appropriate since I'm talking about categories of extremes. As we've seen, feelings and judgments at the extreme are not about the person in front of us. Ultimately, they're about our own feelings and judgments about Fat.

The Lay of the Land

It may seem that all the quadrants are negative and that this map of the Round World portrays an unhappy place. That's not the case at all; people in the Round World are no more unhappy than those anywhere else. But when these qualities of attraction, repulsion, blame and pity are pushed to extremes, extreme things happen. Thankfully, most of us don't dwell at the extremes of the Round World. Most folks are not fat-bigots, and most chasers aren't abusive or self-loathing. Nevertheless you probably know someone who might show up at a different point on the Fat Map than you do. Maybe they live in the same house with you, but they're miles away on the Fat Map.

A person in one of my seminars asked me, "But where am I supposed to be on the Fat Map? Where's the balance? What's healthy?" Well, the Fat Map is just a way to appreciate the landscape of our differences. There's no good or bad place to locate yourself unless you feel you should be someplace else. I suppose if we asked your dog what he thought about fat people, your dog's opinion would probably register right at the cross-hairs: He doesn't love fat, doesn't hate it, and doesn't see any blame or pity for something that's not an issue in the first place. I suspect a lot of people would like to occupy this position. If you find that you have a high degree of curiosity and a low level of judgment about things, then perhaps you're near the crosshairs of the Fat Map. But if we get honest with ourselves, this is probably not where we really are—at least not all the time. If you don't believe me, just think about some documentary you saw about an 800-pound bedridden man who hasn't left his house in years. Still feel neutral? Or what about the enormously fat family you might have seen at the mall recently, hundreds and hundreds of pounds of them, all enjoying their ice cream—the little girl lifting the cone piled high to her chubby cheeks. I would guess that you and your dog do not have the same neutral view of these situations.

It's easy to be neutral about things we're comfortable with. However, the more extreme the situation, the further into your quadrant you'll find yourself pushed. But if you do find yourself deep into a quadrant, don't worry. I don't think there's anything wrong with having hard-and-fast beliefs—or even prejudices—as long as they're recognized as such. That is, as long as you don't mistake your point of view for the only valid point of view—for The Truth. I don't think human beings can ever cure themselves of prejudice. Maybe the best we can do is be aware of our beliefs and prejudices and stop ourselves before we inflict them on the world, before they foul our relationships and make our world into a place we don't want to live.

NOW BOARDING FOR THE ROUND WORLD!

I hope by now you've thought a lot about your opinion of Fat. If nothing else, I hope you've begun to fully appreciate just how vast the universe of opinion is. In the next section, I'd like to take you into the worldviews of chasers (male, female, gay, and straight) and explain what makes us tick. As you can imagine, even among those of us who think fat is sexy and beautiful, there is still a wide range of exactly what that means. Nevertheless, over the years, I've been able to distill some common elements and basic views that help explain how something so reviled can be seen as so beautiful—how something taboo can actually become sacred.

3

Love & Sex
in a Big Fat World

*There is no excellent beauty
that hath not some strangeness
in the proportion.*

—Francis Bacon
from his essay "Of Beauty"
first published in 1612

THE ROUND WORLD

I'm still sitting in that über-fashionable West Hollywood gay bar from back in Section 1, waiting for a hot guy to walk in…my kind of hot guy. It's a long wait since trim or muscular men are the frequenters of my neighborhood bars. There is more variation in body types than you might think, but not quite as wide a variation as I might like, if you catch my drift. But at last a huge, handsome guy lumbers in. He's in the company of several conventionally beautiful guys sporting designer clothes and meticulous hairstyles, and ensconced in their bubble of intoxicated chatter. After scoping the room and assailing the bar, they eventually settle in a clump around a small, high table near the back of the bar, since most other perches are taken. Like most gay men, they begin cruising the room while keeping up their conversation, scanning the clientele to see who's hot, who's not, and what opportunities might be had.

From across the room, I am transfixed by this fat guy. He is beautiful. He's not even very fat, but it doesn't take much extra weight to stand out and impress me in this desert of svelte fashionistas. I stare. I'm staring a hole in this cute chubby guy, who's facing only slightly away from me. I'm spotted by his friend, and he begins to cruise me. I'm spotted by the guy next to the friend, who glances between me and the first friend. Like a herd at a watering hole sensing a ripple of excitement in the air, the whole table is now furtively checking me out—smiling, exchanging banter, then glancing again at me across the bar. I seem to have captured the attention of the entire table except for the fat guy that I'm actually trying to make eye contact with. He is looking at everything else in the bar but me.

Any creature knows when it's being watched. If I had been cruising one of his friends, I have no doubt that the chubby guy would have looked my way. But it is almost axiomatic that if I'm interested in a hot fat guy, he will not make eye contact. He will not cruise me back. And if I go up and introduce myself and attempt to make conversation, he will usually stamp out any possibility of flirtation. I will find out later through mutual friends that the guy was unaware of my interest, or that he didn't know what to do, so he did nothing. That's frustrating for me. Almost all human interaction begins with eye contact, whether it's asking a question in class, joining a group conversation, or assessing romantic interest in a potential partner. Nothing can begin until I have the attention of the other person, which typically starts from across the room by making eye contact.

My friend Cliff and I were on our way to a Halloween party where there would be a lot of chubs and chasers. I was whining about how difficult it is to approach a chub, about how he often won't even look at me. Cliff seemed amused but not convinced of my dating obstacles. He's a good friend of mine and a chub. (Incidentally, he's the one who came up with "the round world" as a term to describe our community). Cliff thought perhaps I was overly aggressive in my approach. I said that I failed to see how eye contact was overly aggressive, but I was willing to get some feedback on the matter. When we got to the party, he watched in disbelief as several chubs in a small room actually turned toward the wall or became focused on their shoes, rather than make eye contact with me when I was near them. If I tried to make conversation, they would look past me, or only glance at me in passing. Cliff said it was really eye-opening to see.

Now, chasers don't necessarily experience what I've just described all the time. In fact, many are just as shy about making eye contact and avoid the glances of men or women they're attracted to. I represent an extreme; I'm in-shape, very muscular, and rather direct. I understand that I probably resemble the jock who made fun of the fat kid in high school. In addition, it is not lost on me that a fundamental reason that I am invited to appear on talk shows, reality shows, and speak at conferences is that I look like the guy least likely to drool over a fat guy. I think a lot of men I approach just don't believe that my attraction to them is real—not that I'm trying to trick them, necessarily, but just that it seems beyond the realm of possibility. Alternately, if my attraction does seem genuine, they think perhaps I'll ignore them after I get what I want. This is often the concern of many BBWs (Big Beautiful Women) I've talked to: They're afraid the guy's a creep, a player, or just playing a really cruel joke. Fat men, gay and straight, talk about this too.

As I say, this is seldom a man/woman issue. The Round World is about Fat much more than gender. A flood of positive attention can be hard to trust, especially if you're not used to it or you've spent your life hiding from *any* attention. But the natural consequence of having such a dating policy is that it excludes anyone who's interested in you. So then you're available only for everyone who's not, saying things like, "Where are the men who like guys/girls like me?" "Where are all these chubby chasers you talk about?" "Why can't someone like me for me?"

I mention my dating experience not because it is typical, but because it sheds light on the primary difference between how the regular world and the Round World spin. In the regular world, Fat is the opposite of sex. In the Round World, Fat is synonymous with sex. That's one thing to read, but it's another thing to experience. Trust me, for fat people and their admirers alike, it's a mind fuck.

Even if you don't believe that Fat is the opposite of sex, this axiom nevertheless pervades the regular world. It's almost like gravity; it operates whether you believe in it or not. So in the Round World, there's often a lot of angst, bitterness, and inexperience when it comes to sexuality—for fat people as well as chasers. The social norms that many people take for granted—dating, clubbing, hooking up—are often unknown or even resented by people in the Round World. Overt sexuality may make us uncomfortable, so we make it wrong. We say things like, "I don't want to be a slut." Or we just exclude ourselves: "It's just not for me." I had a 19-year-old gay chub tell me that he didn't want to meet guys he'd contacted on the internet because he "didn't want to turn into a slut." I told him, "I'm not sure there is such a thing as being a slut, but I don't think you can be one by enjoying sex with guys you like." I suggested to him instead that "Maybe being a slut isn't having sex whenever you want. Maybe it's having sex when you don't want."

We see again that a concern that we typically associate with women—virginity, slut-shaming—is very much a concern for men, both gay and straight, in the Round World as well. Chasers who pursue women particularly fear being labeled "a player." They're quite concerned that their love of fat women will seem like they love *any* fat woman. In contrast, gay male chasers often feel alienated from the gay world's hyper-focus on sex, all the more because it idolizes men whom chasers don't find attractive while disparaging those we do.

Nevertheless, there are men and women in the Round World who know how to have a good time and who actively seek partnership in all its many forms: platonic, romantic, or sexual. I learned long ago that my type of guy was not likely to show up at my local gay bar, or even in my neighborhood. So I took to the internet, where I redefined *local* as any place I can get to.

Putting the *Wide* in the World Wide Web

Whether eagerly or reluctantly, fat people and their admirers eventually find each other and connect as a community. There are half a dozen major websites for people seeking to date a straight fat man or woman (BHM or BBW). There are two or three main sites for gay fat men and their admirers, and their memberships are vast in numbers. Bears constitute a somewhat separate community, although there is considerable overlap, and about four main sites cater exclusively to them. If you're looking to connect, a quick Google search using the key words *chub, chaser, BBW, BHM,* or *bear*—plus the word *dating*—will set you on your way.

Contrary to popular belief, fat people do not represent some glut of unsalable merchandise, and chasers are not some bargain-hunting junkmen willing to take up the slack. Unfortunately, this is sometimes how the rest of the world sees us; occasionally it's even how we see ourselves. For example, some chubs and chasers resist or even resent having to use a website that caters to fat people and their admirers. It's similar to feeling bad about having to shop at a big-and-tall or plus-size store because you can't buy clothes where the so-called normal people shop. As for me, I'm very happy to have been a paying member of several of these sites for decades. (You can join any of them for free; paying gives you access to more services.)

I first started exploring my sexuality—not being gay, but liking Fat—through chat rooms, online profiles, and instant messaging. But eventually the online world wasn't enough. Eventually I had to make it real. I wanted to go to a chub/chaser event. Now, keep in mind that back then I was not experienced. I'd had slightly more sexual partners than I'd had relationships, and both could be counted on one hand. I never went to gay bars or clubs; I didn't drink, didn't smoke. I didn't even dance. I had no idea how to be sexy or what to say to a guy that wouldn't bore me or alienate him. All that was about to change, however.

Events Around the Round World

You might be familiar with the world of gay circuit parties, annual parties held on particular weekends in specific cities across the United States and abroad. They attract the hottest A-gays from all over the world. They're referred to as circuit parties because if you attended them all, you would make a yearly circuit around the globe: the Winter Party in Miami, the Black Party in March in New York City, the

The internet says I'm beautiful, but the internet lives in Tunisia, Siberia, Bahrain, Biscayne, Picayune, Rangoon, Saskatoon...

White Party in April in Palm Springs, and Southern Decadence in September in New Orleans. These are just the major ones; there many others in North America, Australia, and Europe as well.

Although this isn't nearly as well known, the chub/chaser community has its own series of events. Some of the longest-running are Chub-Fest in the spring, MCA in the summer, Convergence over Labor Day Weekend, and Big Men's Weekend in the fall. On the straight side of the Round World, even more events are organized as monthly dances, annual week-long retreats, or occasional weekend sex parties. There's something for everyone's comfort level. Many chubs and chasers also attend bear events, and there are a a few gainer/encourager events that usually fly under most people's radar.

3: Love & Sex in a Big Fat World

The ratio of fat attendees to admirers varies by event, but it's safe to say that in America, the BBWs and chubs outnumber the chasers. However, the reverse is true in Europe. A typical ratio at Convergence might be five chubs to three chasers, but I don't mean to suggest that two of five chubs aren't getting laid. Not at all. It can just as easily be a chaser who doesn't get laid, lacking either the charm or self-confidence to attract the attention of a chub. Many people assume that this unequal ratio means that there are fewer chasers than fat people in the world, but I doubt this is the case. In my experience, this apparent shortage of chubby chasers derives from the fact that many chasers are closeted and don't have a presence in the Round World. They simply don't get counted, so it looks like there are fewer.

I speak about Fat and sexuality at gay and straight events alike. I find the gay and straight events remarkably similar, except that all the participants are men at the gay events. At the straight events, the women tend to be fat and the men tend to be thin. That's what leads to so much confusion when it comes to understanding straight relationships in the Round World. When straight people think about a fat/admirer couple, they usually imagine the woman as the fat one. So most problems are framed as problems that women are having with men. I have to remind them that I hear the same challenges and frustrations voiced by both fat and thin people at same-sex events. Female chubby chasers do exist and do attend the straight events, but their numbers are small. I don't think it's because there's a lack of female chubby chasers. Rather, I think it's because women don't need a special venue to solicit the attention of a fat guy.

Exploring Yourself Through Community

I've been to dozens of these events over the years, and people often ask me what to expect if they go. Convergence is certainly the largest gay event in the Round World, drawing up to 600 chubs and chasers from all over the world. Fewer people attend straight events, but that's probably because there are more straight events around the calendar and around the world.

I ardently encourage men and women to go to these events. The three principal objections I get are time, money, and sex. Time and money are valid concerns, but I often find that they are just ways of disguising a concern about sex or intimacy. "I don't have time for something like that" often means "I don't waste my time looking for sex." Similarly, "I don't have the money for something like that" often means "I'm not going to spend money just to go and have sex." Indeed, most people imagine that the event is all about sex, and some people cast their objection in strong absolutes: "I won't go to an event that's all about sex." And there's the opposite camp: "I have enough friends. I don't want to spend all that money if there's no guarantee I'll get laid!"

So why go? I tell people that these events are what you make of them. No one needs to go to an event just to get laid. Sex is just part of what's on offer. The main reason to go, I believe, is for community and camaraderie. A-gays don't go to a circuit party to get laid. They're already the hottest guys in their town; they can get laid anytime they want. They go to be with their tribe. And for fat people and their admirers, it's about being in a place where being obese or liking obesity is not just normal, it's sexy. The experience is incredibly empowering for fat and thin alike—perhaps even more so for people who face the stigma of being gay as well as Fat. As one reveler told me, "I'm a 400-pound gay man working as a vice principal in a small, Midwestern school. Coming to this event is the one weekend a year when I get to feel normal and be myself."

Perhaps even more importantly, being with your tribe, finding your community, helps you figure out who you are and who you want to be. That's certainly been the case for me and the hundreds of people I've talked to.

My First Time

Convergences are held every year, and local chub/chaser clubs around the country vie to host these events. I remember my very first chub/chaser event: Convergence 1998 in Reno, Nevada. The event was on a scale I had never experienced before. I think it still ranks as one of the best-attended Convergences on record, packed with over 800 chubs and chasers from all over the world.

I drove up with friends from San Francisco, where I was living at the time with my boyfriend, Marc, a beautiful and successful A-gay. Since finding out my proclivities, Marc and I had mutually agreed that sleeping with other people was a great compromise that served us both. For Marc's part, he was amused that there was such an event at all, and I think it tickled him that, for once, I was going to be the promiscuous one.

Arriving at the event was an experience in itself. A-gay circuit parties might feature a host hotel, but people stay all over the city in whatever sort of lodging suits their taste and budget. The dance party and the events before and after are the attraction. However, at a Convergence, the meeting—the convergence of chubs and chasers—is the main attraction. Getting everyone in the same hotel creates the optimal experience, so the organizers tend to go for affordability over glitz, ensuring that as many people as possible can afford to attend. I walked into the lobby and was stunned by the vast number of fat men who had already arrived and were casually ambling through the lobby, on their way to the pool or the casino or some nearby attraction. I was nervous and excited. It was like going to my first gay event all over again.

At that Reno Convergence, I met Vince, a soft-spoken superchub with kind eyes and an easy smile. I'll admit that I was mesmerized by how Vince could walk straight into the swimming pool and the water would buoy him when it reached his shoulders. He could float without the slightest exertion for hours in that standing position. That was the day I learned the paradox of a 450-pound man weighing less than I do when we're immersed in water. Since then, I've often used this irony of physics to enhance the romance and love-making with such beautiful men. The texture and behavior of hundreds of pounds of blubber is quite different when gravity is overruled by buoyancy.

Vince and I have remained friends since that day so many years ago, and I've kept in touch with many friends from events over the years. Vince taught me a lot about myself and my desires. Remember, I had a beautiful, thin boyfriend at the time and no experience being with a superchub. It wasn't just that I wondered what the sex would be like if I had my heart's desire. I also wondered what my life would be like with someone Vince's size as a partner. I wondered if the things I would lose would balance the things I would gain. At the risk of offending some fat people, I think it's important to take a look at what the tradeoffs are, at least in the mind of an inexperienced chaser. As I've said before, just as it takes moxie and gumption to live a full life weighing 500 pounds, so too it takes some special qualities to be the partner of that person. Unfortunately, not every chaser who loves supersized men or women is up for the challenge. I needed to find out if I had what it takes.

The Right Stuff

Vince and I kept in touch after the event in Reno, and many months later he invited me to spend a weekend with him at his house near New Orleans. Vince always enjoyed his size, or—perhaps more accurately—he enjoyed the fact that his size could reduce hot studs to stuttering, adolescent fools. We spent a wonderful few days in the Big Easy, as well as some great times with his friends back in his hometown.

A lot of chasers ask me, "What's the biggest guy you've ever been with?" or "What's it like being with someone over 500 pounds?" Their curiosity is really more sexual titillation, but somewhere in us chasers we harbor a desire to live out a life with such a man or woman. (Some even desire to become that size.) At some point, fantasy and sexual titillation give way to the reality of having such a person as one's partner. I didn't realize it then, but my visit with Vince was an experiment to see what it would be like to live with the day-to-day challenges and delights of having a quarter-ton boyfriend.

What I learned was not what I expected. I thought I would experience a series of pros and cons—burdens and titillations—which I could neatly tot up to produce a mathematical proof of my desires and what I wanted. I've already talked about the pros—the incredible beauty that men like me find in the body of a man like Vince. And some of us, though not all, find greater beauty in even greater obesity. But that's just desire. What about the rest of life? What about the cons?

For example, life with a superchub moves slower, not because he's lazy, but because things just take longer. Showering takes longer because there's more to wash, rinse, and dry. Dressing takes longer, especially when applying talc or antibiotic ointments to soothe the airless creases of his great folds. He may be perfectly capable of putting on his own shoes and socks, or he may not. Either way, there's no denying that assistance would make the process faster or easier. If something is forgotten in the bedroom, he won't be the one dashing back to get it. Dropping him off and parking is faster and more convenient than having him to walk from the parked car to the entrance. The wait at a restaurant is longer if there are no tables available and your date doesn't fit in a booth. If the restaurant has two floors, the stairs are quicker for me but exhausting for him, so I'll ask the host if there's an elevator. (In America, there almost always is; in Europe, there almost never is.) The walk to that table is slower and maybe more circuitous since his girth is no doubt many times bigger than the slim host's. The considerate chaser allows his supersized partner to lead, or cuts a path that his date can follow rather than unthinkingly following the host. And this is what's involved just in going out to eat one Saturday night. Imagine days of this. Imagine a life of this. It's actually a life many wish for.

So here's what I learned from Vince: First, the so-called burdens described above seem like burdens only when I think I should be doing something else or that we should be moving faster. For example, rubbing lotion in the folds of a very fat man is erotic to me, unless I'm focused on the fact that we're late for a reservation. It's erotic like giving a massage, unless it occurs to me that it's wrong of my partner's body to need me that way or for me to be catering to this need. Taking 30 minutes to help him shower and dress is an act of love, unless I believe that 30 minutes is intolerable because my time should be better spent. I learned that, for me, life with a superchub is actually very erotic—all of that life. Life seems burdensome only when I see my partner's size as shameful, wrong, or interfering with how life should be. It can also be a drag if my beautiful obese partner makes himself wrong for the body he has. I don't mean to sugarcoat this. Some fat people have serious long-term or recurring health issues such as diabetes, lymphedema, cellulitis, or gout. Of course, so do many thin people. The difference is that thin people don't usually get blamed for their health problems.

Shame and Blame

Some fat people find it humiliating that they can't do some of the simple things that thin people take for granted, such as those I mentioned above. Actually, some chasers share that feeling of humiliation about being with a supersized partner. What's more, they sometimes experience guilt for feeling sexually attracted to someone who is fat and might have such difficulties. To be clear, chasers are not attracted to these difficulties per se; we're attracted to the person and the body of that person. The difficulties are incidental, as they would be in any relationship.

An apt comparison might be a straight guy who enjoys the fact that his girlfriend has to special order her bras because she needs a large cup size. He doesn't enjoy her difficulty; he enjoys the reason for the difficulty. If her enormous breasts give her back pain, he doesn't enjoy that she's in pain. However, he might be highly attentive to her backaches with massages or making dinner so she can be off her feet, or whatever he can do to make her more comfortable. If she loves her huge breasts, his attention seems erotic. If she's indifferent to the size of her breasts, his ministrations seem like an accommodation: "If I have to be like this, then he has to do that." If she actively dislikes her breasts or their size, then her boyfriend's attentions might seem creepy or fetishistic. He'll never be allowed to appreciate them sexually.

The slow waddle or big-bellied swagger of a chub isn't hot because the chub is hobbled by his weight. It's hot because that sensuous rhythm points to our source of eroticism and becomes emblematic of it. Many people, not just chasers, sometimes find it difficult to separate lust from love. In some chasers, however, lust and love are at odds. We want the best for our fat partner. We want him or her to be happy and healthy, but that noble desire might seem to play havoc with the fact that we are wired to appreciate obesity. Nevertheless, it is a part of our sexuality as strong as (or for some, stronger than) our sexual orientation toward men or women. It is our sexuality.

> **Y**our task is not to seek for love, but merely to seek and find all the barriers within yourself that you have built against it.
>
> —**Professor Helen Schucman**
> clinical and research psychologist at Columbia
> University and author of *A Course in Miracles*

Many people, including some chasers, think our sexuality makes us freaks. Well, how could that be unless fat people are freaks? How could an attraction to obesity be wrong unless obesity itself were wrong? Some chasers are quick to point out that "Hey, I don't like fat chicks, just ones who are thick, curvy, [or some other euphemism]." Usually these men and women are shocked to find out that their ideal man or woman carries about 50 or so pounds of fat. Well, that's clinically obese. If a chaser is uncomfortable with *fat*, it only proves what I said back in "You Don't Know Fat" about how we determine who is fat and why.

Some chasers avoid using the words *fat* or *obese* because it makes them feel like freaks for liking such a thing. They sometimes claim that fat people don't like it, but in my experience fat people are the most willing to use the word *fat* and chasers are the least willing. Some gay male chasers try to normalize their attraction by claiming they like bears. They may indeed like bears, but a chaser likes fat bears. (Bears are not always fat, by the way.) Some chasers deliberately avoid being with fat or very fat people because they're afraid that they might enjoy it. Or they *know* they'd enjoy it, so they dare not risk indulging in that pleasure. What if they couldn't stop? Best not to start down that road, they think.

I think that's such a waste. When people hold back, both sides get cheated. We chasers represent the possibility of loving what the rest of the world considers unlovable. We celebrate as beauty what most people condemn as ugliness.

Passing for Normal

For most gay people, coming out of the closet is an important rite of passage. For some, it's easy; for some, it's hard; for some, it's shattering. Coming out is a transformation that takes us out of secrecy or self-ignorance and sets us on a course to self-awareness and hopefully even wisdom. Gay men and women know what it's like to come out, but gay people attracted to fat people have not one, but two closets from which to emerge. And coming out the second time, as a chaser, feels very similar to coming out as gay. In fact, gay chasers who've told their family and friends that they prefer obese men or women often say, "Oh my god, it felt exactly like when I came out as gay!" So for gays, coming out as a chaser is walking already trodden ground. However, if you're straight, you've probably never had to come out of a closet in your life. In fact, I emphasize with my seminar participants that a white guy attracted to fat women probably has nothing in his experience to prepare him for coming out as a chubby chaser. He has probably never had a conversation with friends or family confessing that he has only been pretending to be like them, that he is actually *other*. We gays at least get a practice run.

Just as some gay men choose to live their lives as if they were straight, some chasers (gay or straight) choose to live life as if they were attracted to thin people—in other words, as if they were just like the majority. In the black community, being culturally black but having skin light enough to be perceived as white is called passing. Chasers, too, can pass. We look like the rest of the population except for our unique proclivity for loving Fat. Being able to pass for a member of the majority makes life seem more comfortable. On the other hand, by passing ourselves off as "normal," we cut ourselves off from others. Pretending to be other than we are cheats us of intimacy and authenticity with those we love. Not only that, but staying in a self-imposed closet cheats us of the challenges and opportunities that would lead to fulfillment and self-discovery.

Fat people, however, have the opposite experience. If you're fat, everyone knows it. No fat teen has ever sat his parents down and said, "Mom, Dad, I can't keep this from you any longer: I'm fat." And if you've been fat since childhood, you probably have an effective way of dealing with the fact that you don't fit into a thin world. You might become the class clown, or the hyper-intellectual, or the good listener. None of these tactics is unique to fat people, of course—they are common ways of coping with the fact that other people often don't seem to accept one's worth at face value. Chasers, however, can pass. We don't develop social strategies for our desires because no one can see our secret. In fact, some of us don't look too carefully into who we are because we're afraid of what we might find. Most chasers are not eager to embrace this part of themselves. Nevertheless being a chaser is a hidden stigma that manifests itself in most social situations whether you're gay or straight.

John E. Panchankis, of the Yale School of Public Health, makes the point that people who can pass are not necessarily any more free than those who can't:

Many assume that individuals with a hidden stigma escape the difficulties faced by individuals with a visible stigma. However, recent research has shown that individuals with a concealable stigma also face considerable stressors and psychological challenges. The ambiguity of social situations combined with the threat of potential discovery makes possessing a concealable stigma a difficult predicament for many individuals.[1]

So even when we chasers know we're attracted to Fat, we often don't develop the skill to stand up to a world that thinks we're abnormal, sexually deviant, or just plain crazy. Instead we may develop strategies for concealing our attraction to Fat, perhaps even from ourselves. As any gay person knows, we can't come out to others until we've accepted ourselves. But even if we are secure in what we like, it's often just plain dangerous to come out and say we like Fat. In fact, the person we're dating probably wants to hear it least of anyone—no matter what his or her size. No, it's far safer to answer, if pressed, that we like people of all shapes and sizes. A chaser might even manage to convince himself of this.

And to be sure, most chasers have dated people in a wide range of body sizes. I certainly have. But as many people have said to guys, "Just because you've dated women, that doesn't make you straight." Chasers are often blind to what we find attractive, in part because we don't want to find out that we're attracted to Fat. We don't want it to be the yardstick of our attraction, the defining characteristics of our relationships. Consequently, many chasers refuse to consider it as legitimate attraction or even as relevant to their sexuality.

To the degree that chasers believe that Fat is a stigma, we believe that being attracted to Fat is a stigma. We often don't deal with our fears and insecurities around sex and intimacy because they're part of the taboo of Fat. So many of us gratefully ride the tide of normalcy. No one suspects that the good-looking quarterback secretly pines for the huge fat nerd in math class. No one suspects that the handsome real estate mogul is cheating on his gorgeous wife with a 350-pound ex-cop who smells of

---

[1] American Psychological Association. 2007. *Psychological Bulletin* 133, no. 2, 328–345.

cigars. No one notices that the cute, shy guy in the corner can't take his eyes off the slow, jostling rolls of a beautiful fat girl as she waddles past. Our desires are invisible. In many cases, we like it that way. We are cloaked in the illusion of normality.

Deep down, however, many happy-go-lucky chasers are dealing with the guilt and shame of Fat. The guilt of "How can I love something that is so fundamentally unhealthy?" The shame of "What kind of sicko gets a hard-on for rolls of fat?" The slings and arrows that society aims at fat people are the same artillery that many chasers fire at themselves.

Coming Out of the Fat Closet

I used to think that only chasers had to deal with coming out of the Fat closet, until a woman in one of my seminars in Germany showed me I was mistaken. I was speaking to a group of mostly straight, fat women in Berlin about chasers coming out of the closet, and she reminded me that fat people often have the same problem. Fat people aren't in the closet about being fat. Their closet is the silent taboo of being fat, the unspeakable stigma that must not be acknowledged. Many fat people are quite aware of their size and comfortable in their bodies. If the chair that's offered them in a restaurant has arms that are too confining, they simply say so and ask for one that will accommodate. To be in the closet about being fat is to pretend that the chair is fine and that there's no discomfort in having your hips and thighs in a vise. Being in the fat closet means being deeply and secretly wounded that the host asked you whether the chair was comfortable. Being closeted about fat means never hearing the word *fat* spoken in your presence because everyone around you knows that you would find it obscene.

Ultimately, coming out is not just a boon to the growth and development of the person coming out. It benefits his or her entire community. I was working on a play with a group of actors I had never worked with before. I don't make a big announcement about being attracted to fat guys, but dating and relationships come up naturally in conversation if you don't actively avoid it. If people see pictures of my past boyfriends, if they ask where I spent a holiday weekend, or if they hear that I've appeared on television, then my sexual tastes eventually surface in conversation. Most people become quite curious, and I consider the ensuing conversation to be outreach for the Round World.

Liz was one of the actors I was working with, and she became quite interested in how an in-shape guy could want to date fat men. She asked a lot of great questions, and we had some good discussions. A few weeks later, Liz came up to me at rehearsal and said, "Dan, I have to thank you. I noticed something I'd never noticed before." Liz lives a short walk from the beach, and she had spotted a couple of guys sitting in the sand being affectionate with each other. One of the guys was young and good-looking; the other was older and obese. "Before I met you," she said, "I would have always just assumed that the big guy was being taken advantage of: How sad that this young gigolo is preying on an older guy who is grateful for the attention. I had never considered the possibility that they could actually be mutually attracted to each other, that they could even be in love."

I get versions of this response a lot. I was working with a director who said that he wanted to do a production of *Romeo and Juliet* in which the young lovers were obese. He explained that when the audience saw the fat couple kissing on stage, that would prove that they shared real love—not just lust. Obviously, he reasoned, there couldn't be any possibility of lust for someone who was fat.

One last example: I remember introducing a professional acquaintance of mine to my boyfriend at the time, who was quite obese. I hadn't talked about my tastes in men, and when my boyfriend was out of earshot, the guy said to me, "Wow, I guess we never realize that even good-looking guys can have self-esteem issues." He had tacitly reasoned that since I was with a fat guy, I clearly had no idea that I was worth more and could do better.

What do these three stories have in common? They share the premise that Fat is the opposite of sex. The one precludes the other. So as chasers, we have a lot of rowing to do against the current. Moreover, since we are born into a culture that believes that Fat is the opposite of sex, we have to find some way of reconciling that on a personal level before we're ready to share it with friends, family, or the world at large. Yet I believe it is through coming out to friends and family as chasers that we will ultimately shift the conversation about Fat. By coming out about our attraction to and appreciation of Fat, we may someday come to see *fat* as simply a characteristic instead of a judgment.

Beyond Shame and Blame

I was leading one of my seminars on obesity and sexuality, and I asked if there was a chaser in the group who could talk a little bit about what it's like for him to be near a fat guy. This was a mixed crowd, mostly gay, mostly fat, but it included some chasers and straight women. Stuart raised his hand. He was a slight man in his mid-20s, very sweet and rather meek. He talked about one of his early experiences discovering his sexuality. He had spotted an incredibly attractive fat guy and was in awe. He watched the fat guy, relished how he moved, how he laughed with his friends, but Stuart didn't dare say anything to the man. He wasn't even sure the guy was gay. The fat man ambled away down the street, and Stuart felt compelled to follow him. He was drawn to the beauty of this man and couldn't bear to let him out of his sight. He followed the man for blocks, always remaining at a discreet distance so as not to be noticed. At this point in the story, a lot of the chubs in the seminar began to get uncomfortable. Stuart's story felt a touch creepy, so I intervened:

"Why didn't you go up to the man, Stuart?"

"What do you mean?"

"Why didn't you go up and introduce yourself to this guy if you were so attracted to him?" Several chubs in the room nodded and muttered in strong agreement. Most of them seemed to feel somewhat slighted: If all these chasers are out there, why don't they make themselves known?

"He was so beautiful," Stuart said. "I couldn't. Why would a guy like that be interested in me? He's way out of my league. I couldn't have handled the rejection."

"What did the guy look like, Stuart?"

"I dunno. He was big and really handsome, and…" He trailed off. I sensed he wasn't used to talking about his attraction to guys, much less the specific parts of their body that attracted him.

"Is there a guy in the room who looks a bit like the guy you're talking about?"

"Ummm…I dunno. I guess he kinda looked like that guy over there." Stuart flushed red. So did the guy he was pointing to.

Stuart pointed to Kevin, a balding man in his early 50s with a button nose, kind eyes, a dapper beard, and a big belly that easily put him over 300 pounds. Kevin began to tear up. I turned now to him.

"What do you think of that, Kevin?"

"I can't believe it."

"What do you mean? Say more."

"I can't believe that I could be that for someone. I can't believe that this attractive young guy would get all hung up over a guy who looked like me."

"Have you never encountered that before, Kevin?"

"No. Not that I was conscious of. But it does explain now why a lot of guys seem to be interested in me online but then don't follow through."

I turned back to Stuart: "Would you ever contact a guy like Kevin online?"

"Yeah. Definitely."

"Would you ever set up a dinner date with him?"

"Me? No."

"Too scary?" I ventured.

"Yeah. I wouldn't know how to do something like that."

The group was flabbergasted. So many of them had assumed that they were the ones who were supposed to be shy and intimidated. It had never occurred to them that they were the supermodels, they were the movie stars, they were the impossible dream. Of course some were equally flabbergasted that something as simple as asking for a date could be a problem for someone who seemed intelligent and otherwise competent. For some, it was the first time that they didn't feel the world's pity and blame focused on them; for the first time, they saw it was a chaser who lacked the requisite confidence, poise, and grace. I drove this home by pointing out to the group, "I know that in a society that looks down on fat people, it seems only fair that a chaser should be required to make the first move. But just because we're not fat doesn't mean we're any better at making the first move than you are. It doesn't mean we like rejection any more than you do. You might remember that the next time a guy you're not attracted to hits you up online or asks you out on a date."

Stuart's story doesn't represent all chasers, but there are many guys like Stuart out there. Gay or straight, his story is hardly unique. I think my interaction with Stuart in that seminar illustrates the upside-down nature of the Round World. It's a great example of what sorts of crazy things happen when you invert the axiom that Fat is the opposite of sex. What happens when Fat is synonymous with sex? In the next part of this book, we'll look at how chasers see obesity. We'll examine closely how and why obesity can be sexy.

LAWS OF ATTRACTION

Now that we're getting into the world of chubby chasers, we're going to keep bumping into the idea of objectification. For most people, objectification means seeing people as objects of sexual desire instead of as unique human beings. I bring up the subject now because if it's not already on your mind, it soon will be, as I talk bluntly about what chasers see—how we perceive an obese body and what it means to us.

In fact, we're going to keep returning to objectification throughout the book because it is one of the main disconnects in the Round World: When people find out that I get turned on by Fat—something that's taboo—they often assume it's all I can see in a person, the only thing I'm attracted to. It's sort of like when a straight guy finds out that one of his friends is gay and then thinks his gay friend must be attracted to him. Since his friend likes men, then he must like any man. Similarly, many people think that those who like Fat must like anyone who's fat because fat is all they see. Of course nothing could be further from the truth. Actually, if you think about it, the person being objectified in that case is the chubby chaser. People objectify me when they reduce me to a mechanism that pops a boner in the presence of enough fat—as if that were my only sexual dimension.

Objectification 1: What We'll Allow

There's a lot—really a lot—to say about objectification, mostly because it's such a provocative issue. Perhaps we should start by talking about what's acceptable to admire. What is it about you that people are allowed to admire? Which aspects of you are acceptable for someone to compliment? You might think that any compliment would be welcome if it's sincere. Many men tend to believe this. However, even men come to see that they have limits on what they're willing to have complimented. Every society has restrictions on admiration and compliments.

TRY THIS AT HOME

Imagine that you're at a party and you've met a few new people.

One of these new people to whom you've been talking for five or ten minutes pays you a compliment: "You know, I have to say I really like your _____." Fill in the blank with each of these items below:

Hair Intelligence Ass Voice Clothes Body Chest Legs Arms Style Eyes Energy Height Walk Belly Skin Color Elbows Nose

Some you find acceptable, some you don't. Is there a rule or test for which compliments you find acceptable? Ask two friends to try this and see what they think.

If you tried the exercise above, you might think that any rule about compliments is elusive, or that it devolves into "Well, the person should just know!" You might think it has a lot to do with whether the two people—the admirer and the admired—are the same gender or different genders, and then whether they are gay or straight.

Compliments and Gender

Certainly gender politics come into play. I think the difference between the way men and women regard admiration versus objectification can be summed up this way: In most cultures and most situations, a man can go up to any other man, gay or straight, and say, "Wow, I gotta say, you've got a great chest." It will be received as a compliment. Maybe it's a straight guy complimenting another straight guy at the gym, or maybe it's a pickup line at a gay bar, but almost universally, the man with the great-looking chest feels empowered and complimented. In fact, it will probably lead to a conversation. I've spoken or received this sort of remark countless times, in many situations and many countries, as have my male friends. None of us has ever reacted with offense. Even a guy who's not particularly proud of his chest will feel complimented to the degree that he believes the compliment is sincere.

But now imagine that a man goes up to a woman in a gym or bar and says, "Wow, I gotta say, you've got a great chest." I think "Thank you" and a big smile would be low on the list of probable responses. To be fair, I have encountered one or two women who say they enjoy this sort of compliment, but even they are quick to say that such a comment is unlikely to leave most women feeling complimented and empowered. Of course, in our society, we perceive men and women in different contexts. Ten thousand years of gender bias reinforces the idea that a woman's value rests solely in what she can do for a man, that her worth is reckoned by men in a man's world that values women for sexual pleasure and reproduction. So that context is present in the moment of the compliment, and may be the only context if no other is present. As a woman friend explained it, "We're so used to having our looks determine our value in society that we hear 'Great chest' as 'You're *only* a great chest.'"

So why am I opening up this can of worms? Well, again, man/woman issues often get mixed up with fat/admirer issues. A lot of guys, gay and straight, don't understand why complimenting a woman's body can be met with such hostility. We don't really understand except with a lot of imagination, and even then I think it's an intellectual understanding more than a visceral one. Similar to this, a lot of chasers have trouble understanding or imagining what it's like to be fat and all that goes with it—that is, the context in which a fat body occurs. In the gay world, there's no ten-thousand-year historical gender context to wrangle with. It doesn't exist between two men; it's shared between two women. Between heterosexuals, however, it adds another level of complication and frustration to fat/admirer dating. Again, that's one of the advantages of this book using same-sex examples.

Compliments and Identity

Let me broaden the point beyond gender. If we receive a compliment for something we value about ourselves, something for which we want to be known, we will respond positively regardless of the gender or intent of the person giving the compliment. As an example, I point to that minority of women who might appreciate a compliment about their chest. On the other hand, if we receive attention for something we don't value or for which we don't want to be known, we hear the remark as belittling or insulting, even if it's intended as a compliment. Okay, belittling or insulting, but why objectifying? Because we don't want to be represented by that characteristic, we feel as if it's not us—not who we really are. At the very least, we feel like we've been reduced to that characteristic, which is not how we wish to be perceived. In fact, for some of us, our whole personality is organized around not being perceived as that characteristic, that thing, that object. So when that part of us gets noticed—positively or negatively—we feel objectified.

For example, imagine that I go up to a hulking bodybuilder in the locker room of a gym or at a gay bar and say, "Geez, man, you barely fit in your clothes." The guy obviously works hard on his body to get it that big. He wants to be known for his body, and he takes my remark as a compliment. But if I go up to a beautiful fat guy in a locker room or a gay bar and say, "Geez, man, you barely fit in your clothes," the remark is likely to shame him. He does not want to be known for his obesity. What's more, mentioning his tight clothes cruelly highlights the fact that he has gotten even fatter, that his stigma has grown worse.

Here's something else to consider: Whether or not the speaker genuinely intends to compliment the person makes absolutely no difference. Any compliment can feel like an insult. If I told a woman at a bus stop that she had beautiful breasts, no amount of explanation, apology, or backpedaling would absolve me of the crime. Even if I explained that I am gay and meant nothing sexual by the remark, I doubt that all would be forgiven. My intended compliment would still probably feel like a violation. Now consider the opposite: An insult can feel like a compliment. I remember working out at a gym in Spain. As I said previously, I appear pretty hulking in most gyms in southern Europe, where they don't have a bodybuilding culture. During one of my sets, I actually displaced the equipment I was using, moving it a foot or so across the waxed hardwood floor. The machine wasn't really designed to handle all the weight I was using, and the floor was equally ill-suited for heavy-duty workouts. The Spaniard next to me got upset. "Go home!" he yelled in Spanish. "You're too big already!" I stared at him incredulously. "No, seriously!" he continued. "What do you mean by coming in here and tearing up the place?"

I suppose it might have seemed scary to him that I could move a piece of heavy equipment by accident. He clearly meant to chastise and discourage me, but of course his tirade had the opposite effect. I simply said that everything was fine, played the dumb foreigner, and smiled happily to myself that my size and strength had made an impression.

Here's another story of my body in context: One time in Berlin, coming back from the gym in a tank top and red gym pants, a little boy saw me and his jaw dropped. He turned to his mother and said in German, "Mommy, look! It's Superman." By contrast, two weeks later I was walking back from the gym in the same tank top and gym pants in Madrid. A man stopped me and asked in Spanish, "My God, what kind of job did that to you?" In Germany I'm a superhero, and in Spain I'm a malformed laborer. But I feel complimented in both countries. Similarly, many fat people feel insulted or objectified regardless of the speaker's intent. That's why they bristle at the word *fat*, whether it's meant to be insulting, complimentary, or merely descriptive. So many chasers, myself included, have learned to watch what we say around the people whose bodies we admire. That may just seem polite or common sense, but in many situations, it takes a toll when someone's admiration is demonized or when we hold parts of ourselves outside the bounds of love.

So where does all this talk of attraction and objectification leave us? Where does admiration end and objectification begin? Why don't we just allow people to compliment any part of us?

3: Love & Sex in a Big Fat World

We're complimented when we're admired for something we want to be known for—part of our identity. We're not complimented when we're admired for something that isn't. I think this is true and fundamental, no matter the context, the gender, or the social norms. I've met chubs who have staunchly argued with me when I've complimented their body, explaining to me why I am in error. On the other hand, I've met a few women who tell me that they quite like getting compliments on their breasts. They tell me that they like their breasts, that they're actually proud of them and feel no shame in that. But clearly we feel that some compliments are inappropriate. We as a society have certain ideas about identity and about what should rightly offend us. Let's look at this next.

Compliments: Personal and Abstracted

For a remark to be taken as a compliment, it must fit with our identity—how we wish be perceived in the world. However, on a societal level, we also make judgments about what is acceptable to compliment. In general, the more abstract the quality, the more we permit its admiration. For example, I don't know many people who object to having their energy complimented: "Wow, I just love your energy," or "You've got this great energy about you," or "Carol thinks you'd be great for the job. She told me she really likes your energy." Other similarly abstract qualities open for admiration might include acumen, point of view, insight, compassion, style, caring, intuition, and sense of humor.

What about aspects that are a little less abstract? "Wow, I just love your laugh," or "You have a really great walk," or "I like your smile." These don't seem nearly as laudatory as the first batch, but they are still complimentary. They are also more intimate, so perhaps we should proceed with caution. It's probably safe to compliment your boss's energy, but what about his walk? What about *her* walk, if you're a man? When compliments become less abstract, gender politics become more relevant.

What happens when we get down to concrete characteristics? For example, "I really like your hair," or "I just love your nose," or "You've got a really great body." These compliments might still fall within appropriate limits, but you also might feel a little uncomfortable about who is paying you such a compliment or the context in which they're paying it. Any time the body is mentioned, gender politics are definitely in play.

But it's more than just how personal or how abstract we are in our admiration. We pass judgments about what is okay to admire, whether it's noble or base, love or lust. For example, imagine hearing someone ask at a party, "Wow, I can't believe you and Bob have been together for ten years now. I wonder, what did you first notice about Bob when you met him?"

If we say we noticed Bob's compassion, we're high-minded. If we noticed his laugh, we're sweet or dear. If we noticed anything about his body, however, we're base—or, at the very least, shallow. I'd like to point out that Bob's compassion, laugh, and body are all very much part of Bob. If you say, "But Bob is not just his body," you could as easily say, "Bob is not only his compassion." They're all aspects of Bob, but we have judgments about which qualities are more or less acceptable to admire.

We tend to think that abstractions are better to admire than physicalities. In fact, physicalities that connote sex are usually the least acceptable to praise. Consider "I fell in love with his eyes" versus "I fell in love with his cock." Both eyes and cocks are body parts. The closer someone's admiration comes to sexual attraction, the more trivial it seems, and the less we approve of it. I don't mean we necessarily consider sexual attraction immoral, but we deem it less noble, less important, less permanent, less valid, less appropriate, less real, less meaningful…just less.

People in my seminars often say, "But I just want someone to love me for who I am." Well, who you are is all of you. Yes, people have their favorite parts, but that doesn't diminish any of the other parts. And really, we don't have parts. Bob is not a collection of parts. He's just Bob. And we notice stuff we like about him.

Welcome to the Minefield

No one ever worries about being misunderstood when they say, "I date only smart men. Intelligence is a huge turn-on for me. If a guy hasn't got a lot going on upstairs, then it's a no-go for me." Despite this strong and exclusive preference, no one assumes from this statement that IQ is the only attractive quality the speaker considers when dating. And certainly no one says in smug condescension, "Oh…you're one of those intelligence fetishists." And if you date an intelligence fetishist, your friends don't caution you, "Be careful. He's not trying to make you smarter, is he?"

But this is almost always what chasers encounter if we say that we date only fat people. We've got at least two strikes against us that the person with the intelligence fetish doesn't have: First, our preference is for something physical. The body is seen as lower than the mind, and the mind as lower than the soul. Second, the physical attribute we prize is stigmatized; we're not supposed to notice it, let alone like it. And third, if you're a man with the hots for a fat woman, then commenting on any part of her body is a minefield of gender politics.

Too often, the desire for a fat partner is dismissed or denigrated. Some people see it simply as shallow objectification. For example, I was invited to give a talk on fat/admirer relationships at the annual conference of the the National Association to Advance Fat Acceptance (NAAFA, a social and political organization founded in 1969). During the conference, I met with a group of FAs (straight male chasers). One of them confessed that he didn't like the term *fat admirer* and felt uncomfortable being identified that way. He readily admitted his preference for "large" women and said that he had no interest in dating "a thin gal." In talking more with him, I found that what he objected to was that the term focused on a woman's physicality. He told me about all the wonderful women he'd dated and took great pains to explain that he hadn't dated them *because* they were fat. Nevertheless, a woman has to be fat to make it into his dating pool. Like so many chasers, he bridles at the idea that fat is the only characteristic he cares about, even though it's the only characteristic that seems indispensible. Necessary, but not sufficient.

Dancing Around the Attraction

What do you do if you're a chaser, but you can't stand the idea of being attracted to something as base as a physical characteristic—especially a taboo characteristic? Well, that's Isaac, a chaser who approached me after one of my seminars. Isaac insisted that even though he was a chaser, he wasn't attracted to fat guys because they were fat. "No," he explained, "it's not that I love fat guys per se. It's that fat guys are less egotistical than thin guys. They don't fit in at normal gay bars, so they have nothing to prove physically. They don't have to bother competing with thin guys, so they're less concerned with primping and having to look a certain way. That's why I like them better than thin guys. It's not because they're big."

Isaac's reasoning is quite interesting, so let's unpack it. "I'm not attracted to fat men per se." By his own admission, Isaac dates only fat men, so I think what he means is, "I don't date a man only because he's fat. It's not the only physical characteristic that interests me." And, of course, he's not attracted to all fat men. Then Isaac says, "Fat guys are less egotistical than thin guys." So it's not the fat on a man—a base physical quality—that he's attracted to. Instead he's attracted to a noble, abstract quality that fat men possess. This is an excellent example of a person inventing an abstract quality to admire because he's unable to face his sexual attraction to physical quality. Isaac constructs fat men as possessing noble qualities: humility ("less egotistical than thin guys") and independence ("nothing to prove physically"). Incidentally, he also attributes masculinity to fat men ("less concerned with primping and having to look a certain way"). I'll have a lot more to say about masculinity later. Isaac says that it's unfortunate that the world sees fat men this way, but it does create in fat men admirable traits worthy of praise and attraction.

When I tell this story at seminars, the fat men in the audience don't seem very complimented. They don't think they are less egotistical and more independent because they have no chance of competing in a thin man's world. They don't feel exempt from the normal standards of beauty. Let's set aside any stereotyping or prejudice you might find Isaac guilty of. Instead let's look at his reasoning. His position would seem quite logically consistent except for the fact that ego-free, independent *thin* guys are outside Isaac's dating pool. Isaac readily acknowledges that a guy has to be "big" to attract his attention. For Isaac, one of two things must be true: Either he believes that thin guys are *always* egotistical and follow the herd of fashion and that fat guys *never* are, or—more likely—Isaac wants to date only fat guys, although other qualities are also important to him. Just as I pointed out with intelligence above, "I date only independent, ego-free guys" sounds far more acceptable than "I date only fat guys."

By the way, Isaac is tall, lightly muscled, and stunningly handsome. His deprecation of preening and following fashion sounds a bit like what he's trying to guard against in himself: If he liked fat men because they were fat, he would have to see himself as superficial and self-absorbed in his own desires. Nevertheless, Isaac does admit that being "heavy" is an important characteristic to him. As with the man at NAAFA, Isaac has little romantic interest in guys who are not fat. So again, noble qualities must be invented to stand in for physical attraction if he is to save himself from succumbing to base superficiality.

Another point about Isaac is that he talks scornfully of men who have sex with each other just because they have a physical attraction. He says, "The physical is not enough. There has to be more." That's true of many (most?) men, but I find it interesting that he feels the need to express his disapproval of people who seek only carnal pleasures. He regards lust as beneath him. This echoes the assertion I made earlier, that the more an admired characteristic is seen as sexual, the more we tend to devalue it.

Finally, and perhaps most significantly, Isaac has a big problem with the word *fat*. In the seminar earlier, when a chub referred to himself as fat, Isaac said with deep concern, "It makes me so sad when you say that word. Don't call yourself that." The chub bristled. He seemed offended that he was being pitied for low self-esteem. "I use the word because it's what I am," the chub responded. "I don't have a problem with it." But in Isaac's face, I could see the pity that he felt for the chub. Isaac told me later that he thinks fat guys use the word *fat* to put a brave face on their insecurity. For Isaac, *fat* is a bad word—just as it is for many chasers, actually. So it makes sense that people like Isaac find it impossible to accept their sexual attraction to Fat if they can't even say the word. How could they tolerate having an attraction for something so awful that it is literally unspeakable? Instead, they will go to great lengths to construct an identity that excludes that aspect of themselves, protesting vehemently when confronted with it.

Isaac would probably want to me to add that he loves that his boyfriend recently lost some weight and that they are both much happier now. He offers this as proof that he's not a fat fetishist, a base creature interested only in the size of his partner. I've already made many of the counterarguments applicable here: Fat is not the only quality that chasers seek, and chasers don't want to see their fat partner suffer. Also, I'll talk later about how chasers are attracted to a wider range of sizes than most people are. However, Isaac says he's happy with his partner's smaller size, and I have no reason to doubt him. Actually, I would offer that Isaac has no choice except to be happy: If he can't allow himself to be attracted to someone for their obesity, then he can't allow himself to be less attracted to them when they lose weight. The cognitive dissonance would be unbearable. Certainly none of this is calculated on Isaac's part. I have no doubt that Isaac is perfectly sincere in everything he says. Indeed, I have heard many chasers go through similar intellectual acrobatics to come to terms with their love of Fat.

Objectification 2: Parts and Pieces

There's a paradox in a book like this one: We look at the parts to view the whole, yet the whole is greater than the sum of the parts. In a moment, we're going to be looking at parts of people, including their body parts. I think there is value in this to the extent that we bring all the pieces back together when we're done.

Earlier, I talked about how women in most societies do not welcome remarks about a part of their body, even less so if the body part has sexual connotations, and under no circumstances if they don't like that specific part of themselves. By contrast, men don't seem to have the same level of concern about being touted for their ass, their face, or their penis. I'm not saying that men never take offense at being objectified, but it seems to bother us less. Maybe we don't interpret a compliment about one feature as being dismissive of anything else about us, or we don't think the person paying us a compliment is trying to pigeonhole us by suggesting that we have only that one attractive feature. Or perhaps we just don't allow ourselves to take offense because it would be unmanly. When I started leading seminars that included more women, I found that objectification came up far more than it did with my gay male participants. Nevertheless, the topic of objectification *always* comes up when I talk about people who admire Fat.

Most people see objectification as bad because it means being treated like an object. That's true, but sometimes we are treated like an object and we like it! We sometimes enjoy being held up as someone's sex symbol or treated like a god or goddess. I've been told this by both men and women, both gay and straight. So I'd like to offer a way to clarify what we mean when we say we dislike being objectified:

> Objectification occurs when what we desire about a person is more important to us than who that person is.

There's actually a lot implied in that statement. "What we desire about a person" means some physical or emotional quality that we want and the other person seems to have. It could be physical, like a big cock, perfect breasts, or a massive belly that drapes exquisitely onto the pulchritude of massive, soft thighs. Alternatively, it could be how he or she makes us feel or what they seem to provide or embody, such as safety, masculinity, femininity, excitement, or stability. What we miss in the equation of objectification is that the other person is not responsible for the perfections and virtues that we ascribe to them. They're just living their life, not trying to fulfill our needs. That's what I mean by "who that person is."

Some men and women are proud of a particular physical attribute—their ass, their chest, their hair—and dress to showcase it. This attribute is part of their identity, part of who they are. On the emotional side, some people genuinely wish to be seen as safe, exciting, stable, masculine, or feminine. Those attributes might be related to their job or even be the reason for their successful career. So when we compliment those people on something with which they positively identify, they don't feel objectified. However, someone who does not identify with that attribute—who does not see it as part of their identity—will find the compliment shallow, objectifying, and perhaps even insulting, because it doesn't fit with how they wish to be seen.

The intent of the comment doesn't matter. You can't insult a bodybuilder by telling him that he's too big, nor will he take it as objectification. Being big is a major part of his identity. Conversely, you can't compliment a man's belly if he hates that part of himself, no matter what you say. He works hard to keep that part of himself outside his identity. He actively rejects it. Your compliment won't land positively, and he's likely to feel objectified or insulted if you persist.

Men objectify. And women do too. (The women in my seminars usually curl their lips into wry, guilty smiles when I say this.) The work I do in my seminars is not about stamping out objectification. I don't think it's possible; I'm not even sure it's desirable. Instead, my work is about people discovering how to integrate their sexual desire for all kinds of beauty, exterior as well as interior, in their own body or in someone else's. I hope to provide an opening for people to see beyond their idealizations so that they can meet the person they are idealizing. I don't think that can happen, however, if people's ideals are considered wrong from the very outset.

Being dumbstruck by someone's outer beauty is not a bad thing just because it might happen before we're dumbstruck by his or her inner beauty. If you look across a crowded room and see someone 40 feet away you'd like to meet, it's not because you're attracted to his eyes. And it's certainly not for his brains. It can't be. You can't perceive those things from 40 feet away. No, what catches your eye is something much more obvious and physical. Except under very unusual circumstances, we meet people from the outside in. We see them, then we hear their voice, and perhaps then we might listen to what they have to say. That's true for both men and women. I hope you'll bear all this in mind as I delve into a detailed analysis of what chubby chasers see when we encounter a beautiful fat person. It's not *all* we see, but it's probably what we admire first.

In short, chasers see beauty and power. We'll start with what chasers (male and female) find attractive about fat men, and then we'll turn to what chasers (again, male and female) find attractive about fat women. We'll see that what people look like is part of a complex web of meaning that forms not only our attractions but also how we see the world.

A Field Guide to Chubby Chasers in the Wild

If you're not a bird-watcher, you may hear birdsong as simply high and low tweets. To a knowledgeable birder, however, the songs of bird species are quite distinct and extremely varied. Similarly, a fat person is not just a person who is fat to a chaser. I remember I was trying to explain to a young chub why he was getting no interest from a particular chaser online. Stephen couldn't figure out why this particular chaser, whom he found drop-dead gorgeous, seemed to have no real passion in pursuing him.

"You're not his type," I explained.

"But he doesn't have a type," Stephen countered. "Look at the men he's friended or favorited on his profile. They're all different."

I took a look at the chaser's online profile. The men he'd highlighted ranged from 25 to 45 years old, from 250 to 400 pounds, mostly hairy but a few smooth, and mostly white, although easily a quarter of the men were black or Latino. "See?" Stephen said. "He likes all kinds. Why not me?" To me, it was perfectly clear what the guy's type was. Every pic he'd highlighted exuded masculine power. Whether it was expressed in size, shape, hairiness, posture, or dress, the admiration of masculine power was consistent and clear. On the other hand, masculine power is not what people saw when they looked at Stephen, a beautiful, 19-year-old, blubbery, fresh-faced doughboy.

Many chasers have trouble articulating exactly what they look for in a fat partner. Some protest that it's not about any particular physical characteristic, but more about the essence or vibe a person gives off. The following models are ones I've trotted out a number of times in front of various chasers from all over the world. I've also tried them out with lesbians who prefer fat women, and with straights of both genders who prefer fat partners. Whether gay, straight, male, female, Eastern, or Occidental—the vast majority tell me I've captured the essence of what they find attractive about Fat in a way that they themselves have never been able to see before.

I want to state straight away that fat people and their admirers don't really see themselves as operating in the way I'm about to describe. That's sort of the point. If they did, I wouldn't need to uncover it. It's not conscious behavior. These are observations of attraction and behavior that I've seen over decades of living in the Round World, and this model seems remarkably accurate in predicting tastes and behavior, which is generally the measure of success of any model. Of course, no one likes to be pigeonholed. So if you go up to a chaser and say, "Ah ha! I read in a book what you like!" you might be greeted with more suspicion than candor. On the other hand, if you happen to be a chaser (or someone who's comfortable dating chasers), you'll probably find that much of what follows hits very close to home. A chaser in one of my seminars told me afterward that he felt so "outed" by listening to what I'm about to say here that he felt naked.

Most of the time, chasers who are presented with this model of our sexuality say they feel not only enlightened, but also lighter. Their concern for their sexual proclivities turns from burden to freedom. Sometimes, however, they react with discomfort, perhaps because I've taken something as personal as sexuality and laid it bare for all to see. An Israeli man in one of my seminars couldn't stop squirming, grinning, and burying his face in the ample shoulder of the chub with whom he'd come. He later came up to me and said, "Wow, you really nailed me. You got it exactly."

In another seminar in a different part of the country, I noticed a young black lesbian who avoided eye contact with me after I started talking about what chasers like. Earlier in the seminar, that same slim, petite 20-year-old had shared about loving her fat girlfriend's body and secretly wishing she wouldn't lose weight. The woman stuck around as people drifted out of the room, and I asked her quietly if what I had said about chasers and our types was accurate. She couldn't look me in the eye, but she nodded. She muttered quickly, "I think I'm that second type you mentioned." Then with the briefest of glances toward me, she said, "I think I learned something about myself today."

Talking about a sexual attraction may be easy for some, confusing for others. But for those of us who like fat people, discussing our attractions is often deeply personal, confronting, and shrouded in taboo—the breeding ground of guilt and shame.

The young woman took a deep breath and mumbled half to herself as she recalled elements of past relationships, old crushes, and even favorite family members that now all had a unifying context she had never seen before. "Thanks. I've got something to think about," she said, and hurried off. Here's what I told her and the others.

The Power of Big

Over decades of observing and talking to many chubby chasers, I've come to find that chasers break down into two basic types. Yes, I am stereotyping, but I think you'll see that such an analysis proves useful.

The first category of chaser is turned on by the power of big. Let's call these people Power Chasers because they see Fat as an emblem of sexual power, physical power, emotional power, perhaps even spiritual power. If a Power Chaser seeks men, he or she is seeking masculine power. If he or she seeks women, that Power Chaser is attracted to feminine power.

Let's start with Power Chasers who seek masculine power. Again, the chaser may be a gay male, a straight female, or transgender. But what's common to all of them is that they seek a fat male (or masculine) partner.

When a chaser sees Fat as masculine power, there are certain aspects of their partner's appearance and behavior that go along with that ideal. What I present here should be thought of as a wish list for this type of chaser. Some of these qualities may be more or less important, but taken together they construct an ideal partner, not just for sex but for a relationship as well if that's what is sought.

The Belly

Foremost among the attributes that a Power Chaser seeks in a man is a fat belly. I know this may seem an obvious feature for a fat person, but Power Chasers are unbelievably particular about the belly. For us, it's just as much an erogenous zone as the ass, the lips, or even the penis. For many, it's even more important than any of these. For a Power Chaser seeking masculinity, the belly needs to befit a "man." So these chasers like the gut to be either firm and protruding like a basketball, or prominent and sagging over the beltline. It's not a coincidence that this is the "apple shape" common among men who have gained weight later in life. The ex-jock who's put on weight is a common fantasy of many Power Chasers.

For chasers who see feminine power in Fat, a woman who enters a situation belly-first is extremely impressive and compelling. It's less about her actual shape than about her higher center of gravity and the way she carries her weight. It gives her a powerful stance and pose. Search the internet for British sumo wrestler Sharran Alexander or United States shot-putter Jillian Camarena-Williams to see this shape of feminine power emanating from the belly.

The Look

Facial hair on a fat man is almost a requirement for many Power Chasers. Some chest hair is usually greatly credited, too. The hair might be close-cropped and militantly neat, or worn irreverently long and messy. The chub's pants must be worn under his belly, rather than across it; the strength and unanimity of this preference among Power Chasers can be seen on countless internet chat boards and personal ads. Suspenders are a further enhancement to the fat man's glory, since they are exclusively menswear. Thick, meaty arms and legs round out the image of this powerful, obese man, sometimes even more so if they're tatooed. As for the face, a good-looking chub for this type of chaser is handsome, but not fine-featured or pretty. Rugged features with a strong jaw count here, or jowls and a double chin if they are enrobed in a beard.

For fat women admired by a Power Chaser, there's definitely a dress-for-success aesthetic. Pantsuits and jackets accent the attributes of feminine power for this chaser more than dresses do. However, a skirt that shows off the belly, or slacks worn over it, can be quite appreciated. Her arms are strong and meaty, though they may sag softly. The face may be pretty, but striking or statuesque is more credited by the man or woman who seeks the epitome of obese feminine power. Rebel Wilson or Camryn Manheim might be good models.

The Demeanor

Power Chasers often look for a fat man or woman who is unflappably calm, maybe even to the point of being taciturn or stoic. Alternatively, he or she may prefer a man who's more open and jovial, perhaps an older Father Christmas type or younger ex-jock who is gregarious and can hold forth on the chances of his favorite sports team. For fat women, feminine expressions of power valued by her type of chaser would include a no-nonsense style of interacting, or the quick wit and sharp tongue of a literary heavyweight who can out-think anyone else in the room. Whether seeking the masculine or the feminine form of power, the Power Chaser is looking for a fat partner who exudes confidence and stability—a fat person who takes action and isn't hampered too much by discussion. The Power Chaser wants a fat man who knows what he likes and goes for what he wants—a man's man. In seeking out a fat woman, the Power Chaser seeks a woman of consequence.

The Job

The fat person who is sought by Power Chasers goes through the front door to get things done, so jobs that reflect that attitude are considered sexy. The attractive fat person holds a position of power at work, perhaps as a manager or supervisor. Or they might work semi-autonomously without much regard for a management structure, perhaps as a trucker or a lawyer.

FIGURE 7: *Jennifer* by Les Toil, pen & ink, digitally colored. Concept and commission by the model.

Jobs that serve as strong emblems of power include the cop, the biker, the construction worker, the bartender, the ex-jock, or the ex-soldier who's outgrown his or her uniform. Most of these jobs are blue collar, it's true. A fat plumber may not seem like a powerful guy in terms of social or economic status, but to a Power Chaser, a wrench-wielding plumber whose belly or ass crack can't be contained by a tool belt is the very picture of sexual power and strength. The hottest, of course, is someone with both social status and sexual power, such as a lover who is really a lawyer but looks like a biker on the weekends. This was the character of Ellenor Frutt, played by Camryn Manheim on the ABC Television legal drama *The Practice*.

The Icon

American culture includes numerous Power Chub examples who appeal to Power Chasers. Actors such as John Goodman, Billy Gardell, Greg Grunberg, and Kevin James are contemporary idols; older idols include Jackie Gleason, George Wendt, and John Belushi. These actors usually play characters with blue-collar jobs, like those described above. Even animated characters such as Bluto and Baloo the Bear are somewhat less popular but still greatly admired by Power Chasers.

FIGURE 8: Illustration by Warren Davis to accompany an erotic weight-gain story.

I've already mentioned some of the icons for Power BBWs, such as Sharran Alexander and Jillian Camarena-Williams. Another sports example is German wrestler Anna Konda. In the world of entertainment, I would point to Camryn Manheim, Queen Latifah, Rosanne, Mo'Nique, and Gabourey Sidibe. Other fat female icons of power might include the sturdy Amazon warrior, the Wagnerian soprano, or the stout barmaid who can carry 12 beer steins in her arms at Oktoberfest. The Power BBW is the conquering heroine who is not afraid to use her size to her advantage. In fact, there is a whole website devoted to fat versions of Wonder Woman. Other characteristics, such as height and strength, may be factors in an obese man or woman's power as well, but they only reinforce the perception of power that derives from obesity; they never overshadow it.

The Vocabulary

If you listen to Power Chasers, you'll hear the same words and phrases uttered again and again: *gut, strong, a real man, a (whole) lotta woman, big, big guy, big gal, thick, belly, he can carry it* (referring to fat), *she carries it well* (referring to fat), *tree-trunk legs, big arms*. The chasers focused on men talk of *filling the gut* or *tanking up,* and having a *keg* for a belly as opposed to a mere six-pack. Again, these are all power references that bespeak masculinity. Eating is less accentuated in the fat female iteration of power, but there is definitely a sense that a powerful fat woman eats what she wants and doesn't apologize for it. As with the men, there is scorn for words like *diet* or *skinny.*

The Power Chaser

The Power Chaser tends to think of himself or herself as supportive and caring in a relationship with this sort of powerful, fat partner. The chaser is typically modest, reserved, or even self-deprecating. A good example of this comes in an email I got from Dale, a chaser in the Midwest. He's muscular, good-looking, and relationship-oriented. In our correspondence, we were talking about how absurd it is that people assume that part of the attraction of

FIGURE 9: Illustration by Warren Davis accompanying an erotic weight-gain story.

being with a fat guy is that it makes us chasers look leaner, smarter, handsomer, or whatever. That's nonsense from a chaser's point of view, as Dale demonstrates in an email: "For me," he writes, "I feel like the lesser person next to a fat man. I feel like they are the more powerful and dominant one. I like making them feel that way. Me? I'm just a lowly average man, and I like that."

I used to think chasers like Dale suffered from a poor self-image, but as I talked to more and more Power Chasers, I realized that was not necessarily the case. Since the Power Chaser admires the size and sexual potency of their obese partner, it makes sense that the Power Chaser would see himself or herself as smaller, less important, and even less potent by comparison—but that's different from feeling inferior. After all, Wonder Woman's admirer is Major Steve Trevor. He may be a war hero, but he's no Wonder Woman. In the real world, the Power Chaser might be a talented neurosurgeon, but it's a guy in a baseball cap with his belly hanging out of his T-shirt who brings this doctor to his knees.

The Power Chub/BBW seems to bring the Power Chaser a sense of grounding or a feeling of home. So in keeping with the fat partner's front-door approach to life as described above, the Power Chaser appreciates their fat partner's taking the lead in decisions made by the couple. If the fat partner doesn't lead outright, they are frequently the decider in the couple—the power behind the throne, so to speak. The undeveloped Power Chaser can feel very threatened by all this. If he or she lacks confidence, they may feel inadequate or overwhelmed by their fat partner. (Remember Stuart, in my seminar a while back?) The developed Power Chaser, however, values the straightforward self-confidence of their fat partner and sees it as a place to call home.

Even if you're not a Power Chaser, you may find many of these traits appealing in a partner. I know a lot of folks who aren't attracted to fat men per se, but they definitely look for a man "with meat on his bones," who looks something like the man or woman characterized above. What distinguishes the Power Chaser is that he or she locates these qualities in obesity. The same qualities in a thin partner wouldn't seem as erotic or powerful.

The Beauty of Fat
The other kind of chubby chaser or admirer can be characterized as Beauty Chasers. (In case you're curious, I'm in this second group.) Again, what I'm about to describe is not a checklist or recipe, but more of a wish list or idealization.

Beauty Chasers aren't looking for icons of power. This leads some people to conclude that we must be looking for something submissive, or nurturing, or feminine—that we seek the mothering security blanket of warm flesh in which to indulge our infantile needs and fantasies. Although we do love soft, ample rolls of fat, it would be grossly inaccurate to create a Freudian pathology of all this.

One year I was home over the Christmas holidays, and one of my relatives, who knows my tastes in men, off-handedly remarked, "Well, you've clearly got some mommy issues." The reasoning goes that a desire for big, soft men is really a misguided desire for a big, soft mother figure. Straight guys who admire soft, fat women get this diagnosis laid on them even more often. It seems reasonable, since women are associated with softness and roundness, two qualities that are definitely attractive to Beauty Chasers. However, this is a misunderstanding of our true nature. It would be like discovering that someone loves the red juiciness of a ripe tomato, and then concluding that it must come from a savage lust for blood and carnage. Here's a more accurate model for the chasers like me.

Beauty Chasers appreciate a fat partner in terms of aesthetics. We admire beautiful lines of soft folds and sagging flesh. We love the sensuality of an inflated form, and we're powerfully drawn to a bright, shining, chubby face. For Beauty Chasers who seek men, a fat guy who looks too feminine may not spark our interest. However, it's probably true that the range of what looks masculine to us is wider than it is for most people.

We're not as concerned about ourselves or our partner looking too gay, too weak, or too pretty. Fat is simply beautiful for us, even to the extent that some of us are not very particular about gender. Even in my case: I consider myself extremely homosexual—I've never been more intimate with a woman than giving her a fully clothed hug. Nevertheless, I'm awestruck by the beauty of some of the supersized women I encounter at some of my seminars. The obesity of some of these women is jaw-droppingly gorgeous to me and stops me in my tracks. I've never had that experience looking at a thin woman.

Let's take a closer look at how the Beauty Chaser constructs his or her ideal.

The Belly

Of course, the belly is important to the Beauty Chaser, but we don't single it out to the extent that Power Chasers do. For the Beauty Chaser, the belly forms part of an overall aesthetic of hanging, draping, and cascading folds. Many Beauty Chasers are turned off by hard, basketball bellies or thin legs and arms even when attached to a doughy abdominal trunk. This holds true whether we're attracted to fat men or fat women.

The Look

Prized among Beauty Chasers who seek men is a handsome, perhaps boyish face, with soft folds of fat abundant on every part of his body. In fact, a clean-shaven double chin and jowls often

FIGURE 10: *Untitled* by Sven Oliver, pencil on paper.

enhance a man's handsomeness for us. Even if the chub isn't really young, being blessed with a beautiful face (usually without wrinkles because of his plumpness) gives him the impression of boyishness. To be clear, I'm not talking about anything prepubescent. I'm talking about the same sort of beauty found in fit college students, stylish club kids, and sculpted jocks…just very much fatter.

In the regular world, people—particularly women—are taught to conceal their obesity or to downplay it as much as possible. In the Round World, however, obesity forms a major part of a fat person's beauty. Again, this isn't about fat women dressing to please men. After all, what I'm saying applies just as much to fat men, and chasers too may be women or transgender. I'm merely suggesting that anyone can dress to showcase beauty, and that beauty comes in many forms.

The Demeanor

There is a dichotomous variation in the personalities that Beauty Chasers esteem in a partner. Beauty Chasers tend to find fat partners based on sociability: their fat partners are either very gregarious and trendy with a large social network, or they're quiet and quirky with a small circle of close friends. As for the fat person, he or she values brains but appreciates brawn. They strategize and talk a lot about options, even though in the end they may act impulsively.

Another characteristic of this type of fat partner is that they try very hard to accommodate people, though not always cheerfully. They seem to fit themselves into society as the jester, the asexual best friend, the den mother, or the good listener. Again when I talk about demeanor, I'm not talking about who these fat men and women really are. I'm talking about a popular role that they are cast in and that they often accept. Of course, no one is just a stereotype, nor are they doomed to play a role if they truly don't want to.

The Job

The fat partners pursued by the Beauty Chaser often have service-oriented careers such as design (clothing or graphic), customer service, computer/IT, academia, social work, or counseling. They are the executive assistants, the number crunchers, the hall monitors, and the evil geniuses. Less likely to kick down the front door, this sort of fat partner prefers using the back door to get things done. Frequently they're the person in the office whom people take for granted but who is key to the smooth operation of the business.

The Icon

The male celebrities admired by Beauty Chasers are somewhat less well known than those admired by Power Chasers. Because of the stereotype described above, these male celebrities tend to be character actors or comedians. If they do star in a show, they don't have a love interest. Notables include Gabriel Iglesias, Ralphie May, Jonah Hill, John Pinette, Louis Anderson, Chris Farley, and even Fat Albert from the cartoons. They play characters who are naïve (a boyish quality) or on the outside (back-

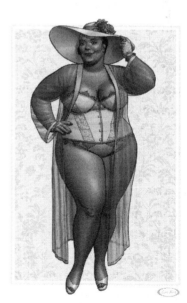

FIGURE 11: *Evon* by Les Toil, pen & ink, digitally colored. Concept and commission by the model.

door approach). Their comedy derives from the hapless situations in which they find themselves.

A vivid example is the actor Chris Pratt. When he was fat, his character on the NBC show *Parks and Recreation* was a comic buffoon outside the main action of the series. The character was married, but his wife suffered his sweet-but-stupid goofs with good humor. When the actor lost weight, however, he became eligible to play leading men and starred as an action hero in the *Jurassic Park* movie franchise.

On the other side of the aisle are the men and women who adore the incomparable beauty of a fat woman. Fat feminine beauty is represented by massively fat hips and breasts, and a beautiful round face framed by chins. She is the round sex kitten, the curvaceous seductress, or perhaps the pendulous ingénue. She, too, conquers, not as the Amazon or the Valkyrie, but as the enchantress or Scheherazade. Icons include actor/comedian Melissa McCarthy and plus-size model Tess Holiday.

The Vocabulary

Beauty Chasers have a vocabulary consistent with their bent. They frequently talk about how *beautiful* a particular aspect of a fat person's anatomy is, and it's not limited to the belly. They speak of a *perfect* ass, *doughy* arms, a *blubbery* belly, and *fat, jiggly* rolls. They express their admiration for double chins, the slow rhythm of waddling, or perhaps even stretch marks. What's deceptive here is that these terms may seem insulting because they conjure images that are ugly to most people, even to many Power Chasers. However, to the Beauty Chaser, they describe a kind of physical perfection.

The Beauty Chaser

In trying to reconcile the drastic difference between society's standards of beauty and their own, Beauty Chasers think of themselves as set apart from the rest—in a positive way as a maverick, or in a negative way as a misfit. Rather than having concerns about power (being a "real man" or "strong woman"), a Beauty Chaser's attention is focused on questioning the status quo and noticing social hierarchies. A Beauty Chaser may seem removed—even aloof or asocial—because they are usually less preoccupied with power and more concerned with appreciating aesthetics or observing how people fit together. In fact, noticing how people fit together might be considered social aesthetics.

Often, these chasers are good-looking. If they are accomplished in their field, they attribute their success to a specialness that sets them apart. If they are not accomplished, their specialness may be a justification for not fitting in or not meeting the pedestrian expectations of the herd. Having a strong attraction to a fat partner is a distinction in keeping with that specialness. In turn, the fat partner confers a distinctive beauty and/or sensuality to the

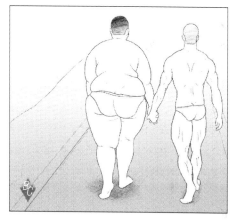

FIGURE 12: *Chaser and Chub* by ButterChuk, digital drawing.

romantic relationship, which the Beauty Chaser sees as a blessing or a curse according to how they see their specialness.

Undeveloped Beauty Chasers can't handle their attraction to someone fat, someone so at odds with society's physical ideals. Frequently they hide, fight, deny, or just ignore their desire for a fat man or woman, even to themselves. Again, they see the attraction as a curse or just a guilty pleasure—not as their true taste. As a diversion, an undeveloped Beauty Chaser might pretend to be a Power Chaser, going after masculine-looking fat guys or powerful-looking fat women who are more socially and aesthetically acceptable than the men or women they truly desire. The developed Beauty Chaser, however, sees their fat partner as someone with whom they harmonize. Ideally, the two see each other as expressing different yet parallel ideals of beauty.

Imagining Fat as Sexy

After all this discussion of Fat as beautiful or Fat as powerful, what about Fat as sexy? Actually, that is probably the most frequently asked question, both inside and outside the Round World—by fat people and thin people alike. It's also the question that's most frustrating for chasers to answer because we don't have the words to do justice to our experience of Fat. I touched on this earlier when I mentioned trying to

FIGURE 13: *Coulter and Emma* by Bonka-chan, digital drawing.

explain the sublime and even transcendent experience of eating fine chocolate to someone who doesn't like chocolate. Nevertheless, I've had some success relating the chaser's experience to people who are not turned on by Fat.

If you're trying to understand how Fat could be a turn-on, you might think about it this way: When most people make love, the touch of a partner and their skin is incredibly sensual and erotic. Think of touching your lover's skin, the texture of it, the pleasure as you draw your fingers across it, explore it, kiss it. Think of how your partner's touch makes you tingle, makes you pound, and how it drives the two of you to get ever closer. Your fingers, lips, and tongue explore the geography of your beloved, a geography mapped by the hand as well as the mind. Thoughts and sensations intertwine and eventually collapse, indistinguishable, one into another as two bodies and souls become one.

Now, what if that erotic landscape were bigger; what if the exploration were vast; what if the sensations too were magnified or even doubled? What if all those sensations were possible at twice the volume, twice the intensity? Or even at three times? Some chasers have told me that the first time they made love to a fat man or woman, they trembled in awe and excitement. Some say they still do, every time. For me, the ecstasy of being with such a man feels like falling and tumbling as if I were a waterfall. We are awed by the sensuous beauty of soft blubber or the enveloping power of massive weight. We play, we revel, we worship. And if we are very lucky, the person we're with can accept this veneration and enter into this sex play with us. For us, making love to someone obese is a kind of rapture wherein we discover again and again what we were made for.

RESPONDING TO FAT AS BEAUTY OR POWER

What does the world look like to chasers when we carve it up into beauty or power? Well, pretty much the same as it does for everyone else. There's nothing new about seeing people as beautiful or powerful. Such representations have been with us a long time, and we're all accustomed to seeing the world in those terms. In the Round World, however, what's different is that beauty and power are represented by elements that the rest of the world considers ugly and weak. In fact, one way to define the Round World is that it's the people who perceive obesity to be beautiful or powerful, and the social dynamics that this perception creates.

A Big *Myth*understanding

At first glance, these two categories—chasers who see fat as power and chasers who see fat as beauty—may seem odd or even arbitrary ways of carving up the world. However, if we look back into antiquity at how men and women were portrayed, we see that these categories are actually clear and meaningful.

People are always pointing back to the ancient Greeks as forerunners of whatever we see in Western society today. We trace our ideals of government and philosophy to the Greeks and Romans. We reason and teach according to precepts set down by the Greeks. And certainly ancient Greek ideals are nowhere more present than in our aesthetics. Even outside the West, ideas of proportion and symmetry are influenced today by the ancient Greeks, who lauded proportion and symmetry as evidence of truth, beauty, and the divine.

Another factor that makes classical culture an apt antecedent for me is that it comes out of a society in which homosexual attraction was not taboo and the power and beauty of both genders was celebrated. So if we want to look back and see where our ideas of attraction come from, classical art would seem to be a pretty good place to look. For example, if we look at classical sculpture, we can see echoes of chasers' ideals of attractiveness.

Masculine Power: Zeus

There are no better representations of masculine power in the ancient world than Zeus and Poseidon. They represent power and strength moving across the face of land and sea. Statues of Zeus are almost always sculpted as an older man with a great beard and muscularity befitting his great strength and power. The Power Chaser is referencing these same ideals, but in an obese version that adds to, rather than contradicts, the connotation of strength and power. Imagine what this statue of Poseidon would look like if the artist had made him fat. Imagine him with a huge belly, fat girdling his biceps, and powerful legs heavy with fat. To some people, that would be desecration. To the Power Chaser attracted to fat men, it would be erotic—and to be taken by such a fat god would be ecstasy.

FIGURE 14: Poseidon/Neptune sculpture in the Port of Copenhagen. Photo ©2005 by Hans Andersen.

FIGURE 15: *Diana of Versailles* © Marie-Lan Nguyen / Wikimedia Commons

Feminine Power: Artemis

Power Chasers attracted to women might find echoes of their desires in a powerful, fat goddess based on Artemis or Diana. (You might remember that Wonder Woman's real name is Princess Diana.) Artemis is often depicted with a deer and a bow and arrow, for she was the goddess of the hunt, wild animals, and wild places. She drew power from the moon and was associated with childbirth, protecting young girls, and the forces of the feminine body. The deer and the cypress tree were sacred to her. It's not hard to see then that with a few hundred pounds, the huntress Artemis turns into the crime-fighting fat Wonder Woman or the massive female shot-putter for the modern Power Chaser attracted to women.

Masculine Beauty: Ganymede

If you know your mythology, you might remember than among Zeus's many lovers, there was a young man who beguiled the great god and drove him to forget all else. The boy's name was Ganymede, and he was the most beautiful person Zeus had ever seen. So seduced was Zeus by the boy that he turned himself into an eagle and bore him up to Mount Olympus to serve as his cupbearer. Statues and paintings of Ganymede lack the age and musculature of Zeus, since Ganymede is meant to depict the flower of youthful

FIGURE 16: *Ganymede and Zeus,* Museo Archeologico Nazionale, Naples. Photo by Miguel Hermoso Cuesta.

masculinity—his power is his beauty, and his strength is his fresh sexuality. I believe this is what the Beauty Chaser is tapping into, albeit unconsciously, when he sees a huge, beautiful fatboy waddling across campus or laughing with his friends at a mall. *Cupbearer* sounds like a servant, but notice in figure 16 how the youth treats Zeus (as the eagle) almost as a pet. The powerful Zeus is reduced to a plaything in the tender caress of the beautiful Ganymede. That's how it is for the Beauty Chaser. All his bravura melts in the presence of his beautiful, doughy fatboy.

Feminine Beauty: Aphrodite

For Beauty Chasers attracted to women, a supersized Aphrodite or Venus is their ideal. In the ancient world, she was the goddess of love and beauty, pleasure and sex. She was the beloved of Adonis, the most beautiful man, and Ares, the most powerful in war. Aphrodite is often depicted reclining, seducing, or just standing and being the most beautiful woman in the world, as in Botticelli's *The Birth of Venus*. In these images we can see the inspiration for the hyperbolic curves of a supersized version of the goddess and her powers.

FIGURE 17: *Venus with the Apple* by Bertel Thorvaldsen, Thorvaldsens Museum, Copenhagen. Photo by Gunnar Bach Pedersen

Why Fat?

You might be saying to yourself, *I understand that someone could be turned on by archetypes of beauty or power. But why* fat *beauty and power? Why* fat *Zeus or* fat *Venus?* Well, the simple answer is that sometime back before we can remember, we chasers associated obesity with attractiveness. For each of us it is different and yet somehow the same. In his book *Lovemaps,* John Money talks a lot about how and when sexual preferences and attractions are formed. In a nutshell, he believes sexual tastes to be a combination of nature and nurture, forming much the way a landscape forms. The land of a particular place has certain inherent qualities, but events and the passage of time forever change the character of that place. That's true of our sexuality as well. We're born with certain innate preferences, but we're also part of a world that plays a role in forming us.

However, it's a thorny business to try to sort out what feature was caused by which source. And frankly, I'm not sure it matters. The vast majority of chasers I've talked to over the years can recount intense childhood memories of attraction to huge fat men or women. Sometimes they remember fat adults who were "so masculine" or "so feminine" because of their size. Other times the memories are of obese playmates or contemporaries who fascinated and beguiled them.

For example, a male chaser might tell me he remembers being four years old on the beach and fascinated by the hairy fat legs of a huge man who ambled by. The memory is so powerful that he can see it vividly 30 years later. The chaser might ask me something like, "Do you think that's why I like fat guys now?" The hypothesis seems to them even more likely if it's not a random passerby, but a close relative or family friend: "My dad's friend Uncle Eli was always over at the house and sometimes bare-chested, like when we would all go swimming up at the lake." The events that these chasers recount, although highly charged emotionally, are extraordinarily pedestrian in nature: a man walking by, or a man not wearing a shirt. As I've listened over the years to these stories of early sexual desire, I've come to suspect that these early memories are not the source of the desire, but rather its reflection.

I find it unlikely that incidents like these can create a desire for fat, hairy men. Rather, I believe the desire for such men is already in place and available for these memories to collect around. It must be like the way crystals form on a string dipped in sugar water. There is a seed crystal to start the crystallization process, but it is so tiny, so lost in the mesh of the string, that all we can observe is how later crystals coalesce around this nearly invisible point of origin. For chasers, I believe this first seed crystal is formed quite early in life. Perhaps before we have language to describe it or even remember it.

The Fat Shaming of Straight Male Chasers

I pointed out earlier that analyzing same-sex male relationships gives us more direct access to the dynamics of fat/admirer relationships and avoids conflation with other issues such as gender roles and identities. When I talk about my desires or those of my straight brethren, a lot of folks (gay and straight) try to bring the old male/female stereotypes to bear on what they consider our abnormal predilection. So often in books and on talk shows, we hear the motives of men impugned because they like fat women. A few FAs whom I've talked to put it like this: People think a man who likes a fat woman is not a real man because either (1) he wants a powerful mother figure to hide behind and fight his battles, or (2) he wants a woman to be a pile of blubber so he can dominate her and make himself feel powerful and in control. You can see here how the notion of obese power and beauty that I described previously becomes distorted and even pathologized by anti-fat prejudice. Not only are these stereotypes unfair, but they also shame the joy that these couples find in each other.

To me, what's most ironic about this interpretation is that while it seems to stand up for women, it's actually just another form of fat-shaming that maligns the fat woman and insults her male admirer. Boiled down to its essentials, the argument is that no man in his right mind could ever be sexually attracted to a fat woman. That is, only a defective man would reject a normal woman and pursue a defective (fat) woman instead. Such a man could only be a weakling or a predator.

I think this is the reason so many men have learned to deny their attraction for obesity, even to themselves. They bury their sexual attraction and instead laud some other facet of their partner: "I certainly don't love her because she's fat. I love her because she's smart." For disavowing any physical attraction to Fat, a chaser's partner and their friends will deem him a hero. Like a chivalrous Don Quixote, he will be admired for being able to see past his partner's unsightly body to find only love and beauty. However, the idea that fat is the very beauty that a chaser sees would be impossible, even immoral to many people. As we saw in our first discussion of objectification, to admire a physical characteristic that is stigmatized would make him a pervert to his partner and their friends, perhaps even to himself. I simply ask, why can't a chaser love both?

Gay & Straight • Power & Beauty

The categories I've sketched here are not boxes for people to live in or aspire to. Rather, these are models of our perceptions of power, beauty, masculinity, and femininity. More than perceptions, perhaps, these constellations of desire form the deepest part of a chaser's psyche and constitute the basis of our sexual attractions. They even inhabit our nervous system.

TRY THIS AT HOME

> ## *What do you see when you look at a woman you're about to meet?*
>
> What assessments do you make? What do you compare? How about when you look at a man? Is that different? How many of your thoughts and assessments are about beauty? About power?

A chaser who's into women will usually see Fat as beauty. A chaser who's into men will usually see Fat as Power. This becomes obvious when you talk with chasers or look at the types of fat erotica that predominate online. Of course, there are numerous exceptions to this generality; in fact, I am one of them.

And yet, is that what chasers really want? For example, do chasers seeking fat men tend to gravitate to power because they like it, or because it's more acceptable than seeking the beauty of blubber? Do chasers who seek fat women really prefer feminine beauty, or is it just that feminine power is too intimidating or unpopular to pursue? I'm not questioning motives here. I'm questioning whether we really like what we say we like at a fundamental level. We could also ask about other limits and tastes. For example, many chasers say there is an upper weight limit to what they find attractive. Is this really true, or does a number on the scale merely constitute a ceiling of what someone thinks is acceptable to enjoy? Can our judgments make us like or dislike something that we really don't? If so, how would we know?

Take the Chub Challenge

I was talking to a chaser at a chub/chaser event in New Orleans. We were chatting on a paddleboat on the Mississippi as it happens, and he was sharing about being out to his friends about his preference for bears, something you hear a lot from gay Power Chasers.

"Bears?" I said incredulously. I'd seen the guys he'd been pursuing during the weekend. They weren't the big, burly, hairy types that most people associate with bears. On the contrary, every single guy he was interested in was boyish and clean-shaven, with little or no body hair on his soft, cascading rolls of blubber. And yet this guy even had a bear flag hanging off the balcony of his hotel room at the event. He went to considerable trouble to associate himself with the *bear* brand, even though none of the men he was pursuing would be seen as a bear. "Bears?" I said. "I think you mean you like fat guys."

"Well," he confessed, "I say *bears* because people know what that means. It avoids confusion."

"So, saying you like fat guys would confuse people?"

"Yeah, I'd have to explain what I mean and answer a lot of questions. Besides, I don't like to use the word *fat*. It upsets people. *Bears* is just easier." He was a Beauty Chaser trying to pass himself off as a Power Chaser, to associate himself with a cooler brand.

"Sounds to me like you just don't want to tell people that you like really huge fat guys."

"Well, some bears are huge…"

As you might guess, I didn't make much headway. Power Chubs are far more accepted than Beauty Chubs. Not all bears are fat, but being a bear is cool even if the guy is fat. You might even say that being a bear is a cool brand. However, Fat is not a cool brand. As we distinguished earlier, saying *fat* is all too often just a more particular way of saying *disgusting*. This chaser says he likes bears because he wants to be associated with a cool brand, not a disgusting fetish.

Now, it's one thing when this happens at the cognitive level, as I suspect was the case with that chaser on the paddleboat. He knows what he likes, but he deliberately trumpets his attraction for something else that seems more acceptable. But for many people, their own deep sexual desires and attractions may be quite different than what they believe they are. For example, I think some guys may actually get more pleasure being intimate with huge blubbery men, even though they say they prefer big stocky bears. What if those things that we think we go for—blondes, bears, or bodybuilders—are just popular brands? A brand associates who we are with what we like. It provides a context for our desires, and it may even give us an identity: A *Marlboro Man*, a *Clairol Girl*, or an *Apple guy/girl*. A brand is a very powerful thing. But what if it's not really true that gentlemen prefer blondes? Can a brand or association really override people's preferences? Can it override our own experience? Yes, it can—according to some neuroscientists who looked into Pepsi's ad campaign known as the Pepsi Challenge.

P. Read Montague and his colleagues, working at Baylor College of Medicine, explored the "Pepsi Paradox" by conducting their own cola taste tests, and they did indeed find that in blind taste tests, about half of the study's participants preferred Pepsi. (Pepsi claimed that "most people" prefer the taste of Pepsi; anything more than 50% is "most.") They also used an fMRI to measure the brain responses of various groups of participants while they were tasting the sodas. In the blind taste test, the pleasure center of each subject's brain lit up on the fMRI in correlation with the sample of soda they preferred. In other words, if someone preferred Cola A, the pleasure center of their brain lit up brighter for Cola A than for Cola B. And as Pepsi claimed, about half preferred Pepsi.

However, when another group was given clearly labeled samples of Coke and Pepsi, the pleasure center in the brain did not correlate with what participants said they preferred. Instead, another part of the brain lit up with a very high correlation to the stated choice: the cerebral cortex, the center involved with learned behavior and decision making. Participants who knew the brand of the cola they were tasting chose Coke overwhelmingly over Pepsi, even though the pleasure center of their brain indicated a clear preference for Pepsi. The conclusion of the researchers was that brand can override our innate perceptions of what feels or tastes good. More generally, Montegue says that context, not perception, determines whether we think something tastes good or bad.

So do most gay male chasers really prefer big-bellied, hairy chunks? Do gentlemen really prefer blondes? Or do they just think they do because they identify with blondes or bears as a brand? Most of us think

Chasers are attracted to a special beauty that a lean body simply cannot express, cannot even contain.

we know what we like, but we underestimate the power of context informing our perception of preference. People do experience pleasure, taste, and sensuality. A brand or a stigma can't change that. However, we can be persuaded that we prefer something when in fact we receive more pleasure from something else. With enough social pressure, we can be persuaded that we don't like something that we actually do like. This is one reason I think there may be many more chubby chasers than people think. Fat is a very unpopular brand. Perhaps it's so negative that it overrides the desires of many who might actually enjoy a fat partner if their tastes alone were the determining factor in whom to date.

Sound far-fetched? Sure, that's what the executives at Coca-Cola thought. They assumed that people drank Coke purely for the taste. And when Pepsi gained market share in the 1980s, Coca-Cola came out with a new product that tasted more like Pepsi. However, the backlash against New Coke—and the company's subsequent apology for the blunder—show the extent to which we are ignorant of how our judgments can dictate what we think we like. The Pepsi Challenge changed marketing forever because it demonstrated that people's experience or preference could be overshadowed by their identification with a brand. You might remember the man I referred to earlier who said, "I'm not a fat admirer. It's just that I only date big women." That's a preference in conflict with a brand. That's an experience of loving fat women in conflict with the brand identity of being an FA.

Brand Fat

Whether chasers see Fat as beauty or as power, these twin aspects of obesity are two branches of the same tree of sexuality. Chasers occupy all different positions in the tree. Some of us go farther out or higher up on a particular branch, but the tree constellates us as a community who loves Fat. For some chasers, having a fat partner is a plus, but not a requirement. A little belly is a sexy thing, they say. They stay down toward the trunk of the tree, close to the ground of normalcy—close to the sidewalk where the normal people go about their day. Others of us are most at home high in the leaves, unable to even see the ground for the foliage; we are unmoved except by the most enormous of men or women. Indeed, these chasers have told me they often have trouble relating to the tastes and norms of regular folks—not just in sexual matters. As one straight white man said in one of my seminars, "The fact that I like 500-pound women…Well, it sets me apart. I find it hard to relate with regular guys a lot of the time."

Many men and women have an interest in dating a fat person that goes unexplored for a number of reasons. Some enjoy a fat partner, but they don't perceive it as an exclusive taste. Other people feel that it's wrong to want to date someone because of a physical characteristic. And some of us find obesity, especially massive obesity, powerfully attractive but too weird or unhealthy to pursue. For all three groups of people, the difficulty is that what we like is tempered by what is taboo. Over the years, I have learned that what chasers say to me about their tastes and preferences is not necessarily accurate. On one hand, it's a bit like the Pepsi paradox. Who they say they like is not necessarily the same as who they have sex with or are attracted to. On the other hand, I've had the opportunity to observe and talk to the same people over many years and watch how their tastes have deepened as their exploration has evolved.

A good example of this is Kirby, a handsome doctor, six foot two with stunning abs. When we met five years ago, Kirby said that he liked fat guys, but only those with "a little belly." When I asked about fatter men, he told me, "Oh no. I just think a little furry belly is cute." Then three years ago, Kirby said, "Well, I may be attracted to fatter guys, but I would never want a guy to be unhealthy because I liked him fat." Finally, last year, Kirby told me that he'd met a great guy who was very fat. He was asking for advice about how to handle his conflict between being sexually attracted to this guy but feeling guilty for liking such a supposedly unhealthy characteristic.

Kirby's story is a good example of a man coming to terms with the conflict between taboo and attraction. I don't think he was lying to me when we first started talking. It was just that "a cute little belly" was all he could allow himself to desire because of his ideas of health and normalcy. Also, his ideas of health limited what he would allow himself to explore. Similarly, you may remember the story I told earlier about the good-looking guy from Colorado who had never had sex with a man he was attracted to for fear of what his friends would say.

The Round World

Of course, many chasers simply like what they like—end of story. I'm not trying to convert anyone or judge them. I'm simply suggesting that it's often difficult to tease out what we like from what we're supposed to like. What the body enjoys and what the mind prizes can often be miles apart. Even contradictory.

Bears, Otters, Cubs and Other Masculine Wildlife

Maybe you're asking yourself, *What's the big deal about liking fat men? Bears are fat guys, and they're all about being masculine and cool.* Perhaps, but not necessarily. It may surprise you that the definition of *bear* is a divisive issue, and I'm opening myself to a firestorm of criticism by venturing to provide one here. What's more, I'm not even a member of that community, so let the drubbing begin.

Historically, bears were gay men who felt excluded by the lean, hyper-groomed, depilated community that defined the urban A-gay scene of the late 1980s and early 1990s. Moreover, many of these men were put off by the narcissistic concern with physical beauty that this urbane lifestyle implied. They held a different image of attractiveness that embodied a simpler and more honest masculinity—a man's man who wore what was comfortable, liked what was practical, and groomed himself as necessary. You can read all sorts of books and blogs about the bear community. You can also read about cubs (younger guys who aspire to bearish manhood) and otters (lean, hairy guys who may or may not be attracted to Fat.) I won't get into that here. I just want to point out that nowhere in my brief description of bear culture did I mention being fat as a requirement of being a bear. Bears come in all shapes and sizes, one of which is fat.

Chubs, however, are fat by definition. A chub is simply a fat gay man who identifies as such. He might have body hair, or he might not. But whether they're hairy or not, some chubs see themselves as bears while others do not. He might be a bear if he fits in with that crowd. This causes a great deal of confusion and even resentment. Some in the bear community resent the fact that *bear* has become so all encompassing that to some it's just a polite euphemism for "fat gay guy." While some in the Chub community resent that some 500-pound guys call themselves bears because they are too ashamed to admit that they're just plain fat. Let's take a closer look at this last point.

The Round World in the Mirror of Media

As I indicated earlier, a chaser who's into women will usually see Fat as beauty, and a chaser who's attracted to men will usually see Fat as power. There are plenty of exceptions, myself included, but the Round World tends to break down this way. I think this has less to do with what chasers want and more to do with how the power and beauty of Fat are perceived in society and reflected in the media.

If I tried to address how the media portrays fat women, I'd have to write two books: women in the media, and then *fat* women in the media. Separating these two filters—how we see fat and how we see women—I'd like to deal only with Fat. To do that, I'm going to talk about fat, straight, white men. A straight, white male character is sort of a neutral in media. Whether you approve or not, that's what people expect. It's *unmarked* as linguists use that term, or *default* as computer programmers use that term. So if we look at a straight white male character who's fat, we can really see how being fat changes that default condition.

It's an interesting dichotomy that male celebrities admired by Power Chasers star in their own TV series as leading men, but male celebrities admired by Beauty Chasers distinguish themselves in self-deprecating humor or stand-up comedy.

All the icons of Power Chasers that I mentioned earlier depict blue-collar characters with loving wives or girlfriends at home: Jackie Gleason, John Goodman, Kevin James, and so forth. They may be fat, but they have solid jobs and solid relationships. Conversely, the celebrity icons of Beauty Chasers tend to play jesters and clowns in TV and movie roles. Even if they are featured in a leading role, they almost never get the girl. More often it's a buddy movie and there is no girl, or they play the hilarious fat friend whose buddy gets the girl. So for me as a Beauty Chaser, the type of guy whom I find sexiest and most desirable for a relationship is usually depicted as the hapless fool who has no hope of getting a date. What's worse, many of the guys to whom I'm attracted carry this negative portrayal of themselves in their own heads. It's no wonder that many of these guys desexualize themselves and won't flirt or return eye contact. It's not surprising that others grow beards and over-amp their masculinity to please Power Chasers and the rest of society. I've had fat men tell me flat out that they can't get laid without a beard.

John Candy was notable because he could look and act like a Power Chub if he wore flannel and a beard, but more frequently he was cast as a clean-shaven Beauty Chub wearing slacks and a sport coat. Candy's characters were usually outright buffoons or clowns with a heart of gold. In *Only the Lonely* (the title says it all), Candy's character does have a romantic interest, but it's clear that since he's a Beauty Chub, any romantic or sexual relationship is a long shot—so long a shot, in fact, that his ineligibility as a romantic partner sustains the plot of the entire movie. As I said, Beauty Chubs are usually sidekicks and rarely the focus of narrative. In the movie, Candy's character is a uniformed cop, perhaps to give him credibility as a romantic leading man and not just a total momma's boy. The icon of a fat cop is from the domain of Power Chubs. At the end of the movie, Candy's character almost apologizes for getting the girl and promises to lose weight to be worthy of her.

A nonfiction example of the Power/Beauty divide can be seen in two states' governors. Before having weight-loss surgery, New Jersey governor Chris Christie was a quintessential Beauty Chub. (Arguably afterward surgery, too.) His great clean-shaven double chin, his enormous pear shape, and his dress clothes that by necessity and tradition are worn over—not under—the belly, all betoken him as a Beauty Chub. Not surprisingly, he was the butt of ridicule because of his obesity. *Time* magazine capitalized on Christie's size, putting him on their November 2013 cover in silhouette. The man had just won re-election in New Jersey, but *Time* called him "the elephant in the room." The magazine claimed that they were only referring to his unconfirmed presidential ambitions, but the nation knows a fat joke when we see one.

Contrast this with New Mexico governor Bill Richardson. To be sure, he was nowhere near Christie's size, but he sometimes sports a beard and could pass for a bear. The press followed Richardson's personal style as they had Christie's, but they never mentioned his weight, which was considerable. Instead, the scuttlebutt was about his beard and whether he

3: Love & Sex in a Big Fat World

should have shaved it or not for President Obama's second inauguration. The media even conducted polls on whether the beard should stay or go. Richardson's obesity was hardly ever mentioned. This demonstrates the double standard in our perceptions of masculine beauty versus masculine power.

OUR SEXUAL DEVELOPMENT IN THE ROUND WORLD

When did you have your first romantic date? Was it before or after your first sexual experience? When did you have your first relationship? Sex, dating, and relationships are all part of the high school experience for many people. But the more taboo the dating, sex, or relationship, the less likely that it will be practiced openly in high school. For example, if being gay is taboo, then you're less likely to see many gay couples at prom. Similarly, if being fat is taboo, you don't see a lot of fat people at prom, and even fewer fat/admirer couples.

Earlier, I said that being fat is a localized event. Someone who's considered fat at one time or place is not necessarily considered fat at another. Sometimes being fat is so localized that only the person himself thinks he's fat. You might know stories about the fat girl or guy who couldn't get a date, but there are also stories about a fat guy or girl who was popular—so popular that he or she was seen as a *catch*. So I don't mean to suggest that fat people are always sad and lonely. Far from it. Nevertheless, to the degree that Fat is taboo, fat people encounter sex, dating, and relationships later in life and with less frequency. So if being fat is no big deal where you are, then fat people date, have sex, and carry on relationships the same as anyone else. But if your community (or just a fat person himself) sees Fat as a defect or disfigurement, then sex, dating, and relationships are less likely. That might not be a revelation to you, but what if I told you that the same is true for male chasers?

Growing Up Chaser

We're all familiar with the stereotype of the lonely and sexually inexperienced fat person. Such people do exist, but today many books, magazines, blogs, documentaries, and talk show episodes point out how that stereotype need not be anyone's life. What's almost never talked about, however, is how feelings of inexperience, inadequacy, and lack of intimacy affect chasers—particularly male chasers, both straight and gay. Just as fat people feel isolated or inexperienced because of their size, many chasers feel that way because of our desires. Not universally, but commonly. Folks in the Round World feel more isolated and more sexually inexperienced to the degree that we experience Fat as a stigma in our lives.

What about female chasers? Here again, gender politics allow a woman's attraction to Fat to fly under the radar. Imagine the lean, pretty, high school cheerleader. Now imagine her dating the 350-pound, big-gutted linebacker from her school's football team. She's dating a Power Chub, so she'll probably not face much stigma. However, what if she dates the doughy, 350-pound computer geek who just published his first app? For dating a Beauty Chub, she'll probably take some flack in the form of teasing or overwrought concern about her self-esteem. Alternatively, she may be seen as the hero who was able to transcend a repulsion for the geek's unfortunate body. Male chasers, however, usually face much harsher reactions from friends and family.

Many chubby chasers have our own issues of identity and sexuality to work through, just as many fat people do. We seem to lag behind our peers, not because being or liking fat makes us asexual or sexually retarded, but instead because having our sexuality linked to a taboo makes the road to self-expression longer and more tortuous. A friend of mine who is a long-time denizen of the Round World says that fat people and their admirers are about five to ten years behind the curve compared with our straight, non-obese counterparts. I think he's right. A lot of the mail I get from fat people and their admirers in their twenties deals with questions like, "Does he really love me?" "How far do you go on a first date?" "Why do I feel the way I do?" These are valid questions, but most people outside the Round World faced these issues five to ten years earlier, perhaps when they were starting to date in high school. For gainers and encouragers, this time lag behind their straight, normative peers can be even greater—10 to 15 years on average.

This explains, for example, why many fat people find that dating a 30-year-old chaser seems more like dating a 20- to 25-year-old. The same age gap is often experienced by many chasers. One female chaser told me how exhausting it was to deal with "the adolescent ideas about love" that her sexy 340-pound boyfriend had. "He's twenty-five. He should be past all this!" When I told her about the five- to ten-year time lag for some of us in the Round World, she said, "Oh my god, you're right. It's exactly like dating a 16-year-old!"

Chaser Adolescence

Psychologists describe adolescence as a period of development marked by emotional sensitivity and/or self-centeredness. It's a period when young people are prone to either explore their sexuality intensively or fail to explore it entirely because of the perceived risk of failure. Everyone goes through this, but perhaps for those of us in the Round World it is delayed or lasts a bit longer. Let's look at three examples of this adolescence in the lives of three gay men I know from the Round World.

Roger is one of the hottest chasers I know. In his early 30s, he's warm and sensitive, with an easy smile and an incredibly beautiful body. He also has a boy-next-door charm and a sexual magnetism that combine to make him almost irresistible to pretty much anyone—men, women, dogs, cats, it doesn't matter. To meet Roger is to be charmed by someone who never seems like he's trying to charm you. He's also well educated and a specialist in his field—quite the catch. Nevertheless, he tends to keep himself at arm's length from relationships. He doesn't really date; he hooks up, and always on his terms. He responds to texts from guys when it suits him, and he doesn't like to make plans with a guy more than a few hours in advance. Roger tells me that he dreams of a long-term, committed relationship with a massive fat guy, yet he has only brief sexual encounters with these men. The men he invests time in are muscle bears, bodybuilders, and power lifters.

Roger and I know a lot of the same people, and they tell me that getting a date with Roger is frustrating. On the other hand, Roger complains that guys don't understand that he's busy. He says they try to manipulate him through guilt or seduction, which he finds desperate and distasteful. If I try to set him up with a guy whom I think will be compatible, Roger often has superficial objections—they're too short, or too dark, or too light, or they don't look masculine enough in their online photos. Roger clearly exhibits two sides of adolescence: a narcissistic focus on personal gratification, and a fear and hypersensitivity that he's being dominated or manipulated.

Another example is Thomas. Thomas falls tragically in love with any superchub he can't have, which is fairly easy since he lives in a rural area far away from most superchubs. He quotes sad, romantic pop ballads on his Facebook page in despair of ever finding a true love who will never betray him. Thomas is 27, but his self-absorption and public pining seem more appropriate to someone ten years younger.

Similar to Thomas, Edgar is stunningly handsome, has a body conditioned by years of competitive swimming, and yet has never dated the kind of guy to whom he says he's strongly attracted: 350-pound bears. I've pointed out that actually meeting such a man might improve the chances of dating one, but he says that he's never encountered anyone who was worth having a first date with. "I'm waiting for the right guy," he tells me. In Edgar's case, his adolescent narcissism will allow him to date only an idealized figment of his imagination, instead of a real guy. His hypersensitivity to failure, too, is evident in his fear of dating a guy who might not be "the one." Though it seems absurd, many men I've talked to see no middle ground between meeting a guy and marrying a guy. Like Roger, they fear that letting someone get too close will start a chain reaction leading sex, then obligation, then a relationship, then inevitably end in betrayal or neediness.

As I said, many chasers struggle with a poor self-image, just as chubs or anyone else might. Remember Stuart? The chaser who followed the hot older chub for blocks without ever saying hello? Many chasers like him feel unworthy of approaching the object of their desires. They feel somehow insufficient—not buff enough, not confident enough, not charming enough. In short: not enough. That's hardly unique to the Round World. Lots of guys feel that way, whether or not they're attracted to Fat. But being attracted to fat may augment these feelings of inadequacy or raise the stakes of failure.

However, I'm sorry to say that many chasers also have a darker side, an abusive side, which comes from a feeling much deeper than a fear of failure. These chasers experience a fundamental feeling of worthlessness, of being defective because of their attraction to fat. This kind of chaser regards sex with a fat person as a guilty pleasure not to be made a habit of. A chaser who is insecure and inexperienced often treats a fat partner as an exciting thrill ride. Again we see here the adolescent narcissism that this gorgeous fat person has been put on earth either for the chaser's sexual gratification, or for their temptation and downfall.

Anal or vaginal penetration is usually the sole ambition of this type of chaser in every intimate interaction he has with a fat partner. It overshadows everything. Sex with him might have the excitement of riding a rollercoaster, but with about the same degree of emotional intimacy. Although this may be fun for a night, it gives many fat people the unfortunate idea that chasers are not capable of love or intimacy. Mikey, the beautiful superchub I was with on MTV's *True Life*, said it best: "I love being with a guy who gets off on my body. I just don't want to feel like I'm a carnival ride."

This goes back to what I was saying earlier about objectification: In this case, what the chaser wants is more important than who the chub is. Maybe you've experienced users, abusers, and cads who have no interest in Fat and who wouldn't be caught dead in the Round World. But I would argue that anyone who treats people like Kleenex—who treats his partner as a sexy meat sack to blow a load in—is actually wrestling with some deeper issues of guilt, despair, or even hatred. Who knows what that particular issue is for them, but in the Round World, there's a pretty good chance the issue is Fat.

Hope on the Horizon

I don't want to leave you with the impression that Fat is hopelessly stigmatized, or that fat people and their admirers are always impaired or second-class. There is certainly a lot of venom out there for us, but the conversation around Fat is rapidly changing.

One of my most affirming experiences was during a seminar I gave on the campus of the University of Southern California for an organization called Models of Pride. The daylong event featured over a hundred seminars and workshops on every conceivable topic of interest to young people in the LGBTQ (lesbian, gay, bisexual, transgender, queer/questioning) community and their allies. With so many events to choose from, I had no idea who would show up to my seminar about fat/admirer relationships. I was stunned when the room not only filled up but we had to turn people away because of fire laws restricting occupancy. It was truly inspiring to see the incredible diversity of young people aged 15 to 24 who showed up for the talk. They certainly covered the LGBTQ spectrum and crossed racial and socioeconomic lines as well.

What heartened me most, however, was that a majority of the participants weren't fat. Let me explain: My seminars are most successful when there is the greatest diversity among the participants. Even when I lead to a group of older, fat, gay, white men and a few of their admirers, there is still enough diversity of experience in the room to produce life-altering results. So when I have a group such as the one at Models of Pride, the depth and variety of our discussion and what they take away from it is exponentially greater. Then consider the age of these participants, and we see that there is something truly remarkable taking place that can alter the course of the lives of these young people—can alter the course of the future.

For me, it felt like a tipping point where the conversation about Fat transcended the concerns of only fat people. (In fact, Section 5 is mostly about that.) What was striking about my audience that day was that they could easily see that the issue of fat/admirer dating is a subset of general issues that all young people deal with: body image, being available for love, sex when your sexual desires aren't the norm, relating to your body when your body feels so far from what's expected. The conversation demonstrated acceptance and appreciation of all people and all bodies. I have been invited back to Models of Pride in subsequent years and found the passion and diversity of the young people in attendance to be nothing short of inspiring.

GAY, STRAIGHT, OR CHUBBY CHASER?

When it comes to romance, we tend to think that gender is primary, sexual orientation is secondary, and preference for a particular physical type comes last. However, this hierarchy of classification is simply not the case for everyone, especially in the Round World where Fat often takes center stage.

Casey is a hot young chaser I met at a chub/chaser event in Oklahoma City. He's a trucker and a part-time cage fighter, which means that he fights other men in a cage in a mixed martial arts competition. This fact alone is enough to seduce a lot of gay men. On the road, he mixes with other truckers who tend to be socially conservative, so Casey doesn't correct them when they assume he's straight. Nevertheless, a lot of the conversations revolve around sex. How does Casey participate in such discussions? He changes the gender of his lovers and tells the other truckers about his love of fat women. He identifies as gay but, he's been with fat women once or twice. Talking about sex with fat women feels easier and like less of a lie, he says, because Fat is primary for him. Gender is important, but Fat is more important.

Jack is a very good-looking bodybuilder who has a slim Asian wife. What he covets, however, are handsome, cherubic doughboys. His wife is beautiful, to be sure, and he loves her and their two children with all his heart. But he also lusts after the jiggling rhythm of hundreds of pounds on a guy as he waddles past. Which to him is more beautiful? His wife or the fatboy? Jack doesn't like to delve too deeply into that question. What he knows for sure, however, is that the jiggly fatboy could never give him the straight, suburban life he leads. A fatboy could never replace the love of his wife and kids. He considers it a question of sex versus love. Jack admits that he got married long before he became fully aware of his attraction to fat guys. Many chasers, including me, never saw ourselves as gay because Fat is so antithetical to the gay male ideal. "You look at these gay magazines, and that's not what I want," he says. "And women just seemed the easier and more natural choice. My wife's my best friend." Jack's never had sex with anyone like the men he fantasizes about. He says he intends to keep it that way.

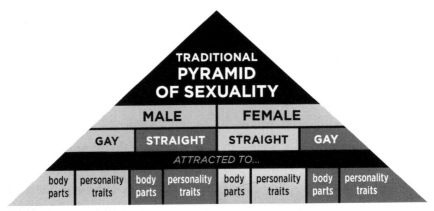

FIGURE 18: Traditional Hierarchy of Human Sexuality

A lot of the one-on-one work I do involves people in picture-perfect relationships who nevertheless are not happy. Worse, they feel guilty for not being happy given their admittedly enviable circumstance. The problem in these situations always comes down to sexuality, but not the typical definition of sexuality. Most people think of sexuality in terms of sexual orientation: gay or straight. Or perhaps in terms of stereotypes: a man's sexuality or a woman's sexuality. Certainly these categories are useful ways of thinking about ourselves to some degree or we wouldn't have invented them. However, they are not useful or even appropriate for many of us. The traditional categories of sexuality focus on genitalia—ours and our partner's. Even when we say that we love smart men or we have a weakness for soulful eyes, it's generally understood that these preferences occur underneath two other layers of categorization: gender and sexual orientation.

Fatsexual

However, when body parts or personality traits are primary in our erotic pleasure, rather than male/female or even gay/straight, where does this

3: Love & Sex in a Big Fat World

leave us? I've found that creating new categories of sexual orientation is a much more useful way for some of us to think about ourselves.

New categories and structures are not easily accepted. We easily accept new elements to fit into an existing structure, but changing the structure to better fit existing elements is a battle hard won. If the only category for sexuality is heterosexual, then anything else is an aberration—an illness, a stigma, or even a perversion. Being gay became a legitimate kind of sexuality in America in the 1980s when the American Psychiatric Association changed homosexuality from an aberration of sexuality to a variation within sexuality. Similarly, I've found that helping couples in the Round World deal with certain problems is much easier when we recognize that for many people, an attraction to Fat is more than an attraction to a body part. It is most usefully seen as a sexuality.

I came to this understanding by analogy. Imagine it's 1957, and Frank and Cathy live an affluent mid-century modern life with their two kids. The only problem is that Frank is anguished by homosexual thoughts and has begun seeing a man who returns his affections. This is the premise of the 2002 film *Far From Heaven*, which received several Oscar nominations that year.

I was struck by the similarity between the relationship of Frank and Cathy and the relationships of the people who were coming to me for help in their relationships, in which one of the couple was wrestling with a burgeoning desire for Fat in some form. Many of the same issues and complaints were voiced: "Why is he/am I like this?" "Why isn't my body enough for him?" "We've tried fantasy and role playing, but that doesn't seem really satisfying to either of us." "I feel helpless that I can't give him what he wants, and I'll never be able to." I've used the masculine pronoun here, but I've met this problem with female chasers as well. A strong attraction to fat operates the same way that a sexuality does, with all the same characteristics, complaints, and pitfalls. Since Fat is stigmatized, it's most visible as a sexuality when we notice its similarities to other stigmatized sexualities.

You might be wondering, *What about fetishes? What about kink? Isn't this all just a slippery slope, trying to distinguish between liking, wanting, and needing?* I'll actually discuss all that a bit later in the next section when I talk about gaining and encouraging (also known in the straight community sometimes as *feedism*). That's all part of the kink side of Fat. For now, however, I'd like to further examine the parallels between coming out as a chaser and coming out as gay, and why a preference for Fat is more usefully categorized as a sexuality than as a fetish or anything else.

Being Out About Fat

There's an axiom about gay relationships: You can't have a relationship with someone in the closet. What you have instead is a sort of entanglement. To what extent are we willing to integrate our sexuality into our lives? Many of us fully embrace our sexuality, and for chasers who are at peace with their desires, the unusual size of our partner is a trivial matter in social situations. My boyfriend, for example, is too fat to be comfortable in the orchestra section of a Broadway theater, so we get box seats. As a couple, we're so physically opposite that people remember us for months or even years. The staff of a Manhattan hotel welcomed us back as old friends, even though we'd stayed there only once and they hadn't seen us in a year. We could feel singled out by stigma, or we could feel special. We choose special.

On the other hand, many couples like us don't move through the world so comfortably. Many chasers are embarrassed to bring an enormous date around their friends and family. And many fat people are embarrassed to expose themselves to social situations where their obesity might take center stage, no matter how supportive their partner is. We could see this as fat oppression, but that doesn't serve us in the situation. I mean, let's say it's all society's fault. Now what? Do we put our lives on hold until society comes to its senses? Do we not date that amazing fat person, or not take our fat body to the beach until fat oppression has ended? Perhaps a fat person might lose weight, but a chaser can't lose their desire for Fat. So whether or not it's correct to blame society for our inhibitions, it doesn't do us much good. As in any coming-out process, the first place to look is within oneself.

Held Hostage by Our Own Expectations

A chaser once told me that he really loves being with huge fat guys, but he hastened to add that he would never seek one out for a relationship.

He told me about a guy he dated once: "He never wanted to do anything. I'm really active. I like rollerblading and rock climbing. He can't do anything like that."

Although there are certainly a lot of fat, couch-loving homebodies out there, there are at least as many thin couch potatoes as well. Moreover, many chubs do lead active, athletic lives. Yes, really. I know lots of guys over 300 pounds who hike, go clubbing, and have an active social life. I have a friend in Chicago who's a 280-pound tennis instructor. My friend Mikey from *True Life* is five foot five and weighs almost a quarter of a ton, yet he is active in his community and keeps up with his young nieces. In fact, he said the whole media fascination with the hopelessly obese shut-in was his major impetus for doing the MTV show. He wanted to show people that just because a person is fat—even massively fat—it doesn't mean he has to live a small, pathetic existence. But no, Mikey does not go rock climbing or rollerblading. (Come to think of it, neither do I. Do you?)

The chaser I describe above knew that he wasn't avoiding 400-pound guys because they are poor rock climbers. I suspect that when he said his fat boyfriend "didn't want to do anything," he really meant that the chub didn't want to venture out to the same social events—or at least not to the A-gay and athletic events to which the chaser was used to going. By contrast, a 400-pound guy that I used to date was far more into the club scene than I was. From his point of view, I was the social recluse who didn't know any of the local DJs and found small talk over loud music tedious. Many chasers develop a negative impression of dating a chub because of the chubs they pick. Like seeks like. A chaser who is uncomfortable being attracted to a fat partner often ends up dating a partner who is uncomfortable being fat. They share an unconscious bond based on the notion that their world would be better without Fat.

Held Hostage by Other People's Expectations

When gay people come out, one of our most basic fears is being rejected by our friends or family. Certainly there are many instances of gay people being shunned, cast out of their homes, or even physically abused. However, the obstacle that most of us face in coming out is not oppression.

It's the fear of disappointing someone central to our lives and losing that person's love or respect. This is certainly what many chasers go through in coming out about our desires. Creating a persona that is lovable and acceptable to others is often preferable to being authentic and risking the love of the people around us. The irony is that when we are loved and respected for the carefully edited persona we present to people, that's not love and acceptance at all. But for many, it's good enough. It's all they've ever known. And besides, coming out just feels too risky. First, what will people think of me? What will they say to other people? Second, what do I think of myself? For example, if a chaser is afraid of what her friends and family will say about her 400-pound boyfriend, she probably hasn't made peace with the fact that she wants one. Chasers often resist seeing their attraction to fat guys or girls as their home base. Moreover, rarely does a chaser have a best friend who says, "Wow, that's so great that you like fat chicks!" Quite the opposite.

Bi-Sizual

A chaser is much more likely to receive praise for dating slim partners in addition to fat ones, because that demonstrates how broad his tastes are and how noble he is for seeing beyond someone's appearance. Of course, there are men and women who care very little about whether their partner is slim or chubby, but they are not chasers. They're simply people who are turned on by a quality that isn't Fat and who have no affinity either way for it. They're the people who are very close to 3 on the affinity and judgment scales in the previous section. But there are a lot fewer of these people than you might think. And remember too that many people who have an attraction to Fat want desperately for it not to be true.

It's kind of like bisexuality: I certainly believe there are bisexuals, but not nearly the number who claim to be. Most people who tell me they're bisexual simply haven't figured out their sexuality or haven't come to accept it yet. Bisexuality is more than simply having experienced sex with more than one gender. Many men think they're not gay as long as they keep having sex with women. They'll even tell you they like having sex with women, even though sex with men is far hotter, more carnal, and feels more like lust. But they continue to date women because it helps them avoid the stigma of being gay and the danger of being swept away by lust, a quality they deem negative. We don't think of men as having a negative attitude toward carnal desire, but it's far more prevalent than you might think—especially when you consider that for a chaser, his carnal desire is bound up with Fat.

For example, I was working with a guy who's not part of the Round World on exploring his sexuality. He was having trouble reconciling his dual attraction for men and women. As he put it, "Sex with a woman is hot and it's fun. But sex with a man is transportive—spiritually moving." He confessed that he felt guilty about having sex with women because he said it felt like he was using them. "Then why not date only men?" I asked. "Because when I'm with a woman, I don't feel like such a pining little faggot afterward."

For me, a true bisexual is recognizable by two traits: First, they have fully actualized their sexuality and find sex and intimacy equally gratifying with either gender. Second, a bisexual relates emotionally to female lovers in the same way that he relates to male lovers. Both men and women are equally capable of fulfilling a bisexual's sexual and emotional needs (though they may not have dated equal numbers of men and women). The same applies to someone who is truly bi-sizual.

But as with bisexuals, most people who claim to be bi-sizual—who date chubs as well as thin guys or bears—are often just dodging the label of *chubby chaser*. Many people who have thin boyfriends or girlfriends are scared of falling into the pit of carnal lust for an obese man or woman. To be fair, a lot of people are truly confused about what they like. Some find clarity in later years. Unfortunately, it may be only after they've taken vows or made commitments that give them no freedom to explore this newly found clarity. And what's a person to do when they find themselves fantasizing about the fat intern at work, rather than about their thin, beautiful wife or husband waiting at home?

What's Your Type?

So if a characteristic like fat can take precedence over something as fundamental as gender, then "What's your type?" becomes a pretty important question, maybe even more important than "Are you gay or straight?" And what if you don't think you have a type? Well, I assert that everyone has a type, but your type is not necessarily a single physical characteristic. Or perhaps you might have noticed that when you were younger, you were attracted to a very specific physical type. To spark your interest, a person had to be dark, or blond, or they had to have features that were just so. As you got older, however, perhaps you noticed that these characteristics became less important. Maybe there was even that one guy, an anomaly, whom no one could have predicted you would go for.

My friend Gabriella had always known she liked dark Latino men, but one day she fell in love with a Swede. What happened? Many people would say that Gabriella broadened her tastes, that she became less shallow and finally outgrew her narrow insistence on a single physical trait. However, I have a different take.

We're often attracted to particular physical traits because we associate those traits with certain feelings and non-physical traits. For example, my friend Gabriella said she always liked "dark, smoldering Latinos" because for her they were sexy, powerful, and very masculine. The only thing that changed was that she recognized those *emotional* characteristics in someone who was neither dark-skinned nor Latino. Her type did not change; what changed was her perception of blond men, whom she had always seen as polite, respectful, and "frankly, a little boring." They weren't necessarily repressed, but when she thought of raw animal magnetism, she didn't think of Scandinavia. Her Swede changed that perception.

However, it is almost unheard of that a person who has been devoted to dating only fat partners, over time comes to see that they can satisfy their affinity for power or beauty with partners who are not fat. What makes a chaser a chaser is that he or she always comes back to Fat. Why? Well, again, if you consider that a person can be fatsexual, it makes perfect sense. Men and women can embody many emotional and physical qualities. However, most gays and straights stick to their gender orientation no matter what new discoveries they make about the type of man or woman they like. Saying that a chubby chaser has a fetish for people who are fat is no different from saying that a heterosexual woman has a fetish for people who have a penis.

For example, Gabriela came to see that a Swede could be counted among the type of man she could go for, but it would be quite another matter for her to discover that a woman could be counted among her type of man. My lesbian friends tell me they can feel the difference immediately between being with a lesbian, being with a bisexual, and being with a woman who is dabbling.

For a chubby chaser, being with a fat partner is like coming home. For some of us, it's so deeply rooted in our psyche that when we see a certain type of fat man or woman, all we are present to is joy. Seen as a sexuality, an attraction to fat operates more like a sexual orientation than simply a preference for a particular physical type. Let's look at a couple of examples.

For a Power Chaser, a bodybuilder might represent masculine power almost as well as a fat, hairy guy. Some chasers try to combine the two by seeking out hairy power lifters sporting a huge gut. Other chasers find they enjoy dallying with off-season bodybuilders or hyper-masculine thin guys from time to time. It's far more socially acceptable to date a really muscular guy than to date a really fat guy, but these chasers always come back to huge fat men as their sexual center. It's not that a bodybuilder isn't masculine or powerful enough. It's simply that the chubby chaser has a sexual orientation to fat. Other types of men might come close, maybe even close enough to make a relationship worthwhile, but it's not the same sexual experience.

For a Beauty Chaser, the case is even more obvious. I can recognize and appreciate beauty in many forms. For example, I think bodybuilders are beautiful. I also think there's an exquisite grace and perfection to the body of a swimmer or a gymnast. But being in bed with a bodybuilder or gymnast doesn't resound in my soul the way that being with an obese man does. Many sorts of men are beautiful, but none create in me the chain reaction of sensations, associations, and ecstasy that a massive, handsome doughboy does.

DATING AND OTHER WEIGHTY ISSUES

I'd like to tackle head-on some of the most frequent issues and questions I get from people both inside and outside the Round World. On one hand, I think it's useful to talk about the issues we face in our community that are different from those faced by other people. On the other hand, perhaps you'll see that these are the same issues you face but in another guise.

Fat and Self-Esteem

I once received a rather nasty email from someone who said that I was wrong to be attracted to fat men because that gave them hope and discouraged them from losing weight. The author explained that if a fat person could be loved by someone thin and attractive, the fat person would have little or no incentive to lose weight and thus would die an early, obese death. Basically, he blamed me for keeping fat men fat and encouraging their demise. I suppose there is a perverse sort of logic to that. If being fat is wrong, and I love fat guys the way they are, then I guess I could really undermine the pain and suffering that would help a fat guy get thin. So many of us—fat or thin—receive and internalize the message that who we are is not acceptable.

Being Unacceptable

I've found that we have two ways in the Round World to deal with feeling unacceptable. One way is to concede defeat: to admit that though we wish we could change, we are in fact unacceptable. This is the chaser who lacks the confidence to go up to a beautiful fat man or woman and make his admiration known because the chaser thinks he is somehow lesser. This is the fat woman who avoids eye contact with a good-looking guy or girl because being sexy and attractive are qualities outside her comfort zone.

The other way fat people and their admirers express being unacceptable is to strive righteously against it: This is the chaser who has sex with a fat partner only as a guilty pleasure and focuses their serious dating efforts on so-called normal people. Typically, they justify their behavior with fat fundamentalism. "Fat people are so unhealthy," they explain, as if health had anything to do with dating. On the other side of the aisle, I'm talking about the fat person who would have nothing to do with a chaser because only a pervert would get off on someone's obesity. "I would never date someone like that," they scoff. This second type of inadequacy is far more pernicious because the feeling of being flawed is usually hidden even from the fat person himself. After all, a chaser can only be a pervert to the extent that being fat is perverted. Refusing to date a chaser and stoop to their "perversion" may seem like confidence or assertiveness, but real confidence or assertiveness doesn't require making someone else wrong.

I certainly don't mean to imply that all of us in the Round World think we're flawed or inferior. In fact, I suspect that feeling flawed or inferior is no more common in the Round World than in any other group of people living a taboo. Nevertheless, the topic of self-confidence does come up a lot in the Round World, and I've even been asked to address the topic head-on by participants in my seminars. While it's easy to say that the bashful chaser or the introverted fat person just needs a shot of self-esteem, I don't find that a very useful prescription. Moreover, the arrogant chaser and the indignant fat person actually suffer from the same problem, but most would never see it as a self-esteem issue. So what's to be done?

Rethinking Self-Esteem

Honestly, I'm not a fan of the whole metaphor of self-esteem. People talk about it as if it were a tangible thing that they could actually measure or physically acquire. It's not real, like a chair or a dog, so wishing we had more of it leaves us no better off than before. It becomes something we "work on" or "try to" yet rarely achieve. Let me suggest something a little more productive by telling you about a date I had.

I was in the Castro, which is known for being the gayest neighborhood in San Francisco, on the night before the Gay Pride parade. People were celebrating, alcohol was flowing, and I saw this beautiful young fat guy dancing with some friends in the middle of the street with his shirt off. As I often say, the greatest gift a chub can give a chaser is to find himself attractive, and I took dancing in the street shirtless as a pretty good sign. I went over to the guy, struck up a conversation, and started to get to know him. He was a bit tipsy, but quite in control of his faculties. Actually, he told me he'd just met the guys he was with an hour or two ago. He was alone in San Francisco for Pride and was having a blast. This was another aspect of him that attracted me to him; he was not only confident but also independent. One thing led to another, and soon we were walking back to his hotel. We continued talking on the way there. He was smart, funny—a law student at a high-powered east-coast university, it turned out. But as we got closer to his hotel, his conversation started to get a bit cynical. When I complimented him, he got sardonic. When I told him I thought he was beautiful, he downright sneered. I had seen this pattern before, and I knew to head it off before the situation became irredeemable.

"Listen," I said, "I know you have a certain opinion about your body. I happen to hold a very different opinion about your body. My opinion is more fun."

He laughed, and his whole mood brightened. Once he got that the matter was a difference of opinion, this law student was able to make the shift. His view of his body wasn't a fact anymore, but simply an opinion that he could set aside at that moment for his own benefit. We had a fabulous time together from there on. We've gotten together since, and we're still in contact off and on to this day.

So what worked about that encounter? First, I didn't treat him as a person with low self-esteem. Actually, he had lots of self-esteem; he just didn't think being fat was attractive, as most people don't. Second, I didn't tell him that his opinion about his body was wrong. When people feel they're being made wrong, they generally pull out all the stops to be right. If I tell a fat guy that it's wrong for him to dislike his body, it will inevitably trigger a response about how being fat is unhealthy. Is that relevant to liking one's appearance? No, but it allows the the fat guy to be right about how bad it is that he's fat, and we enter a debate instead of the bedroom.

I also didn't tell my date that he needed to think fat was attractive. For us to enjoy the evening, he needs only to see his opinion of himself as just an opinion. If only for a few hours, what if he could play with the idea that he is beautiful? He doesn't need more self-esteem. He just needs to give up the righteousness that his low opinion of his body is the *only* valid opinion about his body—that being unattractive is some sort of Truth. He may think my opinion is absurd. That's fine. We believe absurd things all the time in short bursts. We believe eagerly and willingly for a few hours that Jack really will love Rose forever as the *Titanic* sinks. We believe for as long as we're in the dark that the Force really is with Luke Skywalker. What about after the movie? Well, if we're open and generous with ourselves, we might believe that such things as true love and the hand of destiny are possible long after the lights come back on. It is these encounters with the better part of our nature that can show us that maybe a sexual attraction to Fat isn't absurd. Maybe the real absurdity is the crummy way we've been treating ourselves. Maybe all that's holding us back is an opinion. Maybe a low opinion of ourselves is no more true than a low opinion of broccoli is true of broccoli. As I pointed out to the gorgeous chub in San Francisco, "You're entitled to your opinion, and you can have it back when we're done—if you still want it."

> **W**hat we have to learn from chubby chasers is not that fat is beautiful. Chubby chasers show us that ugliness is optional.

Isn't the Person More Important Than the Packaging?

I often get asked why looks are so important—not just fat, but whatever a person happens to look like. After all, beauty—however you see it—is only skin deep, right? It's a fair question and quite a conundrum. I used to think it didn't matter what package love came in. If the right guy came along, I could fall in love as long as I was reasonably attracted to him. I knew that I liked fat guys, but I didn't think it could be a deal-breaker in a relationship. I certainly didn't think it should be. That would be so shallow, right? You fall in love with the person, don't you? Falling in love with a guy just because he's hot is like falling in love with a piece of chocolate cake.

I was actually in a relationship with a wonderful chub—Tony, my first chub relationship—when I met Marc. I did everything I could to avoid falling in love with Marc, but when we were together, it was magical, beautiful—and excruciating because I was already in a three-year relationship with Tony. Marc had been a PhD psychology candidate at an Ivy League university, but he turned his back on the academic world to pursue educational technology in the corporate world. By the time I met him, Marc was a brilliant young executive in a rapidly expanding company. He knew his mind and could share his heart. I'll spare you the blow-by-blow of how I left Tony for Marc. I mention this episode of my life only because Tony was a beautiful, soulful chub, and Marc was a hot, muscular A-gay. I knew I liked fat guys, but the fact that Marc wasn't fat didn't lessen my desire to be with him. After all, how could something as trivial as a physical characteristic matter so much?

Here's how: There eventually came a point in my relationship with Marc when he confessed that he hated our sex life. He said he felt a bit guilty for complaining because every other part of our relationship was great, but our sex life was intolerable to him. I still had relatively little sexual experience at that time; in fact, I'd had about as many sexual partners as I'd had relationships. So I thought the sex with Marc was fine, because I had little with which to compare it. Marc, on the other hand, had thoroughly explored his sexuality, both as an out gay man and more abstractly in his training to become a therapist.

One day, Marc said something that I'll never forget: "Dan, being married to you, I feel like a woman married to a gay man." He went on to explain that he never felt like he was sexy around me—that I didn't respond to his body the same way other gay guys did, even strangers he met on the street. There was lots of love but not much heat. I thought his body was beautiful, though. I started seeing a therapist to see if maybe I was repressed or something. It wasn't a lot of therapy, but it helped me uncover just how deep and how important to me Fat was…is. I should say that Marc never made me feel like I needed therapy to fix myself. I could see and hear from the gay world around me that what I felt during sex was not what everybody else was talking about. In the end, there was good news and bad news: The good news was that I wasn't repressed or defective or unexpressed. I was just turned on by fat men. The bad news was that Marc wasn't fat. It was a level we just weren't connecting on.

Nevertheless we stayed together, because it seemed unreasonable to separate over this one issue. I'll telescope the years here to make my point. We explored the problem from every angle and ultimately decided to allow each of us our sexuality by opening up the relationship to non-monogamy. We could still be a loving couple, but satisfy our sexual needs outside the relationship. That was a big deal for me, by the way. Up to that point, I had been Mr. Monogamy; monogamy equaled relationship as far as I was concerned. It tore me up to think of Marc having sex with other men and enjoying himself with other guys. But then it hit me: I could be having sex and enjoying myself, too. Marc was beautiful, but by this point I knew what I longed for. I had been fantasizing about making love to huge, beautiful fat men all the years Marc and I were together, but I had repressed the idea because I was in a monogamous relationship. So I began to explore my sexuality in bed with other guys. Fat guys, huge guys—I even went to my first Convergence during that time. For the first time, sex was exciting and fun instead of something that was *supposed* to be exciting and fun—and only then if one knew the secret.

That worked for a while, but Marc still wasn't happy. I wasn't either, but losing him seemed far worse. In the end, however, Marc couldn't reconcile the fact that his primary sexual joy would never be in his primary romantic relationship. He would—we would—never have sexual fulfillment with each other. I was willing to sacrifice that, but he was not. I didn't blame him. Today I thank him. We broke up after seven years together. It was devastating, but it was the right thing to do and we both knew it.

The moral of this story is that I didn't leave Marc because he wasn't fat. (Remember, I had left a fat guy to be *with* Marc.) Marc ultimately broke up with me because I was a chaser, and therefore not fundamentally wired for sex with a normal-sized guy—not even a beautiful one.

Sometimes when I tell this story in seminars, someone will come up to me afterward and say something like, "But you were in love! Sex is not the most important thing in a relationship." Well, sex might not be the *most* important thing, but that doesn't mean it's unnecessary. There's a name for a relationship that is extremely intimate and yet non-sexual: friendship. If the sex is bad but you love each other, why not just be best friends? Many straight women and gay men have this relationship. No one expects the gay guy and his gal pal to get married. They have different sexualities. That's not so different from being with a fatsexual.

I think it's also worth noting that the men who come up to me after a seminar to assert the primacy of emotional intimacy over sex are usually hard-pressed to come up with *any* acceptable reason why a couple should break up, except in extreme cases of abuse or repeated infidelity. Also, they typically have not been in a relationship ever or for a very long time. I said to one such man, "I don't think the purpose of a relationship is to last." He seemed puzzled. I explained, "I think a romantic relationship grows out of sex and intimacy; its purpose is for both people to grow and develop together. When that stops happening, the relationship needs to change. Change can take many forms. For Marc and me, it meant staying close friends but not romantic partners." The man disagreed. He longed for a lasting romantic relationship that would endure all time. For him, the success of a relationship is measured in years. According to him, "If it lasts, then I'll be happy."

Does Losing Weight Mean Losing Your Man?

What justifies ending a relationship? Everyone has their own ideas on the question and experiences to back up their reasons. If you've been through a break-up, a friend might have said to you, "I can't believe it took you so long." And perhaps another friend said, "Are you sure you want to throw away all that you two have?" Your friends see the world differently. And chasers see the world very differently, especially when it comes to beauty, power, sex, and masculinity/femininity. The question that I get most often—inside and outside the Round World—is, "So what happens if he loses weight?"

Chasers often get a bad rap here. Most chasers have a broad range of weight that we find attractive, and it's usually a much broader range than the general population has. In my seminars, I point out to chubs or BBWs that any guy they've been drooling over would probably be less attractive to them if he gained 30 pounds. Not to you? Well, what if he gained 50, or even 150? Most fat people in my seminars concede that if their partner gained 150 pounds, they probably wouldn't find him or her quite so fetching. (There is always a holdout, however, who maintains that their partner's physical appearance makes absolutely no difference. It's usually the same person who's never had a relationship and who thinks the goal of a relationship is to never break up.)

So what about chasers? Well, if I think a 500-pound guy is attractive, I'll probably also find him attractive at 400 pounds—maybe even more attractive if he feels better about himself and projects that. Maybe even 350 could be attractive if he's more mobile and we can do more things together. But I'm not so sure about 300 pounds. And at 260...? 200...? Sorry, but I'm a chaser. I like Fat. However, that's just me. Other chasers think along the same lines but with different numbers. Contrast this with most "normal" people, who have a very narrow weight range of what's attractive. If you like your man's muscular 180-pound body, would you like it as well if he lost his abs and his weight shot up to 210? Maybe you wouldn't divorce him, but would you be as attracted to his body? And that's a change of only 30 pounds! By contrast, a typical chaser has a range of well over 100 pounds, and I just gave an example of a 130-pound range. Show me a typical man or woman who would be just as attracted to their mate if he gained more than 100 pounds. Of course you would still love them, but it would change your level of attraction. Let's take a closer look at how the dynamics of the relationship might change.

Trading Places

How would you react if your significant other got really fat? Here's part of an internet blog from a woman who calls herself Matilda Tuesday. She confesses that despite her guilt and her best efforts, she cannot marry the man she loves because his obese body is simply repulsive to her. From the size and response of her readership, I sense she's not alone. This is not some ugly rant about how grotesque fat people are or how horrible obesity is. It's a poignant confession of a person confronting a painful contradiction in her life and the isolation she feels because of it:

When people come to this website for the first time, they are appalled by what they read. They have understandable responses. The responses are the same as those on any other site or blog that discusses obese significant others. They think those of us who are dealing with an obese significant other are being shallow because we cannot love the person the "way he or she is." I read those responses and I think, "Spoken like someone who isn't dealing with an obese spouse (girlfriend, boyfriend, etc.)" If they could walk a mile in our shoes, they would quickly be silent or perhaps join us in our mantra...

I look at my OSO [obese significant other] and what comes to me first is not a thought, but a deep, visceral reaction. I have worked for months to overcome this reaction, and I cannot. I look, and cannot quell the repulsion that rises from somewhere primal within me. I am a woman, and my OSO is a man. What is repulsed by sight is confirmed through touch. Indeed, magnified through touch. His shape, with full hips, buttocks, and thighs, large belly and ample man boobs, is more comparable to a female than a male. I have no lesbian leanings. This repugnant tactile sensation causes me to recoil. I look at his form, as he lay [sic] under the sheets, and what I see is a fat woman, not a man. When I hug him, it conjures childhood memories of my cuddling with my grandmother...

It harps at my mind that I ignore the little signals he sends out that let me know he wants sex or to be affectionate. It makes me feel guilty that there is nothing on his body I long to caress when he comes home after being away. It does not matter anymore how well he treats me, how kind he is, how helpful he is around the house. It no longer matters how much money he makes. The energy about him and around us that always used to be there is still there. These all become horrible teasers. I get turned on by his personality and have nowhere to go with it in an intimate expression. I cannot bond with him. This is absolute hell on earth...

I will always love his person, but I cannot be IN love with him and his fat anymore. My parents think he's great. He has a wonderful personality. My boys wonder when we are going to get married. The neighbor drops hints about it. Most people find him engaging, helpful, smart, witty, etc. He is perfect in every way. I just would have to be okay with a marriage that had no intimacy, for the second time. Don't they see what I am dealing with? None of them have OSOs. None of them get it.[2]

This is the mirror image of what some chasers go through in a relationship with a fat partner who's losing weight. They may not be disgusted by their partner's smaller body or hanging skin, but they are certainly not aroused by it. And they are often unable to respond to it sexually, as I was unable to respond to Marc's beautiful body.

The fact is that many men and women have fat partners, but most take no pleasure in their being fat. In fact, many struggle with being supportive of their partner and not criticizing their obesity while secretly hating the fact that their partner is fat. Guilt and anger are common feelings when you no longer find your partner attractive because he or she has gotten fat. When a man's muscular pecs turn to doughy tits, and stomachs droop and then sag over a pair of jeans, a lot of partners start to withdraw. Although their friends may think they should be more supportive, few of their friends blame them for not being attracted to their pudgy mate. But what if the man gained 100 pounds…? 200 pounds? And then what if your guy said, "I'm 200 pounds heavier and I love the new me. I've no plans to change just so that I can fit your image of me." I think many would understand if one of the couple saw this as the end of their sex life. Yet as chasers, when we lose interest in our beautiful shrinking men or women, we're often blamed and disparaged.

"But I'm still fat!" many people say after losing weight. "I've gone from 500 to 300. I'm still huge, just healthier." Yes, that's true perhaps. And as chasers—most of us compassionate human beings—we understand and commend fat people for getting leaner if that's who they want to be. But when your mate loses 40% of their body, that's a big deal. In reverse, that's like a ripped 180-pound guy stuffing himself until he reaches a proud 300 pounds. And it's not just his increased size. Imagine the stretch marks on his belly and love handles and even on his chest, which has softened

2   Tuesday, Matilda. "Most Painful Thing I Have Lived Through…" *My Fat Spouse…* Blogger, 17 Nov. 2014. Web. http://matildatuesday.blogspot.com/2014_11_01_archive.html

into breasts. That's going to change the dynamic of the relationship a lot. It's not a singular event either. You see him eating and your heart sinks. He cradles a tub of ice cream where he used to sip unsweetened ice tea. It bothers you. It chafes. Even though you know he's never been happier with his body, inside your head you are screaming. That's what it's like for us—some of us, at least—just in reverse.

Crying Over Lost Fat

But here's where this reversal breaks down: Chasers never get to claim the moral high ground. If a person cheerfully gains 100 or 200 pounds, their spouse can always justify their horror by tacitly falling back on fat fundamentalism: Fat is bad because it's deadly. There's no need to explain their disgust, indeed, no need to mention or even examine it; the so-called disease of obesity is justification enough for any and all negativity. Complaints about a partner's weight gain are met with sympathy. Even if what's counseled is to look beyond the physical, no one disputes that gaining 100 or 200 pounds of fat is bad, wrong, or at the very least unfortunate.

Chasers, on the other hand, are never granted that righteousness. We don't have the agreement of society, so our unhappiness seems to have no justification. It's not that chasers don't understand or sympathize with our fat partners. We do. But let's take a less charged example: Think how hard it would be if you hated your partner's new hairstyle, but everyone else told you how great it looked. (Can't imagine that? Just think of the worst hairstyle you've ever seen on a person. Now imagine that your boyfriend or girlfriend insisted on wearing their hair that way.) You probably wouldn't break up over it, but that hairstyle would hit you in the face over and over again: anytime you saw a bottle of shampoo, any time you saw someone in the street who had a hairstyle you liked or disliked. All that upset just over a new hairstyle! So imagine then if the whole world told you how great it was that your guy had buried his chiseled abs under 120 pounds of fat, and how much better he looks now. Imagine a world with little support and even less sympathy for your point of view. What would it take to stay in that relationship when your partner no longer seems sexual, let alone sexy? Could you stay in that relationship?

Perhaps. But *should* you stay in that relationship? Again, perhaps. My purpose is not to answer this question, but to remind people to ask it.

Over the years, more than a few chasers have told me stories about when the men they adored became the men they didn't recognize. My friend James is a particularly poignant example of what many of us go through.

James is a chaser who was in a relationship for almost three years with a handsome chub named Kenny. The two of them were really great together, complementing each other at parties as many couples do. Kenny was witty and gregarious, while James was more reticent with a quiet intensity. Kenny had always been fat, and he knew from their first date that James was attracted to his heft and girth. Kenny admits that James never tried to make him fatter, but "I knew that if I ate more than I should or my pants got a little tight, he certainly wasn't going to scold me."

Over the course of their relationship, Kenny went from 290 pounds to 380. "At some point," Kenny says, "the weight just got to be too much for me. I didn't feel like me any more. I didn't like the way my clothes fit, and how my body moved, and all the new aches and pains I was developing." So Kenny decided to diet and lose weight. "James was very supportive at first. Given what happened afterward, though, I wonder now if it was genuine. After all, he ended up leaving me. My friends couldn't believe it. I mean, everyone thought James was so great. No one thought he'd just go and dump me because I wasn't fat enough for him any more."

That's the story of James, the shallow chaser who never really cared for his boyfriend. What's James's side of the story? Well, he says most people either don't ask or don't understand. James admits that Kenny was never more attractive than when he was approaching 400 pounds. He wrote me the following, and has allowed me to quote him here:

...But I knew he was having some physical problems, and he would complain that things were getting harder to do. I offered to do things for him—tying his shoes, or going grocery shopping for us— but Kenny didn't seem to appreciate the suggestions at all. So when Kenny told me he'd decided to lose weight I totally understood why. I hated seeing him unhappy with his body, and his size seemed to be so frustrating for him. Of course, I didn't turn into some fitness coach. I didn't encourage him to diet, but I never encouraged him to gain the weight in the first place either. Kenny did most of our cooking. He always ate what he wanted.

I admit his weight loss affected me more than I thought it would. The first week of his diet I got this little twinge one night when I saw him skinning chicken breasts. Not only had he never done that before, but I also knew he'd always hated white meat. He wasn't even that crazy about chicken. He started talking about portions and grams, and it felt like that was all he ever talked about now. It annoyed me, but I thought of it like he had a new hobby that I wasn't interested in. Then one night I saw him walking past me while I was on the couch, and I saw how much weight he'd lost. Out of nowhere I heard this little voice in my head screaming, "Noooooooooo!!" I was shocked at my own reaction. I honestly didn't think his weight was that big a deal to me.

I watched him drop down to 360, then 320, then 270, which was lighter than when we'd met. I figured at this point I was justified in saying something. "I just want to get under 250," he said. I swear it was like a bomb went off in my head. I mean, I knew it was his body; he could do what he liked with it. I was mad at myself that it was so important to me. When we were out with friends, they constantly told him how good he looked. "Doesn't he look good, James?" It got so I dreaded people saying it, and they said it everywhere we went. I just had to smile and suck it up.

Sometimes Kenny would squeeze my hand and tease me in front of them saying, "James isn't so crazy about how much weight I've lost." Oh man, that was the worst. For the next ten minutes, I'd have to hear about how weird or unfair I was being. Sometimes it was gentle kidding. Sometimes it was more pointed and got kind of intense. A couple of times I felt like the murderer at the table. As if refusing to turn cartwheels over James's weight loss equaled trying to kill him. Some nights when we got home I'd be seething, but I didn't know why. I mean, nobody likes being kidded, but I was enraged. James and I started having problems. We started arguing all the time over stupid things.

I remember one night on the computer, I was looking at pictures of fat guys and fantasizing. Kenny never caught me, but I started doing it more and more. When Kenny got below 250, I could barely look at him. Not because he was ugly to me or anything. It was just so painful, ya know? This was a guy I was crazy about, but now having sex with him was the last thing on my mind. I felt so angry and betrayed, but also angry and betrayed at myself. His size wasn't supposed to matter to me. How could I do this to him and our relationship? Looking at his sagging skin where there used to be beautiful rolls of fat grossed me out sometimes—and then having those negative thoughts about the man I loved disgusted me. I started going online a lot at work and started chatting with fat guys. I never met any. I knew I'd never forgive myself if I did that. But I came close a couple times.

I know Kenny could feel the distance. I hated myself for creating it, but I didn't know what to do. Finally one day, he said he was going to try to get down to 220 but then stop, he promised me. I told him, "I can't. I know this is right for you, but I can't be your partner any more." I remember the look on his face. He was so hurt when I said that. Then he was furious. Then he tried to reason with me, talk me into staying together—telling me how silly and unreasonable I was being. Everything he said made sense for someone else, but it felt so good to think about being able to be sexual again. (We hadn't had sex in about a year. I actually dreaded him asking for it.) I just wanted the relationship we used to have. I never asked Kenny to stop losing weight. Never. I would never. But I don't think it's fair that I have to ignore my feelings and pretend nothing has changed. When I've tried to explain this to people—even friends—they make it pretty clear that I'm not supposed to be feeling what I'm feeling. I haven't dated anyone seriously since. I just keep to hook-ups.

Notice how similar this is to Matilda Tuesday's story of trying to reconcile romantic love with the loss of sexual attraction. Today, James and Kenny say they don't blame each other, but they still long for what might have been under different circumstances.

Should I Stay or Should I Go?

Lots of chasers have told me stories similar to James's, but with different endings. Sometimes the chaser begins to cheat on the shrinking boyfriend, and they break up over infidelity. In other cases, the chaser stays cheerfully in the relationship; he may even cheer on his partner's fat loss, bragging about how much healthier his boyfriend is becoming. There are no fixed rules here. When I counsel couples, I start with what each person is feeling, experiencing, suppressing, or in some cases actively hiding. Why hide? Because of the usual suspects: fear, shame, and guilt. Again, these feelings aren't unique to the Round World, but the circumstances are.

Let's look at one more ending to the weight-loss story: Tony and Peter. Tony started running into health problems as he entered his 50s. Since he was fat, the cure seemed to be weight loss. He tried to lose weight, doing all the things that are supposed to work. Tony dieted. He tried low-fat, then low-carb, then even severe caloric restrictions. He hired a personal trainer. He altered his lifestyle and eating habits. None of this worked; he had lost no more than 20 pounds after almost a year. Even his boyfriend, Peter, testified that Tony's inability to lose weight was inexplicable, given how little he now ate and how much he exercised. There seemed to be nothing left except weight-loss surgery. Contrary to what we might expect of a chaser, Peter was in favor of the surgery. Of course he was worried about his boyfriend going under the knife, but he thought that a leaner boyfriend would be more active, more social, and less cranky about life in general, as Tony had become. No, it was Tony who seemed to have more trepidation, but he went through with the operation.

The surgery succeeded wildly. Tony dropped weight at an almost dangerous rate. Initially, Tony's weight loss and the operation's side effects (diarrhea, nausea, and vomiting) were so drastic that sexual relations seemed out of the question. But as the reality of a thinner man took shape, Peter and Tony both noticed their sexual interest in each other waning. Peter was not attracted to the sagging skin that made Tony look like a "melted candle," Peter said. He told me that his big, irascible teddy bear now just seemed like a mean, peevish old man. But Tony wasn't all that interested in Peter now either. Tony had once viewed Peter as the pinnacle of unflappable manliness. Now, however, he saw Peter as a closeted coward who had no gay friends or any ties to the gay community, something Tony had always missed in their life as a couple.

Not surprisingly, Tony and Peter eventually split up amid great acrimony. I tell this story not to illustrate how losing weight ends relationships. Quite the opposite. I tell it to show how weight loss revealed how objectification was the only thing holding that relationship together. I said before that objectification is present when what one person wants is more important than who the other person is. Peter was in love with the image of a fat, successful bear. Tony was in love with the image of a gorgeous, motorcycle-racing stud. As I talked about in my field guide to chubs and chasers, masculinity can play a key role for both people in the dyad. Their objectification of each other, their twin fantasies of masculinity, blinded the couple to everything else in the relationship, especially as those other things were brought to the forefront by the stress of drastic change.

I have talked about what it's like for the chaser when his partner loses hundreds of pounds, but it's not only the chaser who can decide to leave or stay. People tend to ascribe the power of choice solely to the chaser, as if the fat person has to take what's handed to them. I also know a couple in which it was the chub who opted out of his relationship after weight-loss surgery. Avery had become more confident in his new, slimmer body. Having felt inferior most of his life because of his extreme obesity, he had never dated or even had sex very often as a young man. His chaser boyfriend was his first and only relationship, and only one of a handful of sexual partners in 38 years. As Avery became smaller and leaner, two things happened: His regard for himself and what was possible grew, and his regard for his fat-loving partner shrank. In the end, it was Avery, not his chaser boyfriend, who called it quits and finally started living the life he had always wanted. His quiet and unassuming boyfriend, who had doted on him, now seemed asocial and introverted.

So it really isn't weight loss per se that brings a fat/admirer relationship to an end. In fact, weight loss may even bring a new beginning. In the Round World, weight loss is bound up in issues of sexuality, fidelity, masculinity/femininity, and attitudes about oneself—issues that are central to any relationship. The couples who come to me for counseling invariably have the specter of a break-up in the back of their minds. In truth, the sooner they can let go of the idea that staying together is the only acceptable outcome, the sooner they can actually work through their issues. I do not mean that these couples should break up. However, I think it is a paradox of life that you cannot freely choose something if you're not equally free to not choose it. On a more pragmatic level, I won't be able to offer any strategy to keep these two together that they have not already thought of. Any new possibility for their continued relationship must inevitably come from a state of not knowing, of discovery. That means no guarantees about how it's all going to turn out, only a commitment that each of them will be happy, fulfilled, and whole by the end. Again, this is true for any couple, but in the Round World we have our particular issues and circumstances to deal with. Weight loss can be one of them.

When we were in the middle of breaking up, Marc said one of the most magical things I've ever heard. I was sobbing over the tragic end of our relationship, bawling over how we would never again have the special kind of relationship we'd had for almost a decade. He turned to me amid all my drama and said quite bluntly, "You're right, sweetie. We won't." And then his smile melted me when he said, "We'll have a different relationship."

I try to pass along that warmth and reassurance when I tell couples that whether or not a relationship is sexual, there can always be love. When we realize that, then we're free to create the kind of relationship that brings growth, freedom, and empowerment.

Love, Loss, and Weight-Loss Surgery

Perhaps because of the life-and-death stakes, the topic of weight-loss surgery is definitely the third rail of the Round World. It's perhaps our equivalent to discussing abortion: Is it a moral violation of the body? The lesser of two evils (dying versus maiming)? Or a quick and lasting route to health and happiness? And the controversy isn't confined to the Round World; weight-loss surgery is heavily debated in our mainstream culture as well. I've even met a bariatric surgeon who considered weight-loss surgery a barbaric solution of last resort.

I've already talked about the effect of weight loss on chub/chaser relationships and the fat-fundamentalist justification that being thin is always healthier than being fat. Now let's put those two ideas together to better understand the conflict that some couples experience when one person goes under the knife to correct a feature that their partner considers attractive.

Weight-loss surgery is usually undertaken only when a fat person feels their life is at stake and there are no other options left. I've never met anyone who considered it cosmetic or elective surgery, no matter how much they weighed. Now, I have talked to 600-pound men who think that a 300-pound man having weight-loss surgery is doing it for cosmetic reasons, but that's not how a 300-pound man thinks of it. If you ask him, he'll tell you he's doing it to save his life.

The difference between weight-loss surgery and losing weight through other means is that the surgery is the most drastic, least wanted, and very last option to be considered by most fat people. This places it on equal ground with some other life-or-death surgeries. I'd like to offer an extreme but apt analogy that highlights how weight-loss surgery affects fat people and their admirers differently from how it affects others.

Let's say that a woman is dying of cancer and is considering a bilateral mastectomy to save her life. This is a serious medical procedure to remove both breasts, and people might debate whether it's the best or only option. Ultimately it comes down to a personal choice. Let's suppose the woman goes through with the procedure. Naturally she does not relish the fact that her breasts will be gone after the operation, and neither does her husband. They may or may not discuss this, but the husband understands it's for the good of his wife. He believes that he may not even have his wife if she doesn't lose her breasts to this procedure. In the best-case scenario, the operation is a success, the wife no longer has cancer, and the couple still enjoy a loving, monogamous relationship. So why shouldn't that also be the case with weight-loss surgery?

The crucial difference is that after the wife's mastectomy, the couple can mourn together the loss of an aspect of their relationship. Maybe the husband adored the wife's breasts—or maybe her breasts were merely incidental to their lovemaking—but the fact is that both partners experience a loss. That shared loss, I dare say, may even bring them closer together. They may fall even more deeply in love, having been through such trauma together (albeit unequally). But the chaser is alone in his mourning. He may even feel guilty about missing his partner's former body, which he associates with ill health.

One man I know even went into deep depression and started seeing a therapist after his wife's weight-loss surgery. Does that seem absurd? When I tell that story in my seminars, it often gets a laugh. To me, the fact that he sought therapy is a sign of his deep commitment to his relationship—to reconciling his sexuality with his wife's well-being. To others, however, the chaser's need for counseling is basically a fat joke in which the chaser's love of fat is the object of ridicule. The punch line of any fat joke involves the idea that a fat person's body is a ridiculous distortion of a normal body. In this case, the fat joke revolves around the idea that adoring a fat person's body is a ridiculous distortion of normal sexual attraction. I think if the relationship between a chaser and a fat person is to survive weight-loss surgery, the chaser needs to be able to say, once in a while, "I miss how fat you used to be." And the fat partner needs to be able to admit honestly, "Yeah, sometimes I miss being fat, too."

Love or Fetish?

One of the most tortured issues for some people, both inside and outside the Round World, is the distinction between sexual attraction and romantic love. There's little question for folks that *true love* refers to something life-giving and pure, and the modifier *true* suggests that we also believe in some inferior type of love that is somehow false. But we never speak of *true sex*. What would that even mean? In common parlance, at least, sex has no such depth or subtly to differentiate, true or otherwise. Sex is just sex. What's more, when most people use the word sex, they just mean penetration. Think about what you really want to know when you ask, "Have you guys had sex yet?" What do you picture when your friend says, "We've messed around some, but we haven't had sex yet." All the pleasure, wonder, and variety of sex we reduce to a single act of anatomical insertion.

Some might claim that *true sex*, if we can admit such a term, might point to something that is not only an intimate physical act, but also a spiritual, transcendental, or sacred bond. But romantics would counter that such a bond is possible only when *true love* exists. Sex is just a physical, mechanical act, they argue, that acquires a higher dimension only when sanctified by love. Indeed, many might go so far as to say that sex without love is simply dirty or even degrading. However, millions of others would strenuously disagree. So you can see the problem in distinguishing love from lust. It's no wonder people work themselves into a lather trying to figure out what they feel.

With so much room for interpretation and disagreement, imagine the mess I'm going to make now when I bring Fat into the discussion—when I ask you to consider that Fat is part of my sexuality and that my sexuality intermingles with love. I think it's extremely important to see how this all plays out in the Round World. Let me tell you about two guys whom I met at two different seminars I led.

The first man is Anton, a 340-pound chub in his late 40s. He didn't have much dating experience; in fact, his sexual encounters only slightly outnumbered his boyfriends. He wrote to tell me that he had gotten a lot out of my seminar, and that he'd since met a great guy who was pursuing him. The guy was very demonstrative and affectionate, and the guy often mentioned how much he liked Anton's body. However, Anton was concerned and wrote to me: "Do you think this guy loves me for me, or just for my fat? When we're together, he can't keep his hands off me, and he goes crazy when I take off my shirt and he plays with my rolls."

In contrast, let's talk about a chaser named Robert. Robert loves fat guys and says that they "really get him going." At the same time, however, he admits that "I'd never date a fat guy seriously." When pressed for his reasons, he told me, "Fat guys are slower, and you can't travel or do as much with them. Besides, how long could it last anyway? I mean, he's probably gonna die sooner than later, right? Why go through that just to satisfy a stupid fetish I happen to have? I'll just have my fun or date a normal guy if I want something serious."

What do you think of Robert and Anton? When I talk about these two men in my seminars, there's usually sympathy for Anton and dislike for Robert. But Anton and Robert actually see the attraction to Fat the same way. They both see the admiration of obesity as something trivial and perhaps even suspicious. Notice that the chaser in both cases, Robert or Anton's boyfriend, is seen as a user despite their completely opposite actions and intentions. Anton's boyfriend is suspected of loving Anton for "only a fetish," which reduces his love to merely lust, an unworthy foundation for a serious relationship. What about Robert? In describing his desires as "only a fetish," Robert freely admits that his attraction is unworthy as the basis of a relationship. He seems to agree with Anton and most "normal" folks who say that you can't base an attraction for someone on Fat. Nevertheless, for adopting the popular view, Robert is seen as cynical and calculating. For rejecting the popular view, Anton's chaser is suspected of being objectifying and fetishistic. It's curious that whether the chaser is sincere or mercenary, he is always in the wrong. His motives are always impugned. Why? Because sexual attraction to Fat is viewed as wrong, so anything that stems from that attraction must also be wrong to the same degree. Love never even gets a chance in the discussion.

People are sexually attracted to all sorts of qualities that may be admirable, banal, or even disgusting. Is that the same as love? No, but it comes with the deal. A romantic relationship is based on both love and physical desire. In fact, in many relationships, sex may be the point from which love grows. When we draw a hard line between love and lust, we're usually just trying to draw a line between good and bad—between what we see as noble and what we see as base. Trying to sort our feelings of attraction into good and bad only leads away from being whole. What's more, it robs us of experiencing the other person as whole while we worry about which parts of them we should or shouldn't admire.

Let's transcend the "love or fetish" question and instead turn our attention to the questions that matter: Do I feel respected? Do I feel valued for the parts of me that I like and maybe even for the parts of me that I don't like. Is there intimacy and empathy in our relationship? Do I feel free to express who I am?

FINDING ROOM
FOR ADORATION

I'd like to return to Anton for a moment to demonstrate how someone might work through that question of love versus lust. You may have recognized that Anton was concerned he was being objectified. If you recall, I said that we objectify someone when our desires are more important than who the other person is—how the other person sees himself, his identity in the world. Here's how I worked with Anton using that definition of objectification.

In Anton's case, I was looking for whether his boyfriend's attraction to obesity was overshadowing Anton's identity—how Anton saw himself in the world. Starting with the second half of the definition, I asked Anton whether he thought his fat was separate from him. Did he feel that his folds and rolls were somehow a separate object that didn't belong to who he was as a person? He acknowledged that his fat was most definitely part of him. But when I asked if it was okay for a man to like this aspect of him, adore it even, he seemed unsure. So I upped the ante. I asked whether there were other aspects of his body or his mind that were also off-limits to someone's attention, admiration...or even ministrations. What were the lovable and unlovable parts of him?

That stopped him. He said he'd spent his life taking himself apart and assessing his pieces. I teased him, "That's fine, but is it okay if someone has a different opinion of some of those pieces?" Then he smiled, as it seemed to dawn on him that he could allow a person to care for any part of him. It didn't necessarily take away from their regard for him as a whole person. We're always attracted or fascinated by certain aspects of a person. Sometimes those aspects are physical and sometimes they're not, but love can be found in any and all of the parts.

But what about Anton's chaser and his view of Anton? Looking at the first part of our definition of objectification, were the chaser's desires all that mattered to him? I asked Anton whether he felt free to express himself, or did he feel like there were right and wrong answers that the chaser wanted to hear. Did he feel valued and heard? What did they do together on dates? Were the dates mutually enjoyable, or were they only enjoyable by proxy, for example, "I liked it because he liked it"? These questions might seem off target since they don't bear directly on Anton's body, but when someone is being objectified, it comes across in every area of the relationship. Anton was able to see that while the chaser was crazy about Anton's blubber, Anton also mattered to him as a person. Anton said he did feel heard and respected. He'd just never experienced anyone so completely enthralled by his body and its hundreds of pounds of fat.

Sexual Inhibition

I recently received an email from a straight woman in her late 20s who described herself as "FAT" in emphatic capital letters. She said that she'd been on dates, but many had ended badly and none had led to sex. She asked, "Can plus-size women get sex? I know it's not the most important thing in the world, but since I am still a virgin, I am extremely curious."

As I've said, outside the Round World, Fat is the opposite of sex. I often encounter people who think that fat people have less sex, worse sex, degrading sex—or just plain don't have sex. However, none of those things are any more true for fat people than for thin people. I think there must be just as many thin virgins as fat virgins, and for the same assortment of circumstances and rationales. The other common misconception is that a hot, young guy must be having all the sex he wants with whomever he wants. Again, this is far from the case, especially if the guy is a chubby chaser.

For many in the Round World, negativity surrounds sex. I've met many chasers who know they have this attraction but have never acted on their "freakish desires." Similarly, I've met fat men and women who have settled for virginity because it seemed to be their only alternative to being someone's fetish wagon. Again, the stigma of Fat suppresses chubs and chasers alike. Some people assume that fat sex is impersonal, fetishistic, selfish, or mercenary. It need not be any of these things.

I've been in bed with guys who just want to worship my muscles. Just like a lot of fat men and women, I know what it's like to be treated like hot, sexy meat. However, I don't see myself as a victim when this happens. I don't feel lonely, thinking that any guy who likes my body must be shallow. Being objectified isn't insulting as much as it is really boring. I have learned to listen better to guys who would objectify me, so we don't get as far as the bedroom. People generally tell you everything you need to know about them within a few minutes. If a chaser gets lost in the ecstasy of blubber and leaves their fat partner behind, they both get cheated. On the other hand, if the fat person resists the fact that their body is beautiful to their partner, then they're opting out of intimacy and some potentially great sex.

Sex and sensuality involve an exploration of the landscape of the body—both bodies. I've been with chubs who feared touching my body because, as they told me later, they were afraid of doing something wrong and ending the encounter. I've been with chubs who didn't want the lights left on, or who were reluctant to take their clothes off. In coaching fat people about dating chasers, I've said this: "A chaser will probably be the most turned on by the parts of your body you are least proud of." Many people—even people who aren't fat—expend a lot of energy protecting, hiding, or downplaying some part of their body that they feel isn't sexy. Some people are actually at war with certain parts of their body. Then along comes a chaser who charges right through all those strategic defenses and not only notices that cellulite, that roll, that fold but who can't seem to keep his or her hands off it. This is another situation of being confronted by a difference of opinion: the fat person's disgust versus the chaser's delight. Of the two, delight is generally more fun.

Most chasers know enough to keep their mouths shut when it comes to expressing their admiration; at the very least, we temper it. Trust me, no matter how much a chaser praises a fat person's body, the chaser isn't saying the half of it. For example, when I'm with a chub, I can't rhapsodize about how exquisite the center cleft in his hanging belly is. Even though telling him might not offend him, a poetic description of the region would probably fall on deaf ears. "I'm happy that you're happy" would be the most I could hope for. Similarly, I have the good sense not to tell most chubs, "I love how deep and red your stretch marks are." Most people just don't want to hear that.

Many people, of course, are more than happy to be admired. My friend Adam, for example, is beautifully and hugely fat, and he has no trouble hearing me gush about that fact. He's quite happy to be the center of my attention. But unless a fat person is sexually aroused by their obesity, they will never see their body quite the way a chaser does. In that way, the fat person and I share something in common: We look to date someone who doesn't look like us. I think I look good, but I would never date a guy who looked like me. Muscular guys are beautiful to me, but not the same way that a huge fat man is. Similarly, a well-adjusted fat person understands that some people find them beautiful, but that doesn't mean that the fat person is going to start looking for other fat people to date.

There is, I'll admit, an adolescent sexual fixation that can take over the mind of a chaser like a fever. I've known chasers to literally vibrate because of the uncontrollable torrent of adrenaline coursing through them when they're naked with a fat partner. This kind of chaser, if he or she is callous and treats the fat person like sexy meat, does so more out of immaturity than malice. Because of that, some fat people find it flattering and forgivable, although others just feel used. It depends on the fat person's own appreciation of his or her body. If he likes his body, he's probably titillated and flattered to be someone's sex object. However, that titillation may turn to boredom if dumbstruck adoration is all that's on offer. By contrast, if he dislikes his body, he's probably offended and may feel like someone's sex toy.

However, when a chaser is ashamed of their desires, then the encounter is more likely to feel negative. The fat person feels slimed and understands, even if only subliminally, that they have been made the accomplice to an act of shame. It can go both ways, though. Chasers also feel used sometimes. When a fat person is ashamed of their body, when they see sexual attraction for their body as a sick fetish or a mercy fuck, it degrades the chaser and casts him or her in a role that is either mercenary or condescending—a psychopath or a sycophant.

Some fat people are simply unwilling to give up their distaste for their bodies to make any room for pleasure. I was in bed with a chub and said to him, "You're beautiful." His response was flat and cold: "Dude, you need therapy." I was with another chub who would laugh at anything

I said that complimented his body. Not a coquettish giggle, but a condescending chuckle that meant, "Don't be absurd." If I got emotionally intimate through eye contact or touch, he would make a funny remark or non sequitur to break the moment. Seeing himself as sexy or desirable was literally laughable to him. Now he was by no means a virgin; he'd had lots of mechanical and sometimes anonymous sex. If I had just wanted to bend him over and bang his lights out, I think he would have been fine with that. But he was very uncomfortable with simple intimacy.

The bottom line is this: The greatest gift a chub can give a chaser is to find himself sexy. The greatest gift a chaser can give a chub is to find himself lucky to be with such a unique, beautiful fat man. And of course this is true no matter what the gender of the partners.

Superchub, Supercool

Superchub is a loose designation that means about what you'd think: He's a gay man weighing over 350 or 400 pounds. In straight nomenclature, the terms are SSBBW (Super-Sized Big Beautiful Woman) or SSBHM (Super-Sized Big Handsome Man). However, as we have already seen, body weight is not a reliable measure of the perception of Fat. If Fat represents a powerful attraction for chasers, then the supersized are the celebrities and supermodels of the Round World. I can have a conversation with a fellow gay Beauty Chaser, and we know and admire all the same guys. It's like we're talking about movie stars that everybody knows: Mikey in Memphis, Nick in Maine, Luke in Canada, and the list goes on. Some people reading these words right now know exactly to whom I am referring, based only on this scant information. Of course, the gay Power Chasers have their darlings as well, whom they all know by name, as do the chasers who are attracted to supersized women of immense beauty or power.

Like anyone else, we all have our celebrity idols, and they are known to anyone who shares our tastes. It's like going to some far corner of the world and mentioning Angelina Jolie—of course people have heard of her! Likewise, many supersized people are celebrities in the Round World with international reputations. They are shadowed by ardent paparazzi (chasers with cameras) and even receive occasional entreaties of, "Marry me!" from anonymous fans.

Sexual Attraction and the Fat Celebrity

Attraction—whether or not it has to do with Fat—can border on obsession in some cases. It's probably just more noticeable and stigmatized when the attraction is based on obesity. People usually form their attractions in one of two ways: additive or aggregate. Some chasers (gay or straight, male or female) have an additive form of attraction. For example, some Fat Admirers see a pretty woman as twice as attractive if she is also fat. Similarly, a fat woman who's twice as pretty and twice as fat is four times as attractive to that kind of chaser. We can see this additive attraction also in some Power Chasers. For example, if a fat guy is handsome, *and* he has a big overhanging belly, *and* he's got a nice beard, *and* he's wearing suspenders, *and* so on and so forth, then the additive effect can be erotically devastating for the chaser.

However, not everyone has this perception of attraction. Many people perceive attraction not as additive, but as aggregate—requiring all or most of a set of desirable traits to be present for a person to be considered attractive. Again, the traits may be physical or psychological. For these men and women, adding traits together doesn't increase the sexual attraction. Rather, *all* the traits need to be present—for example, a masculine demeanor, big belly, and thick beard—before the person is considered attractive.

I point out this difference of attraction—additive versus aggregate—to help explain why supersized people can be so obsessively idolized. For some, their virtues are seen as additively compounding their sexual attractiveness. In other cases, they are seen as possessing the perfect storm of attributes, the perfect constellation that drives their admirers wild. Many obese celebrities can actually earn a decent income from people who will pay to see their pictures, download their videos, or have a one-on-one meeting in person or over the internet.

Supersized Dating

Contrary to their experience in the regular world, extremely obese people in the Round World often enjoy a special status that most people would envy, though sometimes it can be isolating. For example, my friend Matthew is gorgeous. Absolutely drop-dead gorgeous. He's tall, blond, incredibly handsome, with perfect skin, perfect hair, and he's even super smart. He looks like an Abercrombie & Fitch model…if Abercrombie & Fitch models weighed 600 pounds. Matthew has no end of suitors in the Round World, spanning the globe from San Diego to Dubai. Some are ordinary looking, but most are stunning. Matthew is the object of Beauty Chasers, who themselves tend to be beautiful. Two of his admirers have modeled professionally, and others are scientists, lawyers, and even diplomats.

Matthew has taken up Portuguese. He says he loves the language, and I believe him. It's just a happy coincidence that he gets so much opportunity to practice it talking with his many handsome, athletic admirers in Brazil. Men like Matthew can have sex any time, anywhere they want. Really. Men literally fly across the world to meet them; I've done it myself to meet such men. They're just that beautiful. You might think it would be paradise to have beautiful men from every corner of the globe getting on airplanes just for the privilege of meeting you. Perhaps. Some fat celebrities revel in it, but others find it so overwhelming that they can barely deal with the attention and the high volume of email and instant messaging.

I suppose if you think of online dating as a marketplace, then super-sized people are a boutique item. They're like those incredibly expensive Fabergé eggs encrusted with jewels and laden with intricate designs. But if I took a Fabergé egg to the parking lot of a Walmart, I probably couldn't give it away. At best I'd get a few bucks for it as a novelty item. To the general public, it's just a white elephant (no pun intended). But a jeweler knows the true value, and a specialty shop or antiques dealer would ask an astronomical price for such a prize. At auction, that egg would cause a bidding war. So anyone who's 500 pounds and not getting the sexual or romantic attention they would like is just not set up in the right shop.

Supersized Partnership

Believe it or not, however, the adoration and sexual attention of the world's most beautiful men and women can get old when it's all that's on offer. What if you want more than just sex on tap? What if you want a partner and a long-term relationship? Maybe kids? Well, now that partner is harder to find. (But isn't that what thin people say, too?) It's a well-known adage among superchubs that the most ardent suitors live the greatest distance away. Marriage proposals pour in from Rio and Mexico City; offers of luxurious concubinage come from princes in Riyadh. But the hot skater dude down the street is too scared and intimidated to set up a coffee date. He sends love letters, too, but the very fact that his fantasy lives around the corner, just within his grasp, proves his undoing. Still, he pines away, making excuses, somehow convincing himself that wanting is better than having.

It's unfortunate that a lot of chasers can't seem to get over ourselves, much to the frustration of our prospective fat partners. To the extent that superchubs are coveted and revered by some of us, they are also out of our reach because of our own fears and insecurities. It takes something special to live an unapologetic life at 500 pounds, especially when so many people believe your body requires an apology. It takes just as much courage to hold that man or woman's hand on the street, to introduce them to friends and family as your partner, and to make a life embracing all that comes with their enormous, beautiful body. It's not that chasers don't want these things. Indeed, I think many chasers dream of such a life and wish they could have it. Just as they wish they had the courage to live it. But as I say: It's like dating a celebrity. It's a fantasy, but perhaps a stigma too. I mean, if you're Joe Normal, what's it like to be swept up into the world of being Angelina Jolie's boyfriend? Can you handle that much attention, that much scrutiny, that much gossip?

My friend Matthew said something I'll never forget. Like most men his weight, he has contemplated weight-loss surgery. However, he told me something you don't often hear spoken aloud: "If I lost the weight, I'd be appealing to a lot more men, and that'd be great. But then I'd be just another gay guy." This is true. The price of being normal is that you're just like everyone else. Matthew would probably have a much larger dating pool if he were a third of his size. But would those men climb mountains and swim oceans for him as they do now?

Supersized Sex

I'm actually delighted when people have the courage and frankness to ask me about fat sex. I meet a lot of people who can accept that a fat body might be attractive to some people, but when they find out just how fat some of my sexual partners are, that invites questions about the mechanics of sex. "How…?" they ask, dumbfounded. "How do you make love to someone that fat?" Well, my favorite response is "How do you not?" Of course, making love to someone extremely obese is different. But for chasers, the differences are opportunities and challenges, and rarely chores or difficulties.

There are already lots of books and blogs out there dealing with supersized lovemaking techniques, but they're usually written by and for fat women. Some of these are generous enough to include a few words about making love to fat men, but as I've said, fat men barely exist in the literature of the marketplace. There are also sex workshops, but again, these are at BBW events, and only women are allowed in the room to create a safe space. Nevertheless, it's beyond the scope of this book to be some sort of fat Kama Sutra, and reading about sexual techniques and positions isn't nearly as much fun as discovering them. However, I do want to make a few points to dispel certain misconceptions about making love to supersized bodies in general.

Fat and Flexibility

First, getting between an obese person's legs isn't as unlikely as you might think. Even enormously fat people have at least one dimension of extreme flexibility. In talking with BBWs and from my own experience with men over 600 pounds, I've found that extremely fat people are often unusually limber in motion that centers around the pelvic area. They develop that flexibility as a result of adapting to their increasing size over the years. For example, I know a guy who's over 550 pounds at only five foot two, but he can still tie his own shoes. How? The same way a dancer does the splits. He extends his leg straight out to the side, the same way you or I can easily extend our arm to the side. While his massive folds of fat remain mostly in front of him, he leans over to the side and ties his shoes. He looks like he's doing a ballet stretch. Another man I know who's over 600 pounds is able to wash his genitals in the shower by simply resting his foot on the soap dish near his head. This opens up space between his legs for him to soap and rinse there. What works in the shower works in bed, too. Many of us chasers have marveled and learned to take advantage of this incredible flexibility.

Flexibility is a talent that many chasers possess as well, but that frequently goes unappreciated by chubs. A lot of chubs love my bulk and muscularity, and they sometimes disparage the smaller, slimmer guys who pursue them. When I chide them for this, they tell me these young chasers seem like little boys. I always tell them that they're missing out on a great opportunity by ignoring these guys. (By the way, some of these "little boys" look like Calvin Klein underwear models, but for some chubs and BBWs, that's not their idea of masculinity.) "I always feel like I'm gonna break him," they say. "You're not gonna break him!" I respond. "And even if you do, he'll die a happy man." More seriously, I tell them, "You'll both enjoy the contrast of your bodies and the ingenuity that his attraction to you inspires."

But more to the point, a small, lean chaser can get his body into folds and crevices that I would never be able to access with my size and rather inflexible bulk. Some supersized people have come to quite appreciate the unique abilities that a smaller partner often possesses. One of my superchub friends has a name for these lithe, slender men who eagerly pleasure him: "Chub-floss."

More to "More to Love"

Another point about supersized sex is that supersized people aren't just bigger or heavier. Speaking from my experience with fat men, I believe they are capable of more (or at least different) tactile sensitivity and often have erogenous zones that thin people do not. In fact, a lot of huge guys I've played with don't even know this about themselves, which is always wondrous to discover with them. The erotic landscape of an enormously fat person is not just a bigger or more unwieldy version of a thin person's. I've found that generally, the fatter a partner is, the more varied and sensitive their erogenous zones. A very fat person can experience a kind of intense pleasure in lovemaking that arises because of, not in spite of, his or her obesity. Moving into creases, folds, or just an expanse of flesh with the right touch can set off a cascade of pleasure for an obese partner that is beyond the ken of a thin person.

I know this because I've been with men who have gained or lost hundreds of pounds of fat over the years, and we've had intimate conversations about how their bodies experience sexual pleasure differently at different sizes. I'm not saying that thin people don't have intense sex. But the sexual experiences of fat people can be equally intense, and in ways no thin person can really enjoy without having the body to experience it. Making love is like making music. A violin is incapable of making the music that a cello makes, and you don't play the cello the same way you play the violin. Extending this metaphor, I'd say that making love with a superchub is like making music with a vast, sonorous pipe organ.

It may seem to you that sex with a 500-pound person is one-sided, with the chaser doing all the work. After all, 500-pound men or women are not particularly nimble on a mattress, no matter how flexible they may be. True. The reciprocation happens differently but still equally. Male and female chasers have told me that they like their body played with in the same ways as most other men and women do. And most chubs, no matter how fat, are fully capable of this sort of play once the positioning is worked out. If the chaser wants to be fucked, that may prove difficult for some fat partners, but not necessarily depending on how the fat person carries their weight. However, there are usually workarounds that take advantage of the fat person's size, which are as good if not better.

Why better? Because any sexual maneuver that takes advantage of the partner's obesity delights the chaser and pays tribute to the partner. I know many chasers who love bending over to feel a massive belly on top of their back and falling off their hips while that fat man's cock is thrusting into them. I know chasers who delight in pushing their face past the heavy folds of a BBW's thighs to give her pleasure, all the more turned on because he can barely breathe while encased in her flesh and buried under the weight of her massive belly. He may even enjoy impressing her with his expert breath control as testimony to his dedication to her pleasure. Like most pleasures in the Round World, obstacles become adventures. A disability in one context is a unique qualification in another. Sex in the Round World has only one dictum: There is nothing hotter than partners (fat or thin) who see themselves as truly and effortlessly sexy.

From Zero to Hero

Imagine being so large that every movement you make—every step, turn, or lean—has a physical reverberation, even a possible consequence. Imagine that at some level, every day, you are conscious of living in a world that was not designed for your size. How do you deal with that? There are two classic strategies you might employ: One strategy is to simply turn invisible. That's not as absurd as it sounds. I was talking to a guy who was six foot four and about 400 pounds. He said he felt discriminated against in West Hollywood, the gay haven where I make my home. When I told him I am frequently out and about with guys his size and have never experienced anything negative, he recounted a story about visiting one of our gayborhood's swankier bars on a Friday night. As he expected, the bar was packed, but he waited patiently. After a while, however, he noticed that lots of guys were getting served ahead of him. Finally, in frustration, he bellowed at the bartender, "Hey! Do you think I might get a drink?"

The bartender looked up in utter shock. "Oh, sorry, buddy," he said. "I didn't see you standing there."

"Did the bartender seem sarcastic or catty about it?" I asked.

"No, but c'mon! I'm fucking huge. How could he have not seen me?" He acknowledged that the bartender was being genuine, but it seemed impossible to him that someone so immense could be simply overlooked.

One explanation is that a lot of fat guys such as my friend actually do a very good job of hanging back, averting interaction, avoiding eye contact, and generally being as inconspicuous as possible. Eye contact, as I've mentioned before, is often key in trying to flirt with fat guys. Now, my friend isn't a shrinking violet, but he admitted that he's spent most of his life being the biggest thing in a room and trying not to inconvenience people or impose his size on them. I think in this instance, he was even more successful than usual because he didn't want to stick out as the mammoth fat guy in a bar full of A-gays.

The second classic tactic of many fat people is to win people with their charm before they get dismissed for their body. At a seminar in Germany, I talked to a woman who was just delightful. She was the kind of person you feel lucky to meet because of her incredible warmth and charm. She'd gone out of her way to make me feel welcome in a country where I was woefully incompetent in the language and didn't know a soul. When I told her how appreciative I was and how special I thought she was, she said quite naturally, "Well, my grandmother told me when I was a child, 'Sweetie, you have to know that you're more than a little chubby, and you're never going to be the prettiest at the dance. But you can make up for all of that with your beautiful smile and personality.'" She had not taken her grandmother's words as an insult, but rather as sound, sensible advice. She's been highly successful in her career, and as I said, I found her truly and authentically touching as a human being. She wasn't faking it. She wasn't burdened by needing to be sociable and charming. Rather, she saw it as one of her talents that she'd developed.

All of us, no matter our size, develop coping mechanisms for dealing with whatever we consider our defects. In fact, some of us have become our coping mechanism; it has become our whole personality. But what happens when a supposed defect—being fat—is viewed as an asset? What's a mechanism to do? What if you've spent your life trying to stay inconspicuously out of the way, and now suddenly people are turning a sexual spotlight on you? What if you've honed your people skills to the point where they can outshine any physical deficit, but then that physical deficit is admired from across a room before your people skills are discernible? What if someone treated your most glaring defect as your greatest asset?

That's what happens to many people when they enter the Round World for the first time. Overnight they find themselves in the spotlight of a sexual frenzy—as a sex object. Not in spite of their size, but because of it. Dozens of guys click on their profiles, rummage through their online pictures, and beg for more pictures taken just for them. They write sexual messages that sometimes titillate or disgust. (The reaction generally depends not on the message but on what the author looks like.) What do you do when it seems that a whole world you never knew existed suddenly wants a piece of you? What do you do when the strategy that has carried you through the last 15 or 20 years is now totally useless? Well, if you're the type who's accustomed to hiding, the attention might seem like scathing exposure, even violation. If you're the type who's honed other qualities to shine, you might feel objectified because your "real" qualities take a backseat or are even ignored.

It's not that fat men or women are just a fetish to us chasers; most of us don't think that way. True, some of us have to get past our shame of "it's just a fetish," but eventually we come to accept that Fat is a big part of what we're attracted to. But then we encounter that person, that angel, that stud who completely undoes us. It's the dumbstruck awkwardness of trying to talk to your crush, but worse. It's like meeting a favorite sexy movie star. You've seen all their movies, followed their career, listened to their interviews. Now imagine you're actually on a date with this person. How long would it take you to get past "Oh, my god, I'm actually having dinner with this person!!!" How long would it take you to realize that you're on a date with a human being—and not just "Oh, my god! This is the hottest, most amazing thing ever!" I'm sure Angelina Jolie is used to men making fools of themselves just saying hello. However, many obese men or women might infer that such fumbling is some sort of insult or objectification. For many fat people, entering the Round World feels like going from zero to hero, from nobody to celebrity, from sober, asexual professional to scintillating sexpot. Many embrace this change of status, but even so, it can be uncomfortable and disorienting. And this isn't the case only for fat people.

For the chaser, too, it sometimes feels like going from zero to hero. For many fat people, their first encounter with a chaser is the first time they've felt valued rather than pitied, beautiful rather than grotesque. So then imagine a chaser asking them on a date. The date goes well, and the fat person can't believe that such an amazing guy or gal is interested in them, not just personally but also sexually. For some fat people, such interest is rare in their experience, and something they think they shouldn't let slip by for it may never come again. The next thing you know, the fat person is making grand, romantic plans, alluding to making a life together, and feeling hurt when the chaser doesn't want to text multiple times a day. On the other hand, the chaser feels ambushed. From his or her perspective, one moment they're an ordinary person with an okay body; the next, they're the perfect boyfriend or girlfriend, one in a million, too good to lose, and a marriage prospect.

We see this with the sudden celebrity of sports stars, too. One minute he's just a local guy with a talent for throwing a ball through a hoop. The next minute he's the object of public scrutiny, asked to give national interviews, and expected to treat fans with charm and grace—no matter how rude they might be. I can tell you from personal experience going from fat dork to bodybuilder, I had to learn to handle the attention. The first time I was at a chub/chaser event, walking to a lounge chair in a Speedo, it was a bit unnerving to see guys' heads turning to follow me like a flock of seagulls. Suddenly lots of guys wanted my attention, my body, and my love. I had to learn how to be gracious but honest, how to be friendly without leading them on. Maybe the pretty cheerleaders and handsome quarterbacks learned this way back in high school, but for me it was like learning how to swim by falling into the deep end of the pool. You might think it would be different for me, since muscle is generally admired. But I can tell you from talking to BBWs and fat men that being bowled over by attention when you're not used to it—even positive attention—takes some getting used to.

Being a Hero: Coming Out as a Chubby Chaser

Men want to be heroes. We look for opportunities to demonstrate our heroism to our partners. We are the protector, defender, role model, breadwinner, dragon slayer, gallant, savior, adventurer, mariner, and standard-bearer. Women can be these things, too, of course, but many men feel it's our job—perhaps even a burden more than an aspiration. The more inflexible the gender roles in a particular community, the more the men in that community feel it's their job, their duty, to be the hero—whatever a hero looks like for that community.

So, too, a male chaser wants to be a hero in the eyes of his fat partner. He wants to be the gallant helping his fat date through the crowded restaurant. He wants to be their protector if someone makes an unkind remark. He wants to go on adventures with his friends, but still have his best friend—his partner—with him forever.

Most people think of heroes as having two physical characteristics: they are athletic and they are male. That's not always true, of course, but it is what comes to mind when people hear the word *hero*. So in the

Round World, we struggle a lot against this stereotype. Fat women often feel the least empowered—people aren't likely to look at them as heroes since they are less likely to appear masculine or athletic. This struggle to be recognized as heroic is actually part of what makes Fat a feminist issue. However, fat men often don't have it much easier. They may feel slighted because they don't look athletic, and doubly so if they're gay and don't feel that they're man enough either. Thin women are more likely to be viewed as heroic than fat men or women, especially in the Round World if they have the gumption and poise to walk with a fat partner by their side.

But let's focus for a moment on lean male chubby chasers because we can look the part of the hero even when we haven't earned the title. And as I said, men strive to be heroes even when no woman is involved. As men who love Fat, we want—we need—the opportunity to be heroic for our fat partner. Many fat people in my seminars, particularly women, nod their heads when I say this, testifying to the degree of devotion they experience from some of the chasers they have been with over the years.

Most of a man's adolescence is spent working out what it means to be a man—how we should look, what we should pursue, and who we should be. And yes, we come up with some pretty ridiculous answers sometimes because that's what adolescence is for. Also, I've noted that people in the Round World tend to lag five to ten years behind our straight, normative peers. What's more, if a man (straight or gay) choses to ignore questions of adolescence—his sexuality, his arousal, his place in the world—then this process takes even longer. So adolescence, for some of us in the Round World, may carry far into our 20s or 30s. The hero takes that much longer to develop.

Ultimately, however, the only thing that stops chasers from fulfilling our role as the hero is fear. Circumstances will never stop a hero—only fear can do that. The difference between the hero and the ordinary man is that the hero does not allow his fear to stop him. He knows that a person who waits for courage waits forever. When chasers ask me how to get up the courage to come out to their friends and family, or how to know when the time is right, I sometimes remind them of the Cowardly Lion in *The Wizard of Oz*. The Lion is petrified at every turn, at every single step, as he makes his way with his friends to face the Wicked Witch in her castle.

At no point is he brave, though he is ultimately successful. He simply does not allow his fear to stop him. His courage comes only afterward, in the form of a medal bestowed upon him by the Wizard. That's the first time the Cowardly Lion feels brave. We feel our courage only after the scary deed is done. That's when we look and feel brave. In the moment of crisis, however, there is no such courage. All we have is what the Lion had: a commitment to something more important than our fear.

Anyone who has come out as gay knows that you don't suddenly get courage and then fearlessly come out. Some chasers are very open about their attraction to Fat, but many more are still in the closet or hiding behind euphemisms. Over the years, fat people have told me stories of chasers who adored their obesity but lacked the courage to brave the stigma and social pressure that comes with having a fat partner. Many times, these chasers justify their cowardice with fat fundamentalism. Since obesity is an abnormal and unhealthy condition, they reason, enduring the stigma of having a fat partner is a fool's errand. Since they believe the stigma of obesity to be justified, they see no sense in going against it.

Sometimes our coming out as chasers happens by accident, and sometimes it's meticulously planned. But coming out—as gay, as a chaser, as whatever—always happens when who we are no longer fits with how our community relates to us. And then our community, our relationships, our priorities, our whole world has to align with our new identity. I have heard some horrific stories about what happened to people after they came out of whatever closet they were in. However, even when coming out resulted in homelessness, shunning, or unemployment, no one has ever told me that they regretted it. None have wished they could go back to the way things were.

In the previous section, you had the opportunity to distinguish a lot of what you think and feel about Fat. If you live outside the Round World, the Fat Map with its extremes of blame, pity, loathing, and ecstasy is a tool to help visualize what you think of fat people and their admirers. But for those of us inside the Round World, the map locates what we think of each other and ourselves. It locates where our relationships fail or flourish. So, in a larger sense, the Fat Map is a way to listen to the conversation that we're all having about Fat. By allowing us to be honest about what we think and feel, it may also be the way we'll start to change how we see Fat and have a conversation that empowers us. All of us.

Entering a dark forest

Now I'd like to take you to a part of the Round World that most folks hear about but never get to understand or explore. It's a place supposedly inhabited by monsters and demons, a place that righteous folk prefer to stay clear of. I'm going to take you there next, and you'll meet the men and women who are sexually aroused by making themselves fat or even fatter. You'll also meet their partners.

The terrain we've covered so far in the Round World has been the geography of our thoughts and feelings around Fat, fat people, and the upside-down notion that Fat can be synonymous with sex. Now we go to a dark forest, so to speak, where the feedists live. They are called *gainers* and *encouragers* in gay parlance, *feedees* and *feeders* in straight lingo. I do not call the forest dark because it is evil. Rather, I call it dark because it is not well illuminated. Indeed, it is unknown, feared, and misunderstood even by those of us who live there.

4

Fat Kink and the Drive to Get Fatter

Each of us is born with a box of matches inside us, but we can't strike them all by ourselves.

—Laura Esquivel
Like Water for Chocolate

THE FOREST OF FATTER

As I've said throughout this book, people's prejudices about Fat inform what they believe about fat people and their admirers. Nowhere in the Round World is this more evident than when I take people into the Forest of Fatter, where the feedists make their home. These are the people who are sexually aroused by making themselves or someone else fatter.

I call this region of the Round World a forest because it is not well mapped; there are few roads here, and exploring the psychological terrain can be disorienting, baffling, and even upsetting. Compasses, magnetic or moral, seem to spin here. There's a lot of wandering too, as people try to find their way in or out or just make a home where they are. In fact, the folks who live in this forest mostly have to make their own trails, although sometimes they run across someone else's and follow that for a while. But as in any forest, the exploration of this terrain is rich with personal insight and natural beauty. That's certainly been the case for me, for this is my place in the Round World. It's where I make my home.

Gainers and *encouragers* are the traditional terms referring to gay men who wish to become fatter or make someone else fatter; *feedees* and *feeders* are terms that grew up separately but in parallel in the straight community. This convention is not strictly observed, however. The terms *feedist*, *feederism*, and *feedism* have recently developed in response to the fact that, as we've seen elsewhere in the Round World, one's gender or the gender of one's partner are not always what's most relevant. This is particularly true as we enter the Forest of Fatter. As we'll come to see, genitalia are even more likely to be incidental, rather than definitive, here in the forest than anywhere else in the Round World.

I don't particularly like any of these terms; they're not very accurate as labels and actually bring a great deal more confusion than clarity. But like all the other terms in the Round World, these are the ones we've got until someone can come up with something that people agree is better. Again, I won't bother referring to every possible combination of sexual orientation and gender. Anything I say about gainers and encouragers applies equally well to feeders and feedees. I'll address any differences in the cases where they may arise, but really there's an amazing consistency in what people feel when they are sexually aroused by weight gain, whether they are male, female, gay, straight, or transgender.

Again, most of my examples are gay men. This is partly for simplicity's sake, since the many variations of gender and sexual orientation make little difference in our discussion. However the greater purpose is to eliminate the gender bias that occurs when we look at heterosexual feeder/feedee relationships.

TRY THIS AT HOME

1. A man is taking care of his 700-pound wife. She is too fat to leave the house and requires a great deal of care. Is the man...

    a) an enabler?
    b) an abuser?
    c) a loving husband?
    d) a victim?

2. Now the man tells you that he is sexually aroused by his wife's obesity. Does that change your choice? Does he seem a better person to you if he disapproves of his wife's body? If he pities her? If he suffers while caring for her, rather than enjoying it?

3. Okay, forget all that. Reverse the genders and go through the exercise again: A woman is taking care of her 700-pound husband. How do you see the woman? Do your answers differ from those you chose before?

The common image of the gainer/encourager relationship is of a slender person shoving food into a desperate, deluded fat person. The relationship is assumed to be that of oppressor and victim because it is very hard for most people to imagine someone wanting to be fat. It's similar to the misconception that dirty old men seduce innocent young boys into something called a *gay lifestyle*, the allure of which is apparently so powerful that newcomers can never escape. Also, we tend to cast men in the role of the fattener and women in the role of the fattened. However, many fit young women are sexually aroused by feeding and fattening their boyfriends or husbands. Likewise, many men yearn to be fattened by such women, just as many women long to be fattened and cared for. People seem to think that women with such sexual desires are rare, deviant, and therefore irrelevant. Setting that sexist view aside for the moment, there are actually many more female feeders than people suspect. I think this dismissal or ignorance of female feeders and feedees has more to do with the fact that women's sexuality is often marginalized and their role in kink is typically considered rare or unwitting.

Many TV documentaries and talk shows have featured people (mostly women) who are actively pursuing so-called super-morbid obesity with the avid encouragement of their partner or online fans. If you're not from the Round World, you probably know about erotic weight gain from an episode of some shock-TV show. Even when abuse is not the focus of people's horror, disgust often takes its place. When I talk to regular folks about gaining, they often jump to the example of an 800-pound, bedridden man who had to be rescued from his own filth by a demolition gang, a paramedic team, and a documentary TV crew. But most gainers and encouragers lead far less dramatic lives. Most people don't suspect that the chubby guy next door loves how well his girlfriend is fattening him up. Most don't look at the fat girl down the street and wonder how many men she's invited over to feed her and help fatten her that month. And frankly, you'd probably be right in not suspecting your neighbors; it's a comparatively rare kink. Most 800-pound shut-ins are not gainers. Conversely, most gainers do not grow to be 800-pound shut-ins. And yet, obviously, gainers and encouragers are someone's neighbors, so they could be yours.

A New Terrain

Gainers and encouragers are quite different from chasers. I suppose you could say that we are a subset of chasers because all three groups are turned on by Fat. But though gainers and encouragers share a lot in common with chasers, we are in fact quite different in our sexuality. Again, this is true regardless of gender or sexual orientation.

Despite the fact that they like fat men or women, chasers have a pretty basic and normal sexuality, whether it's gay, straight, or in between. They like fucking and sucking and ass play or tit play. Some people like one thing more than another, but chasers like most of the normal sex stuff; they just like it with a fat partner. These partners—chubs, BHMs, and BBWs—are simply fat folks who have come to see the sense of owning their size and seeking the romantic attentions of men or women who can appreciate it. Again, the sexual acts they enjoy are pretty much the same as those enjoyed by most gays or straights.

However, those of us who are gainers or encouragers are a bit more complicated sexually. Many of us enjoy the traditional sexual acts, but as we mature, we find that those acts are less interesting—perhaps even totally bankrupt—without the presence of weight gain in reality or in fantasy to drive the act. By the same token, many gainers and encouragers practice sexual acts that wouldn't seem sexual at all to most normal folks, including chubs and chasers. I've never done a rigorous count, but I would wager that the majority of erotic weight-gain stories (gay or straight) don't even mention penile penetration of the ass or vagina. Because of this, many of us have the mistaken notion that we're not interested in sex. I have to remind many of my seminar participants and clients that fucking is not the same as sex. It's just one particular sexual act. And for gainers and encouragers, fucking is somewhere between secondary and irrelevant when compared with getting fatter.

But I'm getting ahead of myself. The way we talk about sex—gay/straight, top/bottom, gainer/encourager—you would think that what people do in bed completely defines their sexuality. In fact, I think this is the greatest handicap we face in talking about any sexuality. As we'll see, *gainer* and *encourager* are names for acts: gaining fat or encouraging more fat. Although this distinction appears more or less accurate, it is far from useful and leads to much more confusion than enlightenment. We aren't defined by any particular act, sexual or otherwise. Rather the key to ourselves lies in the exploration of the desires that lead us to these acts. For most of us, these desires start in early childhood, even before memory.

Growing Up Gainer

Jeremy was 14 when he started thinking seriously about making himself fat. Though he had fantasized about it since as far back as he could remember, only in adolescence when his hormones started raging did he begin to strategize how he would transform his body from average to obese. He had always been fairly normal in weight, but that was mostly because his parents refused to keep anything in the house more fattening than an avocado. It was a struggle to gain weight back then; he was fighting not only his mother's pantry, but also his own naturally lean body. Still, by sneaking candy bars and taking advantage of endless 2-for-1 deals on offer at fast food restaurants, Jeremy at 16 had put on a lot of soft flab that he was proud of. It was even worth the hectoring of his parents. He couldn't wait for college, where his food intake would be unsupervised. Money for food would be tight, but at least he wouldn't have to worry about his parents discovering his food stash or walking in on him while he was drooling over the online pictures of fat men whom he longed to become.

Jeremy came to see that he had no control over this desire—or, rather, only the control that any of us has over any primary sexual desire. He described it as entering another world—a rush and also a relaxation—when he would stuff himself with food, especially junk food or decadent pastry. He learned that he could bring himself to climax by jiggling his belly fat and fantasizing about his body ballooning with fold after fold of soft, heavy blubber. Still, even with the sheets wet with cum and the occasional chocolate smear, he wouldn't admit for many years yet that his obsession was his sexuality. For a very long time, it was all just a "really cool hobby" that happened to get him off.

At 17, Ben was a bright, promising, high school junior who induced sighs from female friends beguiled by his shyness and sexual ambiguity.

Tall, slender, and handsome, he was able to earn some money from local modeling gigs. Though family and friends told him he as meant for greatness, he feared that he would disappoint them—that he'd never make it into a good enough school, get an impressive enough job, or do all the great things he believed people tacitly expected of him. He told me that he felt totally inadequate to his destiny. He felt like a little kid, not like a man. He fantasized about having a huge gut that entered a room before he did—a big swag of a belly that would give him size, import, and manliness. His secret desire was for someone—a man—to mold him into that image of confident manhood. To Ben, that looks like a huge beer gut offset buy thick, solid arms that have at least as much muscle as fat. He dreamed of having the courage to become the big-bellied stud but…well, "I'm only a kid," he thought, and he didn't have the courage to ruin his future and break his mother's heart by getting fat.

Geoff thought he was possessed. Not really, but the urge to eat in order to become hugely, jaw-droppingly fat was overwhelming sometimes. In junior high, he stuffed himself for a few months and put on almost 50 pounds. Then his panic, even louder than his family's protestations, finally reached a fever pitch. He crash dieted his way back past normalcy and even started working out. He buffed out and got himself a set of abs and cut pecs. Then began college, and the cycle of fattening up and slimming down began again. Yet the desire to stuff himself with food and become immensely fat was at times so overwhelming that he could barely concentrate on anything else.

Whenever he allowed his desires to hold sway, he would spend hours eating and masturbating. He decided to allow himself some pudge, but the fatter he got the fatter he wanted to be. The mad testosterone storms of late adolescence might have pushed other guys to hit the gym, but Geoff's sexuality pushed him to eat and eat until his gut ached and he could barely move. Then he would orgasm. At one time, the guilt following an orgasm would wrack him with guilt. He'd regret what he had eaten and what he had fantasized. But now in his early 20s, stuffing himself has become so common that the guilt and shame are pretty much gone. And the bloat and lethargy of his gluttony only slake him for a few hours before he goes off on another binge of junk food and ecstasy. In fact, Geoff has found that he can pre-cum just standing in front of a pastry case. He gets an erection when pants that used to be loose now refuse to button.

Many adolescent boys go through a period where they are basically nothing more than spooge monkeys, running to lock themselves in the bathroom several times a day to jerk off. But for guys like Ben, food and fat is their porn. They don't play with their dicks nearly as much as they play with their fat. Their blubber or their gut is a far more sensitive sexual organ for them than their penis. Geoff weighs over 400 pounds today. He says that he hates being fat in the circles he travels in. He works for a swanky, multi-national business consultancy. But when pressed, he says it wouldn't be so bad if he weren't single—if his sexuality weren't almost entirely online. He loves his body, his size, and even the limits that being so obese brings. He just wishes he had someone at home to share it with. At a meeting full of pretty, young interns and sexy power brokers, he's chagrined that his ass and back fat engulf the chair that strains to hold him. Yet when he gets home, he'll jerk off to that image of being the fattest one in the room and how everybody knew it. There's a cold soberness in the moments when he realizes that no matter what he weighs, whether he decides to lose weight or gain even more, this peculiar variety of sexual ecstasy will be his for the rest of his life. Nothing else will even come close.

Funhouse Fat Mirror

When you look in the mirror, what do you see? You may have noticed that what you see depends a great deal on your mood, and vice versa. For example, if you step on the scale and it doesn't say what you'd like, perhaps you feel a pang of disappointment in the bottom of your stomach. Maybe you poke yourself unkindly because your body is not as good as you wish. Or maybe your body seems emblematic of a more general sense of dissatisfaction with your whole life. For some people, that feeling will last the whole morning. Then just when they've forgotten about it, lunch rolls around and kicks up the issue again. Bargains and recriminations swirl in the minds of some people as they glower at the menu: *I can have a good dinner tonight if I have only a salad now.* And *I've been a pig all week. It's no wonder I'm so fat. I'll just have something light.*

The process can flow in either direction, however. Sometimes our emotions affect our judgment about how we look. Perhaps we're feeling down about something, or maybe we just have low blood sugar—so when we look in the mirror, we denigrate what we see. Last night in the club's restroom mirror, we looked pretty good. But this morning, the closet mirror shows someone fat and unattractive staring back at us. Well, it's exactly the same for gainers. Exactly the same, but in reverse.

When a gainer is having a bad day, he sees himself as unattractive, too. But in his case, he sees a thinner or smaller version of himself. He beats himself up if the scale starts creeping downward. He vows not to slip back into his old eating habits, which kept him small for so many years. He tries to eat as much as he can, but he is thwarted by a high metabolism, or a stomach that just won't hold enough to allow him to balloon, or a lack of discipline to stuff himself with frequent, large meals. Losing weight can be a terrible blow to his or her self-esteem and even self-confidence. Many gainers tell me that they felt unattractive or even inadequate before they got fat. After gaining 100 pounds, however, they say that they feel so much better about themselves, more at home in their bodies, and more secure when they meet people. And just as most people feel sexier when they lose weight, a gainer feels sexier when he or she gains weight. They might even put off buying bigger clothes because they enjoy the feeling of a shirt stretched across their belly or pants cutting into their love handles. The fact that only a few weeks ago the pants were loose can set a gainer on a high that lasts for days.

My friend Clark is a gainer, and we were out shopping for some bigger clothes for him since he was nearing 400 pounds and very excited about breaking through to a new range on the scale. A young guy just out of college, Clark said that now that he's getting so fat, he really wanted to start dressing with some style. He'd gotten by with sweats and T-shirts in college. When he weighed only 330, he didn't want to spend money on clothes to show off a body he wasn't proud of. But now that he was getting so obese and looking and feeling better about himself, he wanted stylish clothes to reflect his new confidence and self-esteem. He added that since he works in the world of computer art and design, he wanted his burgeoning sense of style to be as apparent as his burgeoning fat body. It makes sense, right? No one likes to invest in new clothes when they don't feel attractive. In the end, we had a very productive shopping trip. It was erotic to Clark to find that he fit into sizes that previously he'd only dreamed about being fat enough to wear.

THE LOVE AND EROTICISM OF FAT

Clark is a good example of what I mean by gender prejudices and how they obscure our view of the Round World. Typically, we think of women as concerned with fashion and self-esteem. A man who's concerned with these things is seen as weak at best; at worst, he's shallow, effeminate, or vapid. We see a man getting fat differently from how we see a woman getting fat.

When I talk about gainers and encouragers, I'm talking about both genders and any orientation or combination. I emphasize this point because so often when erotic weight gain comes up in my seminars, my straight participants seem to automatically picture a woman getting fat for a man. First, they assume that the woman is a victim and derives no enjoyment from her obesity. Second, people seem shocked when I tell them that there are men being eagerly fattened by their fit girlfriends. Even if my participants can bring themselves to picture such a gender role reversal, most do not view the men in these situations as victims. Of course this all disappears when I talk about same-sex gainer/encourager relationships. People may still see a victim and a victor, but at least then it comes from a prejudice about fat, not gender.

The Sexuality of Getting Fatter

It's unfortunate that all the terms surrounding erotic weight gain—*gainer, encourager, feeder, feedee, feedist, feederism, feedism*—all focus on a sexual act rather than on our sexuality. This causes profound and even damaging misunderstandings in trying to understand ourselves. As the terms imply, we tend to believe that we *are* these acts. I'm a feeder if I feed a partner fatter; I'm a gainer if I gain weight. Conversely, many gainers think that if they stop getting fatter, then they're no longer gainers. Many encouragers think they've stopped being an encourager when they no longer date someone in order to fatten them.

It doesn't make sense to define gainers as people who are gaining weight. If that were true, then anyone who got fat would be a gainer. The act of gaining weight does not make one a gainer. The sexual context is what's decisive. Imagine identifying ourselves by the sexual acts we perform. Guys might say, "I'm not really gay anymore these days. I haven't had a dick up my ass in months." But that's not how it works. You can't stop being gay just because you stop performing a particular sexual act. And as many adolescents discover, you can be gay even if you've never had sex at all.

Being gay or straight is a constellation of erotic ideas and impulses plus an identification that they are one's sexuality. Sixty years ago, a man might condemn himself: "I have to stop having sex with men! It's ruining my life." He thinks it's a bad habit or even an addiction, but not an identity. Another man of that era might say, "Sure, sometimes I like to unwind by letting a guy blow me at the bus station, but that doesn't make me a homosexual." Again, this man confesses a guilty pleasure, but not a sexual identity. Though sexual acts flow from one's sexuality, an act is different from an identity.

For gainers and encouragers, getting fat or helping someone get fat is actually a combination of many acts that are sexually arousing to us. Getting fatter is a long process; a gainer/encourager encounter is a mere episode in that process.

Being a gainer or encourager has nothing to do with actually gaining weight. It's about whether getting fatter makes your dick hard.

The encounters themselves involve gorging, jiggling, caressing, kissing, feeding, swallowing, and maybe even fucking. These for us are sexual acts, and we may practice some, all, or none of them. However, many gainers and encouragers mistake these acts for their sexuality. No set of erotic acts defines our sexuality. Rather, our sexuality dictates the acts that we find erotic.

Put simply, a gainer or encourager is a person who has the sexual desire to grow fatter, to be grown fatter, or to grow someone else fatter. As with any sexuality, it makes no difference whether the desire is actually fulfilled in reality. Consider two people: Both think of themselves as chubby and are trying to lose weight. However, one of them fantasizes about becoming immensely fat one day, but knows they will never really do it. The one who gets sexually aroused thinking about getting fat is the gainer; the other is not. And the one who's a gainer, will be a gainer for the rest of their life, whether or not they gain or lose an ounce of fat.

Sexuality is a chord struck deep within the mind and sung by the body. No set of acts, behaviors, or decisions defines our sexuality. Again, this is the problem with most terms for sexual kinks because they focus on what people do in bed. Instead, consider that our sexuality is expressed through these acts.

As I said earlier, an attraction to fat often transcends gender and frequently includes acts that other people consider nonsexual. So, being a gainer or encourager is not a feature of being gay or straight. It's not an additional component, not like leather seats that we can purchase or decline when we get a car. Being a gainer or encourager is the car itself. It is our sexuality. It doesn't matter what you weigh, or what you will weigh, or whether you will ever indulge this desire, or the gender of the person with whom you indulge it. The erotic desire itself gives you membership in our tribe, even if you choose not to accept it. A good example of this ambiguity is a man I talked to named Greg.

Greg is married to a woman. His wife is fit and very pretty, and they have a daughter in kindergarten. Greg loves his wife and generally finds women attractive. But when he sees a massive, hairy, fat guy lumbering down the street, he just can't stop staring. It's almost a kind of rapture. His mind goes fuzzy, and he can't separate the tangle of feelings. It doesn't seem sexual. He says he doesn't want to have sex with the guy, by which he means penetration. Nevertheless, his desire is far more intense than curiosity. It's a strange and powerful urge that Greg feels to be with such a man, to be his pal, to be his. He's had these feelings off and on over the years, but they never seemed to lead anywhere that Greg was prepared to go. They certainly never competed seriously with his attraction for women.

At one point, Greg tried being bisexual, but that worked out poorly. However, the guy he tried it with wasn't fat—not really. Certainly the guy was not as big as what Greg thinks about in the privacy of his own mind. Still, Greg doesn't identify as gay or bisexual. He doesn't want to have sex with that hot fat man. No, he wants to *be* that hot fat man. Greg wants the fat man to transform him; he wants to be his apprentice or protégé. It wouldn't be the same if it were a fat woman. A fat woman is not what he wants. Neither does he want to be a fat man in his current life with his attractive wife and daughter. He just wants to be in the thrall of that hot fat man, to be nurtured and guided by him. But that's not gay, right?

Trying to get to the heart of Greg's sexual attractions, I asked him once if he wanted to be fat and to have sex with women as a fat man.

"No," he said flatly. "That wouldn't be hot at all."

"What about being fat and getting with a hot guy? What about having sex with one of those muscular navy guys when they come into town on leave?" Mike lives near a naval base.

"I wouldn't want to have sex with them. Besides, they'd probably make fun of me if I were really fat."

"Maybe you would enjoy that."

Greg thinks a long while. "Yeah," he admits finally. "Yeah." He grins as his eyes sparkle. "I think maybe I would."

When we expand the definition of *sex* to mean something besides penile penetration, many gainers and encouragers see their sexuality begin to emerge and make sense.

At some point a man may become aware that male bodies arouse him. At another point he may become aware that obesity arouses him. And at yet a third point he may become aware that becoming obese or making someone else obese is a sexual ecstasy like no other. However, these three do not have to occur in any particular order. That is, realizing you're gay, realizing you like Fat, and realizing you want to be fat or to fatten someone, can happen in any order.

In my case, I knew that a man gaining weight was hot, but it never occurred to me that I was gay. To me, gay guys were handsome men with sculpted bodies who put their dicks in each other's asses. By contrast, I was fascinated by bodies that gained extreme amounts of muscle or fat. Nothing gay about that, I thought. Besides, an asshole never seemed a rational place to put a dick. I wasn't in denial exactly; it was simply a lack of recognition. Then I came to see that the majority of the weight-gain I fantasized about was in men, and that fat men fascinated me. And finally I saw that this fascination was undeniably sexual and almost always involved men, so I reasoned this was a kind of gay I had never heard of.

Attraction and Identity

I'd say the most common question I get in interviews is this: "If you like fat so much, then how come you're not fat yourself?" My answer is fairly simple: "I know a lot of men who are attracted to women, but no one asks them, "If you love women so much, why don't you want to be one?" I know many people who say that intelligence is sexy, but no one says, "If you like smart guys so much, why aren't you trying to get smarter?" Having a sexual attraction to a characteristic is not the same as wanting to be that characteristic. Let's take a closer look at how that works in a person's dating history.

You may remember that I said I never recognized my desires around muscle and fat as being sexual. As a fat kid, I always felt strangely, intensely uncomfortable around bodybuilders; even the sight of one used to intimidate me. Perhaps many people feel drawn to or repulsed by extremely muscular men. In my case, however, I think I was attracted to their physical beauty and status, but also envious and fearful because they had something I so conspicuously lacked. That reconciliation has been part of my journey. But back then, I was the fat kid. Okay, but if fat was such a turn-on—or at least a fascination—then why didn't I stay fat or get even fatter? It wasn't just because fat kids don't get much respect or power. It was because of a feeling that the fit guys and the bodybuilders had something I wanted. It wasn't a sexual need; I didn't want to have sex with a bodybuilder. No, I wanted to *be* the bodybuilder.

So I transformed little by little. I began to lose weight after high school, came out as gay after college, and got into bodybuilding in graduate school. It was a complete shift in my identity, so of course people related to me completely differently. Then, well, I've told you the rest of the story already: I discovered that I like fat men, and later that I am something called an encourager. It's been a tortuous path, but that's how we move sometimes. Yet with each step, I was uncovering my core sexuality and moving toward identifying as an encourager.

Many gainers go through the same process in reverse. For example, my friend Scott had always been an athletic guy, but he had to fight to keep his weight down. That personal struggle led him in elementary school to befriend the fat kid in his class, for whom Scott felt an affinity and even sympathy. Scott was the all-American jock in high school and college, yet he eventually came to date fat guys. He found superchubs to be especially beautiful. Then one night he was sitting across from his date, relaxing after a big meal. The guy was very obese, and Scott marveled at his size and how this guy could allow himself to just eat and eat. As usual, Scott found himself thinking about what it was like for that guy to be so fat—what it was like to carry all that blubber, to live in a body so huge and soft and fat. It was a pleasant thought. It was an erotic thought. It would have passed unnoticed as it usually had, but instead Scott had a realization. He didn't want to have sex with this fat guy. He wanted to *be* this fat guy. In the years that followed, Scott began to eat as he'd always wanted to. It was terrifying and erotic for him to see his body change. Gradually he stopped thinking of himself as a chaser and grew more comfortable thinking of himself as a gainer.

Scott's shift in identity took only a few years. For others, it can take decades. When such an identity shift is so protracted, it's usually because of one of two causes: Taking on the identity of a gainer may be actively resisted out of fear, shame, or guilt. Alternatively, as in my case, the journey takes decades because there are no labels for what we feel. We have to invent ourselves. Only then do we discover other people who share our feelings and identity, and we become a community.

Gainers and encouragers, like anyone else, develop over time. Often, we mistakenly perceive this gradual development as a change in a person's sexuality. Though I'm frequently challenged on this point, I continue to assert that a person's sexuality does not change during one's life; it only deepens or constellates differently. You might look at a tree over a span of 50 years and say the tree has changed. The tiny sapling bears little resemblance to the immense sturdy oak. Even though the tree seems to have changed radically over the years, it would be more accurate to say that it has grown to become what it always was.

The change occurs in our perception of ourselves or others, not in our sexuality. For example, you might think of sexuality as a cluster of stars in the night sky. One society sees the stars as forming a bear; another, a dragon; a third, a trident. Have the stars changed positions? No, the stars are where they have always been. Different peoples give them different contexts, or even include neighboring stars which another group of people saw as irrelevant or perhaps part of some other constellation. Similarly, a person in his life has the same innate sexuality, but over time and experience he perceives his sexual attractions in different contexts. Attractions that were once seen as opposite may now be seen as complementary or even parallel. Particular sexual acts or attractions may change, but they are expressions of a particular sexual drive that is based deep in our psyche, incorporated into our nervous system, and that stays constant through our life.

Like the tree in my example above, we are all in the process of becoming who we already are. Scott came to embody his childhood love of fat. I came to embody my childhood fantasy of gaining muscle while my partner gained fat. What's more, we eventually came to see how things we once repudiated were actually aspects of who we've always been. Although gainers and encouragers have different tastes and quirks, our differences are less consequential than what we have in common. We're each on very different paths along our particular journeys, but all our journeys lead to the same place. All our roads lead us back to the same home.

Sexuality as Identity

Framing gaining or encouraging as a sexual identity, and not a sexual act, is a useful way of seeing ourselves that empowers us and creates us as a community. That's part of what any identity can do for people. For example, there was a time when left-handed people were shunned and denounced. As a young child at school, my uncle's right hand was tied to his pencil so that he would not transgress and write with the wrong hand. His teachers were trying to stop his deviant acts of left-handed writing. For him, it always felt wrong, even felt unnatural, to write with his right hand, but that only proved to his teachers how very deviant he was. Years later as an adult, my uncle was able to locate himself in the identity of a left-handed person, meaning that he became "a leftie." Writing with his left hand was no longer the transgressive act of a deviant, but the natural and expressive act of a leftie. This is what it means to take on an identity, and how identity in a community can normalize what others consider deviant. Gainers and encouragers often ask me whether their desire to bury themselves or someone else in hundreds of pounds of fat is "normal." I tell them, "Of course it's not normal. But it is for us." That is identity.

I've mentioned before that when we think of sexuality, we usually think of gender as the primary category of preference. In seeking someone to date, we first think about whether we want someone who is male or female. Next we think about whether a person should be gay or straight. Perhaps then we think of acts or roles we can perform with that partner: Are they a top or bottom? Lipstick lesbian or butch? At some point, many people start answering, "Um…none of the above." Well, what if not only the choices, but also the whole hierarchy were up for grabs? This reshuffling of the order of categories happens even more frequently in kink. Many times, kink trumps sexual orientation (gay/straight). In fact, in some cases it might even *dictate* a sexual orientation.

For example, if you're a guy and your kink is to submit to extreme, masculine power, then you find yourself having sex with guys to fulfill this kink, which means you probably see yourself as gay. If you're a woman with this same kink—to submit to extreme, masculine power— you'll also find yourself having sex with men but see yourself as straight. More intriguingly, many of these people tell me that when they have sex outside their kink—for example, if the element of extreme, masculine dominance is removed from the encounter—they find men and women equally appealing, so they view themselves as bisexual. These people often invent elaborate labels for their sexuality that try to encompass their seemingly complex, contradictory, or capricious desires for men or women on different occasions or circumstances. For me, however, it's simpler and more accurate to see their kink as primary and the gender of their sexual partner as secondary.

I know more than a few chasers and encouragers who'll tell you that although they think of themselves as gay men, they sometimes think about having sex with a fat woman. I know some straight guys who are confused by their lust for a particular fat man, or by their occasional fantasies of being fed by a dominant fit man. When I suggest a dominant woman instead, these straight guys answer that, no, a woman wouldn't be the same. So if you have a kink, it's often simpler and more useful to see the kink as your primary sexual driver.

You can see this reflected in the way people go about dating. If you think of yourself as gay or straight, you might go to a gay bar or a straight bar to meet a compatible partner. But if you know you have a kink, then you know the problem of trying to find a partner who shares your kink among such a general population. You may tolerate dating in bars if you believe your kink is just a feature of your hetero- or homosexuality. But when people discover how central their kink is—how it's actually the basis of their sexuality—they increasingly find themselves going online to find compatible partners.

Kink: A Distinct Realm of Sexuality

When I use the word kink, I'm referring to a driving sexual obsession with an object, ideal, or situation that is not typically considered sexual. A kink is an intense sexual desire for something that is almost always considered taboo or transgressive by society at large. Gainers and encouragers have a powerful sexual kink centered on Fat. How is this different from being a chaser? Well, chasers simply prefer a fat partner. Even if they prefer them exclusively, kink is present to the degree that sexual acts and fantasies outside the normal locus of sexual interest are hotter and more satisfying than all other erotic acts. Most people, for example, come back to the tried-and-true sexual pleasure of the erectile tissue and other sensitive areas. For example, the clitoris, the penis, the nipples, even the anus and some internal structures have a myriad of sensitive nerve endings, which may extend to the immediate surrounding areas as well: breasts, penile shaft, butt cheeks, perineum. That's all well and good, but for those of us with a kink, the stimulation of those areas does not fully arouse us.

Those of us with a kink usually have other erogenous zones that rival or even surpass the usual ones in their ability to give us intense physical pleasure. In fact, one of the ways I can tell whether the man with whom I'm in bed is a gainer or a chub is by how his body responds to my touch. For example, if I jiggle the belly fat of a chub, he might find it cute, ticklish, or embarrassing, or he might find it sexy that I find it sexy. However, if I jiggle the belly fat of a gainer, it will create waves of delight, the pressure in his penis will surge, and he may even moan with pleasure as I jiggle him more vigorously. This will happen to his body even if he does not think of himself as gainer. Of course, I don't use this as the sole determiner of someone's sexuality, but it is a melody I listen for in the music of making love to a fat man. A surprising number of fat people have a kink involving Fat, but whether such a person chooses to identify as a gainer is another matter. (Similarly, plenty of men have homosexual sex but don't identify as gay.) But as that fat man's lover in that moment, I'm interested in bringing about his fullest sexual expression, for it will in turn bring about mine. My purpose in such exploration is to listen and delight, not to diagnose.

The Cathedral of Fat

Having alternative erogenous zones, however, is only the beginning of what it means to be a gainer or encourager (or feeder or feedee). These erotic sensations mingle with images and assemble into narratives that most people would not find sexual in the least—and might even find horrific. Even when our acts are sexual by the standards of normal folks, the context of that act is unique to our own kind of sexuality. For example, feeding a lover a chocolate-covered strawberry might be erotic for almost anyone. However, doing so because it will make them fatter is something only gainers and encouragers delight in.

I'd like to draw the analogy of entering a cathedral. For some people, the religious objects, vaulted ceilings, and stained glass of a cathedral are architectural curiosities at best, representing a foreign time and place. From their outside perspective, a cathedral might represent an impressive commitment to faith, a foolish devotion to superstition, or even a willing servitude to religious oppression.

To the devout, however, entering that same cathedral couldn't be more different. For the devout, the sacredness of each object within the cathedral—individually and collectively—points to the divine. The devout glimpse the divine in the soaring architecture that transports us to an ecstatic realm outside time, in the stories painstakingly told in light shining through shards of colored glass reassembled into stories of profundity and significance. This sense of meaning and ecstasy is incomprehensible to the outsider.

In a similar way, a roll of stretch-marked blubber sagging over a tight waistband is a collection of unfortunate images to the outsider: stretch marks, a roll of fat, and the unsightliness of ill-fitting pants. The chaser appreciates the beauty of such obesity—again, the way someone might be awestruck by the impressive beauty of a cathedral. However, just as devout worshippers contemplate a stained-glass narrative of religious truth, a gainer or encourager assembles these three images into a single, erotic narrative of increasing obesity. The stretch marks tell the story of a once slender body that has grown fatter. The roll of fat speaks of the full flourish of obesity in the present. Finally, the straining waistband conjures the hope of future growth and the idea that these pants will eventually fail and become useless relics of the fat person yet to be. Weight gain is a process. Gaining or encouraging is, by its nature, a story or narrative that is present for all gainers and encouragers when we regard Fat. We differ only in our awareness of the narrative.

As with the ecstasy of the cathedral, the joys of our kink are incomprehensible to normal folk. It is not too much to say that gainers and encouragers inhabit another realm of sexuality, just as the devout inhabit another realm of consciousness when they enter the cathedral.

Only the devout are transported to ecstasy as they immerse themselves in the features and architecture of the cathedral. Similarly, only gainers and encouragers are driven to ecstasy by things that the rest of the world doesn't even consider sexual and usually finds repulsive. We are the devout of the Cathedral of Fat. People with other kinks worship in different cathedrals, but this one is ours.

Operating with a Kink

Of course, there are many other kinks in the world. Kinks tend to fall into one of six categories, as taxonomized by sexologist John Money. For example, smelling a woman's unwashed panties or caressing her high-heeled shoes might be deeply sexually arousing for some people attracted to women. For those attracted to men, the equivalent objects might be an unwashed jock strap or athletic socks. A person who gets off by smelling women's panties has a kink if they find the panties are necessary—in reality or fantasy—to reach sexual climax. The panties are central to the orgasm. They recall the woman herself, to be sure, but it's the panties that push him over the edge of orgasm.

This particular kind of kink involving an object is called a fetish, which is why I'm not using the word *fetish* in relation to gainers and encouragers. Our sexuality doesn't revolve around an object. In the strict psychological definition of *fetish*, most kinks are not fetishes, because most don't revolve around an object or a body part treated as an object. A fetish is simply one particular subcategory of kink. Another kink that's not a fetish is flashing. The flasher is a man who needs the shock and humiliation of publicly exposing his genitalia to unsuspecting women in order to reach sexual climax. If you are really interested in the world of kink, I can recommend a couple of books.[3] But for my purposes here, I only need to make a distinction between a sexual taste and a kink.

The way I'm using the word, a kink is something that you need, in reality or in fantasy, at the moment of climax in order to reach orgasm.

---

[3] John Money's *Love Maps* (1984) and Katharine Gates's *Deviant Desires* (1999). The former is an excellent psychological treatise on the nature of sexual paraphilia (kink). The latter is a more general survey of strange things that human beings have come to sexualize.

Sometimes when gainers or encouragers are young, our thoughts of weight gain are fleeting or not very defined. If we've never had sex with someone who shares our kink, we may not even be aware that we're employing these touchstones of eroticism—little images or fantasies—in order to climax. We might step into our minds for a moment, right before orgasm, to push us over the edge. For others, the technique for orgasm is more like an overlay that's present from beginning to end of the sexual encounter. It's like an ideal or narrative that we lay over our partner to bring the passion to sexual fulfillment.

I realize this may sound dishonest or objectifying, but in many cases we don't even know we're doing it. I'll talk later about how we can transcend such objectification. However, right now, I only want to point out that this is the only way some of us have ever known sex. Also, if the gainer or encourager is resistant to emotional intimacy, then not being present for their partner is nothing unusual. It's just the air they breathe. In fact, it's unlikely they'll even realize they're using a touchstone or an overlay to orgasm. The kink may go unnoticed. On the other hand, some people I've talked to are quite aware of doing it; they think it's just what most people do to climax, or at least what they have to do. This artifice and complication starts to drop away, however, when we're with someone who shares our kink.

The Agony & Ecstasy of Kink

I can't really describe what it's like to have a kink. When I try to tell someone what it's like, they often say, "Oh sure, I have a kink. I have a fetish for blondes," or "Big round asses drive me wild." Yeah, sorry. That's not quite it. First, the rush when you're in your kink is all consuming. Most scientists writing about the subject use the word *intense* quite a bit: "intense sexual feelings," "intense arousal," "intense sexual fantasies." But again, the word *intense* is far too pale and clinical to capture the experience. I describe it as taking the flow of regular sexuality and putting it through a high-pressure nozzle, putting it under such pressure that it drives out all reason—all other thought.

A kink flows powerfully out of a highly focused act, object, or idea. The drive to experience the kink is so powerful that some people describe it as almost painful in its ecstasy. When you're in your kink, time stands still. You can be in it for hours—online in a chat room or in bed with a like-minded partner—during which you experience nothing but drive. The needs and limits of your body fade into the background; there is no need to sleep, no awareness of anything in the world beyond. One man said it was like being on crystal methamphetamine in that respect: There's no guilt about the past and no fear of the future, just the hard, pounding excitement of now.

When people feel guilt and shame about their sexuality, they often experience a hard-edged downside after they orgasm. This is particularly observable in men. You may have noticed that everything changes in a man after he ejaculates—both biologically and psychologically. If he has a kink, this change might be even more noticeable. Now, many men are sweet as pie after they orgasm; some grow even more intimate and cuddly (perhaps right before they fall asleep). Yet we always hear of those jerks who treat their partner like a stranger after orgasm or who rush away to avoid the awkwardness of being a naked human lying next to another naked human when the party's over, so to speak. Again, if the person has a kink, such behavior may be magnified as well.

Because kinks are usually based on taboos, feelings of shame and guilt often fall like a rain of bricks upon men or women who haven't made peace with their kink. We're talking about the most powerful psychological and biological force I know. Think of a firefighter who hasn't learned to control the high-pressure flow of a fire hose. The water in the hose can actually lift them off the ground and pummel them badly if they're not trained to handle it. So it is with kink, too. And if just having the thoughts of indulging in a kink can be shameful, then the guilt of enacting those thoughts can be absolutely brutal for some men and women.

We've discussed the guilt and shame of being fat. We've also broken open the guilt and shame hidden in liking Fat, as chasers do. Now imagine raising those feelings to a fever pitch and you can begin to fathom the guilt and shame that some experience about wanting to become fat or make someone else fatter. Though what I describe here may be more observable in men, many women have told me about the shame and guilt they go through after sex. The timing and drama may differ between men and women, but the physical and psychological mechanisms are generally the same. I'll discuss men here because all my direct experience is with them and because the onset and duration of male orgasm is so clearly defined and observable.

On the way up to orgasm, the fantasy takes hold of us. We spiral higher and higher until we can no longer contain the ecstasy. But for some men, the higher they go, the more devastating the fall after orgasm. So great is the fall, that a few men I've been with have asked if it would be okay if they didn't orgasm. When I asked why, they told me it was because they feel so horrible afterward. The collage of thoughts and images that drive them to ecstasy suddenly disgusts them after (or even simultaneous with) ejaculation. It's as if their rationality has been locked out of their brain for the sexual encounter, but it rushes back in after orgasm. Afterward, they are horrified by the sight of spent food containers, the feel of aching torpor, and the shame that such deep debasement is the source of such intense pleasure.

I was with one man who had to be out my door within minutes of his orgasm. We had a handful of sexual encounters, and each time I tried to get him to stay. I almost succeeded once, but then his eyes began to well with tears, and he jetted out the front door. I learned from him later that he would sit in his car sobbing for half an hour after our encounters before he regained the composure to drive home.

Another man I was with actually disassociated during sex. When the passion and eroticism of obesity got to a certain fever pitch, he would enter a fugue state—meaning that he would seem to fall asleep. His eyes would dim, then the lids would close and his breathing would slow. It was like someone unplugging a phonograph that had been blasting at high volume and hearing it wind down in a few seconds to stillness. His erection would dissipate, and he would lie as though lifeless. Then after about 15 or 20 seconds, he'd snap back to consciousness—but with no memory of what we had done or said immediately before the break. Perhaps it's only coincidence that this guy was totally closeted about being gay and grew up in a devout Catholic family in Mexico. On the other hand, maybe the guilt of being gay and wanting me to make

4: Fat Kink and the Drive to Get Fatter

him massively obese was so painful that his psyche would spirit him away, rather than let him drown in the annihilation of orgasm. Indeed, his body would never let him cum. In our times together, I was able to reduce the depth, duration, and frequency of his fugue states, but he never ejaculated.

Another guy told me that before he made friends with his desire to be fat, he used to go through cycles of ecstasy and panic. He'd binge for weeks on end, growing fatter and fatter. He'd cancel his gym membership and throw away his skinny jeans. He'd eat with abandon and thrill to the numbers on the scale as he gained 20, 25, 30 pounds. But then one day, he would see himself in the mirror. Disgusted by how he'd deliberately destroyed his physique, he would break out in a cold sweat, panicking over how fast he could regain his once beautiful body. He said that one time the panic was so bad that he broke out in hives for a week, as his body manifested the intense guilt and shame of what he was doing to himself and where it was leading. Then he'd rejoin the gym, pound his body with intense workouts, and starve himself in what seemed like repentance for the weight he'd gained. He went through this cycle two or three times in high school and into college. Today, 15 years later, he tells me he's made peace with his desires and is very happy with his 340-pound body. His boyfriend of almost ten years also delights in his size.

The Resistance and Persistence of Kink

My purpose in mentioning these extreme cases is to demonstrate how very powerful a kink can be and how it is so much more than what most people are capable of experiencing or understanding. Of course, most gainers are not as tortured as the men I just described. Actually, most gainers and encouragers come to embrace their kink to some degree. Some even thrill to the new limitations and even the maladies of their obesity. However, when gainers and encouragers contact me, they usually do so to seek out my advice in dealing with what they perceive as the inherent conflict of their desires. They often have very dark fantasies, not just about gaining many hundreds of pounds, but about all the limitations, risks, and even afflictions that might accompany such obesity.

I mentioned earlier that having a kink is the most powerful force I know. What else could cause a beautiful, muscular young man to bury himself in hundreds of pounds of blubber, despite every rational thought telling him not to? One such guy put it beautifully: "Every night I dream of getting enormously fat, and every morning I wake up to the nightmare of having six-pack abs." Many of us come to accept and understand what arouses us, and even to embrace it. However, too few of us finally come to make a life that integrates our sexuality rather than isolates it. Some people practice their sexuality openly, and others are more secretive. Some even channel their energies into erotic art or fiction, or hours of online chat. You can't stop the flow of sexuality; all you can hope to do is direct the current.

Actually, I find that comparing sexuality to water reveals a number of surprisingly apt parallels. For example, one of the physical properties of water is that it cannot be compressed, as a solid or a gas can be. If you try to force water into a small space—try to make it behave—it will only push back with equal force. That's true no matter how much force is applied, even if the quantity of water is small and the force is monumental. Water can be partitioned, diverted, even dammed, but you cannot diminish it or get rid of it. Sexuality behaves along similar lines. People often redirect or dam up their sexuality. They may even try to resist it, only to find it pushing back with equal force. Another curious property of water is that if you do manage to put it away somewhere and try to ignore it, it tends to corrode or degrade whatever is trying to contain it. Tanks rust. Ponds fester. Even rocks wear away.

Many gainers and encouragers see damming up their sexuality as the only alternative to letting it flood their minds and wash away their lives. I know people who have proclaimed themselves "former gainers" or "former encouragers." I've seen that status last for a few months or even years, but being a former gainer or encourager is like being a former gay. The desired reform never lasts. Of course the person may not gain any more weight, but gaining is not about what you weigh, and encouraging is not about whether you put food in someone's mouth. Sexuality cannot be pushed away, any more than you can push away the tide. As cities like Venice and Amsterdam have known for centuries, water is something you live with and even celebrate. The specific engineering of just how to do that with one's sexuality is the basis of my seminars and private work with people. There's no universal solution; it depends on the person. This is without question an instance in which one size does not fit all.

GAINING & ENCOURAGING 101

Most gainers I know get sexually aroused when they've grown too fat to button their pants. Most encouragers I know get a sexual thrill when they see a guy or a gal who's gotten too fat for their clothes and become aroused by helping them continue the process. People vary greatly in their specific pleasures. Many gainers can get aroused just walking into a grocery store. Some, like Ben, can even pre-cum just by standing in front of a pastry case and fantasizing about all that food being inside him. For these gainers, eating is central; for others, it may be incidental. This applies as well to the encourager—the gainer's counterpart. Encouragers are also intoxicated by weight gain, but we express it differently. Gainers and encouragers are two sides of the same coin. As children, we have almost the same fantasies; we have the same wiring in our bodies that makes us thrill to the amassing of fat. The difference between gainers and encouragers is our sexual role. This may seem trivial, but just as a coin must have two sides, a gainer must have an encourager, and an encourager must have a gainer. It's inherent in the design of the kink. As with any sexuality, playing alone amounts to masturbation or exhibitionism.

To be a gainer or encourager is to be sexually aroused to some degree by the distress of obesity. Quite simply, the downside of obesity—whether physical or psychological—is in some way erotic to all gainers and encouragers. In fact, it's the very thing that separates us from bears, chasers, fat admirers, or others with normative sexualities. The gainer or encourager is turned on by at least some of the downsides of being fat: the social stigma, the physical limitations, the sloth, even the maladies. That's why it's kink: it's a kind of pain or distress that has been sexually transformed into pleasure—even ecstasy. The only difference among us is the point at which a gainer or encourager taps out, so to speak—the point of "too much."

Many gainers and encouragers become alarmed and a bit defensive when I start talking about liking the distress of obesity. They protest that they don't even want stretch marks, must less to get sick and die. Perhaps, but those things are toward the deeper end of the pool. I remind them that I'm talking about a very broad range of distress. For example, I remind them that "normal" people are embarrassed when they pop a button on their pants, and they certainly don't see it as an achievement, as most gainers do. Gainers may say they don't like their stretch marks, but they love that they no longer have a flat stomach and that their belly is starting to droop over their belt. Again, I have to remind them that "normal" people would find such a development distressing. It's simply a matter of when the distress ceases to be erotic and starts to become frightening or disgusting. And that's a line drawn in the sand, because it usually moves during a gainer or encourager's lifetime.

Many gainers and encouragers try to see the distress of obesity as a necessary evil or as the price of glory. However, I believe it is far more central and stems from the root of the kink itself. All gainers and encouragers dream of the distress of obesity, whether physical or psychological. A few examples of psychological distress that gainers and encouragers eroticize include breaking a chair, not fitting in a restaurant booth, or being the fattest person among their friends. Examples of physical distress that arouse us might include being out of breath at the top of a flight of stairs, having less energy, or a general feeling of being heavier and slower. Many gainers say, "But those things are hot! They don't distress me at all." Well, yes—that's my point. To be a gainer is to find arousal in what others find would find distressing. To be sure, the feeling is double-edged: fear is intertwined with excitement. We differ only in the degree of distress that we consider sexy, extreme, or disgusting.

What's more, we change our minds about it. What was disgusting may become sexy years later. What was sexy may become unmanageable. Gainers who once vowed utter immolation by their own gluttony when they were 20, sometimes retreat in terror when their doctor gives them the news of diabetes at 30. But we see the opposite trek too. Gainers in their 30s who swore they would never compromise their health "for just a fetish" find themselves with greater and greater tolerance for taking medications so they can continue getting fatter and fatter.

Of course, the same is also true for encouragers and where we draw our lines in the sand. Perhaps you remember my story about getting with Vince, that superchub whom I met at Convergence, and wondering whether I could handle having such a person as a partner. That's a window into how encouragers experience and savor our distress of obesity. Examples of psychological distress that arouse us include being out dancing with the fattest person at the club, bringing a fat date to a family dinner or work event, or being seen as subservient to our fat partner and having to tie their shoes or help them up. These situations are both scary and erotic to us. As for physical distress, injuries for encouragers are fairly rare, but they do occur: I know encouragers who have suffered sore backs, cracked ribs, and blown out esophageal sphincters. But they might add, with a bashful grin, "Yeah, but it's kinda hot." A chaser might suffer these cheerfully, but an encourager suffers them erotically.

Encouragers sometimes experience terrible guilt in discovering that a fat person's distress—their difficulty walking, labored breathing, inability to fit through a turnstile—is erotic to us. Of course, gainers may find a fat person's distress to be intensely erotic as well. However, if the gainer experiences guilt, it's because they feel ashamed of their desire to suffer likewise from such obesity. It is true that the immature encourager may objectify the fat person, savoring the distress while ignoring the sufferer. But the more developed encourager can set aside their desire and see the obese person who embodies it. For example, the sight of a fat man struggling to make it up the stairs is erotically beautiful, but the sight of a person in distress elicits in us sympathy and assistance.

When pity and arousal collide, the result is sometimes guilt. This is a paradox inherent in any kink. So, let's gain some more insight into this by using the Fat Map. Looking at the diagram on page 98, we can see how gainers and encouragers vary in our desire for fat (the Attraction side of the Affinity axis). Also, we vary in how we express our desires according to where we fall on the Judgment axis. When we're toward the extreme end of Blame on the Judgment axis, we can be cruel. When we're far toward the extreme of Pity, we tend to feel guilty or deny our desires entirely.

More generally, I've explained how the Round World spins on the axis of shame and guilt. The rotation around that axis is actually the sexual dynamo of gainers and encouragers. Those who have explored and embraced their kink spin the guilt and shame of obesity into ecstasy and empowerment. This is not some rationalization on our part, some way we explain it to ourselves to make it okay. There is no faculty of reason involved. We experience ecstasy and empowerment just as anyone who experiences their sexuality does—in our bodies and our psyches.

POWER & BEAUTY IN GETTING FATTER

As I mentioned earlier, I consider gainers and encouragers to be a subset of chasers—chasers with a particular kink involving the distress of obesity, whether someone else's or their own. A lot of what I said about chasers applies in part to gainers and encouragers, but there are also some important differences. In this section we'll see how all that plays out. Again, I'll be dealing with gay men, but we can easily analogize this to the straight or lesbian feeders and feedees by simply focusing on whether the desired quality is power or beauty, rather than on gender or sexual orientation. For example, a straight woman who loves fattening up her big bear of a husband is a Power Encourager. A woman who loves being the growing goddess of her attentive girlfriend is a Beauty Gainer. In the Round World, it's perhaps best to see gender and sexual orientation as accidents of anatomy.

Power Gainers & Encouragers

Gainers and encouragers cleave into the same two groups we saw with chasers: Power and Beauty. Just as most chasers are enamored of the power and masculinity of a fat Zeus, many gainers desire to become that icon of power and masculinity. At the same time, most encouragers see their role as serving to augment such a powerful man. Gainers and encouragers seeking feminine power are rarer. However, I suspect this is because such desires in or for women are not seen as sexual. I knew a New Zealand woman who loved power lifting and made sure she ate enough "to keep her weight up." She was about five foot four and already well over 200 pounds. I remember her being adamant about drinking lots of organic whole milk. I don't know if her desire for a bigger, fatter, stronger body had any sexual resonance for her, but I could well imagine it. I could also imagine a man who would be attracted to such a powerful, obese woman, wanting to help her train and fatten.

Turning back for a moment to masculine power, you may remember that I talked about the hot young stud who dreamed of obesity but awoke every morning to the unfortunate reality of his chiseled abs. That kid, Kurt, also had a number of other wishes for his genie. He wanted a big gut, a man's gut that people could see coming from 50 feet away. Kurt also wanted big, thick arms; he was even willing to go to the gym to get a set of big, bloated arms that would be strong but show no signs of definition. And above all, he wanted a beard. In fact, Kurt told me he fantasized about having a beard even before he fantasized about having a huge gut rolling over his belt. The two for him are almost inseparable elements of his sexual identity. I should say, however, that as much as Kurt's fantasies sound like the pursuit of masculinity and bearishness, it would be inaccurate to think of him as simply wanting to be a bear. Unlike bears, Kurt thrills to the distress of his obesity. Over the years, he has fattened himself slowly and steadily to over 600 pounds. He tells me that he loves the physical limitations that his body imposes and that he and his partner are sexually aroused by the effort it takes for him to live at his size.

Kurt's masculine ideals are typical in a way. If you look at be-fore-and-after pictures of Power Gainers, you'll see not only a huge gut that wasn't there before, but also almost inevitably a beard that gets longer or thicker as the man gets fatter. Tattoos, suspenders, or a trucker's cap often finish the look. The pictures Power Gainers post of themselves are almost exclusively of their bellies; no other view of themselves seems to matter as much. Just as chasers are sometimes criticized for objectifying chubs as bellies with legs, Power Gainers seem to willingly objectify themselves the same way. A photo of a headless chest and belly is a common self-portrait. Certainly a desire for anonymity plays a role in such editing. Gaining weight is quite stigmatized, and doing it deliberately is anathema. Nevertheless, it is worth noting that if these guys are going to post one picture of themselves, it will be of their belly.

The focus on the belly holds true for female Power Gainers to a lesser extent. Women wishing to symbolize obesity as power will often do it through a stance or a pose that seems aggressive or challenging. The images are never coquettish except as deliberate irony, such as a black lace teddy on a 400-pound woman in an authoritarian stance, with a sly grin offsetting her thick, black tattoos. Such images dare the viewer to take on such powerful and massive womanhood.

For the Encourager who seeks power, that belly-centricity often translates into feeding and belly rubs. It's all about feeding the belly, feeding the tank, keeping the tank full, filling the gut, pumping up the gut, bloating and maximizing the capacity of the stomach. He or she is likely to see themselves as subordinate, supportive, and attentive—like being present at the training of a star athlete.

Eating and feeding can be a very physical and literal drive for Power Gainers and Encouragers—consuming mass to attain mass. The more he grows his belly, the sexier and more masculine the man. The larger her girth, the more her presence dominates. As one Power Encourager put it in an online posting, "I am a gaining coach. I like to see men grow HUGE GUTS on themselves. It is very masculine." Those are his capital letters yelling, not mine. You can't get much clearer than that.

Strength in Numbers

Another facet of the Power Gainer is the way he seeks community and partnership. Though he certainly welcomes encouragement from smaller men, that typically occurs as a form of worship of the big man. As in the case of the Power Chaser, the Power Encourager often sees himself as "just a guy" in contrast to his idol. He may wish to get fat himself to become like his idol, in which case his idol functions as a kind of mentor or coach. Alternatively, as in the case of the gaining coach mentioned earlier, a Power Encourager may see it as relationship of equals—one man helping another, each to achieve his goal. More often, however, Power Gainers tend to prefer the company of other big-bellied men. Smaller men, even if they are fat, tell me they sometimes feel dismissed as less masculine, less powerful, or just less sexual.

I confess I've never heard of a bunch of female Power Gainers getting together to storm a buffet. However, I have heard of a female Power Gainer joining male Power Gainers in an eating foray. It seems like such a male-oriented setting, but a female Power Gainer in this context is simply one of the team. Membership, status, and respect come from gluttony and mass. You can see this at gainer events where the fattest man has an unmistakable cache of power. Among the Power set, he is the alpha male, whether he accepts the mantle or not. (Again, Power Gainers are typically male.) Similarly, the biggest eater is also lionized. If he's not also the fattest, he might be seen as an up-and-comer. Think junior varsity.

That last metaphor should not be underestimated. The mentality is of competition and camaraderie. One now-defunct gay male gainer website used the extended metaphor of guys in a frat house to organize its content. Members were called brothers, older members were designated alumni, and communications were in the form of FratNotes and Bellyrubs. Another site makes the analogy in its title that belly building is like bodybuilding: the pursuit of a hyper-masculine body as represented by a huge, bulging belly rather than lean, bulging biceps. In some men's fantasies, the two are even conflated. They dream of behemoth muscle men dwarfed by their inflated guts that defy gravity as if they were balloons. These are fantasies and cartoons, to be sure, but they eloquently express the desires and physical ideals of such men and women.

Eat to Win

For the Power Gainer, there's great pleasure in consuming large quantities of manly foods. How can a food be manly? Think of meat and potatoes: pot roast, mashed potatoes, slabs of ribs, corn on the cob, Thanksgiving dinner, and Fourth of July picnics. You can man-up an androgynous green vegetable if you cook it long enough with lots of bacon. Desserts? Maybe pie. Fuck yeah, real men definitely eat pie. Cake? Sure, why not. Now, éclairs? Hmm…Cream puffs? I'm not so sure…Ladyfingers? No fucking way. Actually, I've noticed that many Power Gainers often say they're not really into desserts. Some say it's just that they don't love sweets, but I suspect that meat and potatoes is also more manly and therefore more erotic than cupcakes or puff pastry.

Beauty Gainers & Encouragers

Now we come to me and mine. As you may have guessed by now, I count myself among the ranks of the Beauty Encouragers; I'm the counterpart of the Beauty Gainer. Guys like me see a man getting fatter primarily as an act of erotic beauty and not necessarily as the basis for masculinity. Take Leonardo da Vinci's David and fatten him until he becomes another, even more breathtaking, work of art—a beautiful youth no longer chiseled, but heaped. Not surprisingly, it is generally the Beauty Gainers rather than the Power Gainers who long to be 500 pounds of soft, gelatinous blubber. They find an erotic satisfaction in developing a slow, heavy waddle—not a tough-guy power, but the power that comes in expressing the beauty of who you truly are and long to be.

I don't know whether most female gainers are Beauty Gainers, but they are certainly far more visible and overtly sexual in their imagery than female Power Gainers. Women who've deliberately made themselves fatter tell me that they feel more feminine, more confident, and more attractive—not just to men, but to themselves when they look in the mirror. They also find their fat sensuously erotic, and they incorporate it into seduction and sex play just as male Beauty Gainers do.

Dark Seduction

There's something more forbidden about the imagery of Beauty Gainers, but we should expect this. Remember when I talked about the language of chasers? The language of Power Chasers was all about masculine or feminine power: *big guy, big gal, thick, tree-trunk legs, swagger, strut, big-bellied.* By contrast, the language of Beauty Chasers seems insulting: *fatboy, fatgirl, doughboy, blubbery, blob, waddling.* But while these are simple descriptors for the Beauty Chaser, Beauty Gainers and Encouragers see these words as aspirations or achievements. A Beauty Gainer, for example, might thrill to have earned the title *fatgirl, doughboy,* or even *blob.* Such language is not insulting, but erotic. Since gaining and encouraging turns on the distress of obesity, terms that would be hurtful to ordinary folks resonate seductively to gainers and encouragers.

Acts of Daring

We see this more forbidden aspect played out in socializing and eating habits as well. Power Gainers often congregate in bars and buffets and enjoy a friendly competition to out-eat each other. The gathering could be easily mistaken for an outing of bears or fraternity brothers. The atmosphere is a bunch of guys going out and getting pizza, wings, and maybe some beer. Encouragers are not particularly welcome except as appreciative onlookers. Beauty Gainers might be there, but you can sense the difference in their interaction with the group. In fact, Beauty Gainers are less likely to go out and eat in groups. It's an entirely more private affair and hardly the competitive sport that it seems to be for the Power Gainers. A Beauty Gainer is more likely to eat alone or to be fed by a zealous encourager.

Fed what? Well, they might enjoy the same macho cuisine as the Power Gainers, but they often harbor a secret desire to eat the least healthful food they can lay their hands on. Remember the guy I described who can pre-cum looking at a pastry case? That's a Beauty Gainer. It's no wonder he doesn't usually carouse with Power Gainers at barbecue joints. His idea of eroticism is to lose himself, not just stuff himself. His ecstasy comes from surrendering to a massive amount of food, not from conquering it. The Beauty Encourager also often places a greater emphasis on his partner's eating unhealthful foods. Giving a guy a single bite at a stick of butter can have more erotic resonance than feeding him an entire pizza. Although a pizza is more fattening than a stick of butter, the latter is more transgressive—more sinful and therefore more erotic.

Side by Side

As you can see, I'm dealing in gross generalities here. However, gainers and encouragers have told me that it's been useful to see themselves delineated and contrasted so exactingly. They tell me it's helped them answer questions of why they feel that they don't fit in with this group or that group when it seems on the surface they have everything in common. It provides insight into why we do and don't like certain things. It helps us see community where there was only strangeness.

You can see also that eating is a highly charged, erotic component for both types of gainers and encouragers, but in different ways. Eating represents mass, achievement, and dominance for the Power Gainer. But for the Beauty Gainer, it means decadence, abandon, and seduction. If you see getting fat as a dangerous sport, then Power Gainers are the boxers and hockey players. In contrast, Beauty Gainers are the cliff divers and daredevils. That analogy goes a long way, actually.

	POWER GAINER	BEAUTY GAINER
Social Scene	Social group or team	Loner or individual
Relationship to Getting Fatter	Risky sport	Daring act
Relationship to Eating	Conquering a mountain of food makes me powerful	Giving in to gluttony makes me beautifully obese
Milestones	Achieving a weight, measurement, or capacity	Experiencing a sensation, identity, or limitation
Focus	Doing	Being
Goal	Winning	Surrendering
Risk Assessment	Powerful men and women putting it on the line, breaking a record	Beautiful men and women pushing the limits, entering a new realm

FIGURE 19: Power Gainers versus Beauty Gainers

5 WAYS INTO
GAINING & ENCOURAGING

Gainers and encouragers come to our sexuality in different ways in different periods of time. Nevertheless, to be a gainer or encourager is to arrive at our sexuality through one of the following portals or on-ramps. Some large cities, such as Dallas, Washington, D.C., and Paris, are surrounded by a superhighway, sometimes called a ring road, which encircles the city. In Washington, D.C., for example, it's called the Beltway. What if a ring road surrounded gaining and encouraging? People could access the ring road from different on-ramps, but eventually they would all get to the same central destination?

Obviously there are many ways into gaining and encouraging, but we cannot take any journey all at once. We have to start somewhere. Each of us generally starts down the road to our sexuality from one of five portals or on-ramps. For most of us, one of these five is how we first become aware of our sexual desires. Often it corresponds to fantasies that we've had since early childhood.

Taking the On-Ramp

Let's look at me as an example. My earliest memories of gaining and encouraging had to do with blubber. As a kindergartner, I remember a girl saying to our teacher from across the playground, "Mrs. Dunsmore, look how fat I am!" The girl wasn't fat at all. She was eating a cupcake and sticking out her abdomen. I still remember how her avocado-green jumpsuit hugged her slim body. (It was the 70s.) I was looking for her to be fat—scrutinizing her shape and her lines—but she was lean and fit. I was not, however. I was a fat kid and I knew it, yet I was fascinated by Fat. I remember thinking that girl had no idea what fat was.

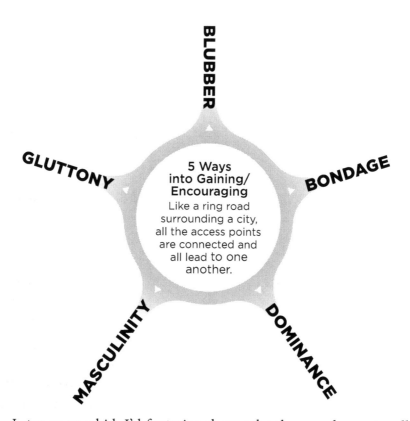

BLUBBER

GLUTTONY

BONDAGE

MASCULINITY

DOMINANCE

5 Ways
into Gaining/
Encouraging
Like a ring road
surrounding a city,
all the access points
are connected and
all lead to one
another.

Later on as a kid, I'd fantasize about other boys and occasionally myself getting very fat or very muscular. I remember when I was about ten, daydreaming about the boy next door. He was about my age, handsome and athletic, but his body was already taking on that V shape that looked so good to me. I imagined that I had a machine that would make him extremely fat or extremely muscular. I didn't think of these thoughts as sexual, even though I knew about sexual intercourse and I knew what it meant to be gay. In fact, the gay couple living next door to us were friends with our family. But my fantasies didn't match any notions of sexuality that I knew anything about.

But my feelings were sexual, of course. Men have a built-in barometer for such things. The first time I ejaculated, I was thinking about a cartoon I had seen in which the main character gets fatter and fatter. As I entered adolescence, I thought more and more about guys' bodies, but I just thought it was body envy. I was fat, so of course I wanted to look like them. *But that's not gay*, I thought, and I never wanted to get naked and jump in bed with them. Of course, I didn't think about doing that with girls either, so I just went through adolescence as asexual. Meanwhile, life at school was hell because of my obesity. It could be fairly said of my time in junior high that the only time I wasn't ridiculed for being fat was when I was the only person in the room.

This conflict might be hard to understand: How could I hate being fat at the same time that fat formed the basis of my sexual fantasies? Well, I didn't hate being fat per se. I hated not having friends. Many gainers feel this acutely too until they find community. As for my sexual fantasies, it would still take many years before I realized that blubber was central to my sexuality. When I tell the story this way, it sounds ridiculous that I didn't know, but remember that Fat is the opposite of sex for most people. In fact, even today I talk to many young gainers who don't relate to their desire for obesity as primarily sexual. Overeating, jiggling their rolls, bloating their bellies with air or water, or stuffing pillows under their clothes and pretending to be obese just seems "really fun." Only when pressed will they admit that these forms of play also give them an erection. But once they admit it, the conversation turns easily to all sorts of things they do or fantasize involving obesity to get sexually aroused.

I wanted to tell my own story here to show that these on-ramps are not necessarily obvious or traveled easily. However, we can describe some basic touchstones of eroticism that correspond to each of the five ways into gaining and encouraging. Again, straights and lesbians will probably recognize themselves here, too, if they have such a kink around Fat. Just change a few pronouns.

Blubber

As we can see from my own example, the route to gaining through blubber represents a focus on body composition: fat and its opposite, muscle. The fascination is physical, tactile, and often involves body measurements such as weight, BMI, body fat percentage, or circumferences. Blubber is usually the first way in for a Beauty Gainer or Encourager, because both the quality and the quantity of obesity are seen as primary measures of beauty. One Beauty Encourager captured it brilliantly: "I like two things: Fat and Pretty. The more of one I have, the less I need of the other. If I can get both, I'm in heaven."

Gluttony

Blubber is one way in, but it's not the most common one. For Colin, a very good friend of mine, the way in was food. He remembers being eight years old and discovering that food was available not just when it was given to him at mealtimes, but anytime he wanted it by sneaking down to the kitchen. He talks about how he would fantasize about eating as much food as he wanted, whenever he wanted, and no one would know to stop him. He had fantasies of being stuck in a room full of food and having to eat his way out, growing fatter and fatter as he did so. For an encourager at this on-ramp, there is a thrill in seeing a partner consume more and more food, their capacity increasing over weeks or months.

Masculinity/Femininity

For gainers and encouragers who seek men as sexual partners, it's often masculinity that dominates their view of obesity and how they originally came to love Fat. Kurt, whom I talked about earlier, wanted a beard at least as much as he wanted a belly. This is particularly common for gay male gainers: As their bellies grow, so do their beards. They caption their photos with slogans such as "From boy to man." They leave approving comments for each other: "Great beard with that gut. You look like a man now." Or "You've got a real man's gut now."

These gay male gainers and encouragers often tell stories about a fat uncle, or Dad's fat friend, who looked like the pinnacle of what a real man should be. As kids, they fantasized about growing to be as fat and masculine as that man someday. At the very least, they had an inexplicable fascination for that man every time they saw him. If the gainer is thin, he tells me how someday he hopes to have a huge gut so he doesn't feel "like such a little kid" even though he's already in his 20s. Likewise, many lean young men are not seen as manly enough to be credible encouragers. They often try to put on weight—muscle or fat or both—so that gainers will see them as sexier, more masculine, and more credible in their sexual role.

For gainers and encouragers who seek women as sexual partners, this on-ramp is all about femininity. When femininity is the way into gaining, fat makes a woman feel more sexual and her partner more aroused. As with the before-and-after pictures of fat men who grow beards, you can see a subtle change in the photos of female gainers who make themselves fatter to become more feminine. Their poses become more sexual, more inviting or seductive, and frequently their clothing becomes more revealing and titillating. A *before* photo of one particular feedee shows her at 130 pounds wearing a T-shirt and jeans. The photo of her 100 pounds heavier shows her in full makeup with her hair styled and dressed in a frilly blouse. She shows off how her last pair of jeans no longer buttons, leaving her soft belly fat exposed as she smiles at the viewer.

Bondage

Ryan loved the marks a rope could leave on his skin even hours after sex. He found gaining and encouraging by accident. He stumbled on a website and felt like he'd finally come home. Being tied up was great, but how much more binding would it be to be encased by hundreds of pounds of fat. How much more powerful to be restrained not by rope, but by the weight and lethargy of one's own body. How much more insidious to be rendered helpless not by physical force, but by the addiction of gluttony and the atrophy of muscles overburdened by fat. He was amazed by how obesity and force-feeding could bring him to ecstasy by pushing his body—his whole body, inside and out—to its limits. The pain of being fed to almost bursting was exquisite. The restraint of not being able to tie his own shoes was delicious in its humiliation. What's more, the tokens of this pain and bondage remained on his body: his sagging gut, his soft rolls of fat, and the angry red stretch marks that were terrifying and thrilling in their permanence. Pain and pleasure, bondage and beauty had been conflated for him since early childhood, but it was not until he discovered gaining and encouraging that he found his true sexual ecstasy.

For the encourager at this on-ramp, their job is to bind the gainer in fat. It's thrilling to make your partner so fat that they need help, or so full that they can't be moved until the food settles. I should remind you of two things now: First, this is consensual; the gainer in this situation wishes to be bound by fat. Second, few people understand that the more a gainer is bound by fat, the more the encourager is bound by servitude. It may be as innocuous as paying for an extra dessert or fetching a box of cookies—or as drastic as helping his partner out of bed or washing him. The encourager's bondage becomes more restrictive, more demanding, and more degrading as his gainer gets fatter and fatter. The symbiosis between a gainer and his encourager is perhaps seen most clearly at the on-ramp of bondage.

Dominance

Jason was the son of a war veteran. He was never sexually excited by pain; in fact, he considered it weak to complain about physical discomfort or even acknowledge it. He was proud that he was good in a fight. Any guy who got the upper hand with him usually regretted it by the end. But what Jason thrilled to was how a man could rule over his mind with only the power of his words. He enjoyed playing mind games and various forms of psychological seduction. But the form of control he found most intoxicating was when a stranger, typing from across the country on instant message, could make him eat and grow fat. He thrilled to the intensity of a man controlling him by getting in his head. He adored the subtlety of having his body ruined from the inside out, of having the strength of his body and his will fall weak as he grew fatter and more obedient at the hands of a powerful man. It made him run hot and cold to know that he was being pushed to erase himself pound by pound and turned into a soft, weak pile of lard. For the boy who worshipped power and control, nothing could be more erotic than being lured to perform this debasing transformation on his own body.

Riding Down the Road Toward Desire

If you're a gainer or encourager, you might be aware of early memories of one of these five on-ramps. In my case, blubber was my first access to my sexuality. However, you can see that things get complicated quickly. When I started fantasizing about putting muscle or fat on the boy next door, I was discovering masculinity and a vague sense of dominance and submission.

It's important to see that these five on-ramps are merely access points, a way of grouping sexual acts and ideals—they are not the sexuality of the kink itself. We arrive at some on-ramps before others. Some we embrace, some we resist or repudiate, and some we're not even aware of. But all are always present. No matter how we feel about any one, all five on-ramps lead to a single road toward our sexuality. All the entrances are connected. The level of attraction to each is usually not equal, but neither is it constant. In the people I've talked to, any of the five on-ramps may seem more attractive at one time or another, but they are all manifestations of the same central sexual desire.

A fully actualized gainer or encourager will pass through and ultimately come to embrace all five on-ramps in their journey toward their sexuality. However, it can take a gainer or encourager a lot of time and experience to perceive this unity. So our response to a particular onramp is often to strenuously denounce it, to disavow any connection it might have to us. But as my friend Jason puts it, "You can't be that upset about something unless you've got some skin in the game." As gainers or encouragers, the skin in the game is ego, or self, or identity. Even if we fight against or disavow one or two of these on-ramps, most of us come to see our resistance as fear, and the fear eventually turns to eroticism. That process is difficult for us to recognize sometimes because it happens over years or even decades—so slowly that we forget that who we were and think we've always been as we are now. Also, we tend to forget that what we thought of as "going too far" a few years ago has now become a goal or even not going far enough.

For example, I used to disparage and downplay the whole idea of masculinity. To me, machismo and images of hairy bellies and ball guts are a complete turn-off and even a ridiculous preoccupation. But as I began to write this book, I came to question why I spend so much time at the gym. Why do I devote so much time to making my muscles big? Why is it so important to me to look a particular way? I used to think that it was just a feature of being dominant or assertive, but the first time a guy called me *sir* in bed, I almost laughed, and it took me a long time to understand why guys sometimes call me *daddy*.

What turned the tide was simply embracing the fact that the men I was with thoroughly enjoyed my body as a construct of masculinity. It's similar to my story about meeting that gorgeous chub in the Castro who gave up his opinion about his body in favor of one that was more fun. Being a bodybuilder, being hyper-muscular, implies hyper-masculinity. The fact that I had built my body for other reasons entirely didn't matter to them. So when I was with these guys, I gave up my opinion of how I saw myself in favor of something more fun and empowering. Embracing masculinity as a facet of being an encourager also allowed me to be intimately tender and nurturing, like a father, as well as stern and unyielding, like a football coach.

I finally recognized that masculinity is an on-ramp to my sexuality just as much as blubber is. The two are not just two routes of getting there. The routes themselves are connected. Even though I resisted the whole cult of masculinity, it most definitely has been a part of my sexuality. And today, I embrace and take advantage of it with guys who enjoy it.

So why did I get into bodybuilding, if not for the masculinity or power? In looking back, I can see that my initial interest in bodybuilding was in part a resistance to the on-ramp of blubber. Having been the fat kid, I saw bodybuilding as blubber's antithesis. Of course, blubber was also my initial way into gaining and encouraging. This conflict eventually resolved itself when I became an encourager, embodying the antithesis of my obese partner. We'll talk more about the gainer/encourager dynamic later on in this section, but for now, what's important to see is that gainers and encouragers express the two parts of a sexual dyad that is rooted in physical transformation. I am the most perfect partner for a blubbery doughboy when I am his complete opposite. To understand this, however, we must first look at how a kink works—its architecture and design.

At THE HEART OF THE KINK

A burning question for many gainers and encouragers is "Why am I like this? Why do I want this?" If you're reading this book and you're not a gainer or encourager, I suppose you might be pretty interested, too. What makes someone desire such things? Ours is arguably a hazardous sexuality and certainly an inconvenient one. People ask me all sorts of questions about their sexuality and the Round World, but this "Why?" question is like a drumbeat behind all the others. I've worked out my own answer based on a lot of reading about sexuality, and it fits with the experiences of the men I've talked to over the years.

I used to unwind a long explanation when people would ask me about why they were gainers or encouragers, feeders or feedees. However, I have found that my explanation—any explanation, really, whether right or wrong—does not give people greater access to love, their sexuality, or peace of mind. Of course, some people want to know the answer just because it's an interesting question. You can tell who these people are by their nonchalance when I say, "It's a long explanation, and it won't change anything." They respond with detachment, saying something like, "Yeah, I figured. I was just curious." On the contrary, I've discovered the question of "Why me?" burns hottest when people hope the answer will confer blame or grant forgiveness. If you think back to that axis of blame and pity, it is the gainer or encourager whose own sexual desires are set upon that scale. In asking, "Why am I like this?" many gainers and encouragers hope to finally settle the question of their damnation or absolution. Let me give an example.

I gave a talk that was quite well received at a gainer/encourager event, and one participant commented afterwards that he wished I had addressed *why* we want to fatten ourselves or others—why it is so central to our sexuality. He told me he had struggled with his desire to become enormously obese for decades—almost his whole life, in fact. He said that maybe if he knew why, he could finally find some peace. I told him I would share my thoughts on the subject with him, but that they wouldn't change his desires.

"Oh, I know I'll always want this," he said. "I always have. I just think I could stop feeling so guilty if I knew why."

I asked him to explain a bit more what he meant, and in the end I said this:

"I think you just want to know what to blame." He was taken aback, but I continued. "I think that whatever I tell you, you'll just add it to the pile of evidence against yourself that makes you feel guilty. Any answer I give you will just be one more club in your arsenal. For example, if I tell you that your drive to get fat is a genetic or brain defect, you can blame nature and be its victim. If I tell you that your drives come from early childhood trauma, you will struggle to recall the trauma and ultimately blame people in your family. If I tell you that it's right and natural for you to want to fatten yourself to 600 pounds, and there's no one and nothing to blame, you won't believe me. In short, you seek an *explanation* for the guilt, not relief from it. So there is no explanation I can give you that won't serve as a way for you to make yourself bad, wrong, or defective."

I suggested that what might be a more productive line of inquiry would be how to transform the guilt, to have it disappear and leave him with more freedom and peace of mind.

Harsh as that may sound to some, he actually thanked me. He saw the truth of it, and we had the transformative conversation instead. So many times in life, we think that explaining a problem will help solve it. We see the world as a place to corroborate our feelings rather than to transform them. So while I'm not going to bother about explaining how I think we gainers and encouragers got this way, I think it might be worthwhile to explain some of the biological and psychological mechanisms that underlie our desires and in fact underlie all kinks. After all, knowing who built your car or how the car was invented doesn't make much difference while you're driving it. However, knowing the principles behind its operation—what makes it go, what it needs to run, whether the motor is connected to the windows—is very helpful indeed. Let's look at that next.

Finding Answers in Sexual Conflict

On the journey toward my sexuality, I met with a sex therapist a couple of times. I had figured out that I liked fat guys, that I was gay, and even that my greatest sexual gratification involved men getting fatter. Given all that, how could I have been sexually attracted to Marc, a man who wasn't even fat, much less a gainer? Granted, our sex life never worked, but how could I have fallen in love with someone so sexually incompatible at such a fundamental level? And why, if I'm so one-dimensional in my sexuality, do I find myself staring at muscular men? Even at hot, slim guys who look like underwear models? Why does a spike of adrenaline shoot through me when I see a fitness model. I had figured out, as many men do, that I could fake an orgasm. I had learned that I could step sideways in my mind into a weight-gain fantasy at just the right moment to ensure a proper orgasm with these guys. I think many people do this in various situations, but a classic one is when you're having sex with someone who does not share your kink.

The therapist explained that my erections and orgasms resulted from impulses transmitted along my parasympathetic nervous system. However, the adrenaline rush that came from lean, beautiful men was carried along my sympathetic nervous system. That rush was a learned response based on what I saw in the world; I had formed the opinion that lean, beautiful men were attractive and exciting, but my body was not in full agreement. If you remember the Chub Challenge, we saw that what we like is not necessarily what we think we like. In my case, a learned preference happening in a particular part of my brain was in conflict with the pleasure that was happening in another. In other words, my excitement at pursuing a beautiful, thin man, was happening through a particular part of my nervous system. However, the arousal leading to ejaculation was carried through a different part of my nervous system, and that part did not respond particularly well to thin, attractive men. That's why I would get a hot guy home, but then be mostly incapable of turning the encounter into passionate, orgasmic sex. Well, I could—but first I'd have to mentally *step outside* and fantasize about the guy telling me how fat he wanted me to make him. Then I would mentally step back into the encounter as I orgasmed. As I said, many of us do this so easily that it is beneath notice, particularly if we don't wish to examine our sexuality too carefully.

How We're Wired

To sum up, I discovered that my sympathetic nervous system had been trained by experience and expectation to respond to traditionally beautiful guys—the guys you see in mainstream magazines. However, my inward nature to revel in a man's fat and push him to get fatter is expressed physically in my body through my parasympathetic nervous system. Let's take a closer look at this biology.

Parallel Systems

The sympathetic and parasympathetic nervous systems are responsible for how emotions feel in your body—how emotions manifest as physical signs. For example, think of a time when you were really stressed or excited: You're driving along, and a child runs out in front of your car. Or you learn some great news and start screaming and jumping up and down. Or you're home for the holidays, and your uncle starts talking about "those people." What happens?

Sympathetic Nervous System

That fear, excitement, or anger is translated into physical sensations by your sympathetic nervous system. You feel your temperature rise, your muscles tense, your heart pound, or your stomach sink. You don't decide to do those things; they are physical sensations manifested by your sympathetic nervous system in response to stress or excitement in your environment. Notice that it happens even in the absence of the real thing. For example, maybe something made you angry while you were reading some words in this book. Even just the mention of certain words—Democrats! Republicans! Fat!—can trigger a physical response.

Parasympathetic Nervous System

You also have another nervous system, which operates in a complementary fashion. Rather than responding to external demands and concerns, the parasympathetic nervous system focuses mostly on your own biology, keeping your body on an even keel as it goes about its most basic functions: digestion, excretion, and reproduction. Yup, how perfect is this for gainers and encouragers: Eating and sex. Of course, I'm not suggesting that eating and sex are somehow fused together in the nervous systems of gainers and encouragers. After all, the parasympathetic nervous system is also the pathway that signals the eyes to tear as an expression of deep sadness or joy. Actually, I think it's more interesting that sexual arousal, intimacy, and being moved to tears are all transmitted along the same network. So anyone having meaningful sex—with or without a kink—is playing on their parasympathetic nerve strings.

Normally, the sympathetic and parasympathetic nervous systems complement each other: the former speeds us; the latter soothes us. Notice how some people use masturbation as a technique for relieving anxiety. However, others can't perform at all sexually if they are nervous or stressed. Some people eat when they are nervous to calm themselves, but others can't eat a thing when they are anxious. This shows how people are wired differently. Think of your physical experience of emotion as a matter of circuitry. When we experience various emotions, these two systems bring about the physical sensations that we feel in our bodies. To be clear, these two branches of the nervous system do not *cause* our emotions or desires. They just carry messages about emotions and desires to the rest of the body, which we experience as physical responses such as erections, vaginal secretions, goose bumps, or butterflies in the stomach.

Short-Circuited Desires

For the sexually conflicted person, these two systems end up antagonizing each other. You might recall the earlier example of a guy who reveled in making himself fatter, but then felt so ashamed and guilty that he would break out in a rash and hit the gym intensely for weeks to lose all the weight. That's a clear illustration of the two nervous systems in action. It would be like trying to drive a car by alternately stomping one foot on the brake and the other foot on the accelerator. The car lurches, and stalls, and races forward. The ride is terribly uncomfortable and perhaps even scary, but the car is simply carrying out the instructions transmitted along two different systems: the braking system and the drive train.

First, as he gets fatter, he gets more turned on. It feels good, his erections rage, and eating is erotic. In a gainer, these physical responses are all manifested through the parasympathetic nervous system. This is the system that looks inward, keeps the body in tune with itself, and conveys physical manifestations of biological needs or desires. But then one day he is horrified by what he sees in the mirror. He fears he's gone too far and is out of control. The stress is so intense that he breaks out in hives as his heart pounds and his mind races to engineer the fastest way back to normalcy. Hives are a skin rash mediated by the sympathetic nervous system in response to extreme external stress. The rash, the rush to the gym, and the blood pounding in his ears are bodily responses manifest in the body via the sympathetic nervous system in response to his panic. This is the system that is outward-looking, that learns to respond to stimuli as interpreted by judgment, fear, and guilt.

Orgasm in the Nervous Systems

Here's a more common and less dramatic example of how our nervous systems act out our conflicting desires. Some men and women are pummeled by guilt and shame after sex. It could be the guilt and shame of their kink, or of being gay, or of just having sex at all. The journey to the orgasm rides on the rails of the parasympathetic nervous system; it coordinates the organs and glands of the body to release hormones and neurotransmitters. Orgasm then engages the sympathetic nervous system in addition, as muscles contract rapidly and powerfully to ejaculate semen in men, or deeply and rhythmically with vaginal secretions in women. At that moment, however, if there's any panic, fear, or anger, the sympathetic nervous system is more than ready to flood the body with cortisol, adrenaline, and other chemicals. The conflicted man or woman might have a feeling of only restless unease. However, if his or her conflict is desperate, the body is flooded with hormones resulting in a fight-or-flight response. Remember the man who had to be out my door within five minutes of ejaculating? That's a pretty good example of a flight response triggered by deep feelings of guilt and shame in the mind, and made physically real in the body via the sympathetic nervous system.

I don't mean to suggest that this explanation lets people off the hook for rude behavior after sex. The root of the conflict is in the mind, in the unresolved elements of one's identity. But the body doesn't understand such abstractions. It experiences no difference between a threatening attacker and a threatening ideology. Our body interprets all threats as real because it knows no other kind.

When we feel a pang of guilt in the pit of our stomach, that is a judgment about ourselves or the world, transmitted along the sympathetic nervous system to the adrenal glands, to give us a burst of energy. The body is simply preparing for the action that would logically ensue from encountering something bad. It's preparing to fight or flee from that bad thing. And just as the body acts to preserve the body, the identity acts to preserve the identity—who you think you are and are not. When your pleasure is in conflict with your identity—*I shouldn't be like this! I'm not this kind of person!*—the parasympathetic and sympathetic nervous systems bring the mental conflict into the body.

The Firmware of Our Sexuality

Where does kink fit into this explanation of sexuality? What's different about gainers and encouragers, or feedees and feeders? Well, if we imagine a person to be like a computer, then the conscious mind would contain all the data and software. All the skills you have learned, all the knowledge you possess would be like applications and files on a computer. Things you consciously learn, such as playing the piano, doing algebra, and writing an email would be like software. It would also include learned ideas such as sex is wrong, fat is ugly, men are liars, and women are unknowable. And like software or data, the knowledge and skills you possess can be installed, modified, upgraded, or lost—and perhaps it gets reinstalled or relearned.

Meanwhile, your physical body—your arms your legs, your tongue— would be like computer hardware. Hardware is the physical equipment of your computer system, including your printer, scanner, and monitor. Software controls the hardware as your conscious mind controls your body. For example, you know how to operate a book, and you can command your hand to hold it and your fingers to turn a page.

However, there are deep parts of consciousness that the software has little or no control over. In some cases it has no access at all or is completely unaware. This is the system of communication throughout the body that allows software to be understood by the body and the whole apparatus to work in harmony. Computer people call this firmware. It's not complicated, highbrow software that we have to install, and it's not dumb mechanical hardware that obeys commands. It's the underlying communication system that makes it possible for us to function. Hardware can be connected and disconnected. Software can be installed or deleted. Firmware, however, is far more integral and far more necessary. Most firmware is designed to run on the circuitry of your particular machine.

If you are a gainer or encourager, in fact if you have any kink, that kink is part of your firmware. The only way to shut down a kink is to shut down that part of your operating system—the whole psychosexual system. The only way to "cure" someone of gaining or encouraging is to cure them of sexuality altogether. That's another reason why I say that being a gainer or encourager is a sexuality. The desires of kink work in the body exactly the way the desires of being gay or straight work. At the deepest level, they are the same for us. The only way to stop being gay is to stop being sexual. That's why the only successful so-called treatment for homosexuality has been chemical castration. That's why I say that gaining and encouraging is not something that operates on top of or beside our sexuality. It is our sexuality.

Some gainers and encouragers tell me that they go through periods when they feel more or less affinity for their desires. Gainers get bored with stuffing themselves or begin to see it as lonely and pointless. Encouragers feel deprived by the seeming lack of suitable partners and yearn to connect to a more normal dating pool. I think there are two reasons why our desires seem to wax and wane.

First, most human beings experience periods when sex is more or less important to them. The drive to have sex waxes and wanes in all of us, and those fluctuations have nothing to do with any kink. Second, gaining or encouraging is sexual, and sex is best enjoyed with a partner. Eating alone and fantasizing is simply masturbation for a gainer. For the encourager, searching night after night for a like-minded partner online and finding only cybersex seems equally pointless and masturbatory. But here again, we see the parallel with homosexuality of another era. Many men of 1950s America used to say the same thing about the desperation and loneliness of being gay: "Why should I waste night after night trolling for a man in a park to have sex with, when I could be having a great time with a girl at the movies or at a dance? I mean, is sex really all that important?" The key to personal fulfillment lies in partnership and community. Through understanding and accepting our sexuality, we come to locate ourselves in a community of like-minded people. Within that community, we come to know friendship, partnership, fulfillment, sex, and love.

A LOVING RELATIONSHIP AND A FATTENING KINK

You might have noticed that since I started talking about gaining and encouraging, I haven't said much about love and relationships, which was a key component of the previous section. That's because gaining and encouraging (or any kink) operates in a field separate from love and the usual erotic centers of attraction. Now, I certainly do not mean to imply that those of us with a kink are incapable of romantic love. I just think that for various reasons, it takes us a little longer to bridge the two dimensions of sex and love. If you think back to my own history, I seemed to understand how to have a loving relationship long before I understood how to have fulfilling sex. For other young gainers and encouragers it may be the other way around. They figure out their sexuality in early adolescence, but they are unable to have a loving relationship that incorporates their sexuality until much later in life. I think there are several reasons for this.

First, as I said earlier, chubs and chasers are generally five to ten years behind the norm when it comes to sexual experience and/or the maturity of their relationships. This is even truer for gainers and encouragers, who tend to be 10 to 15 years behind. As in my own case, it takes longer for us to figure out who we are and how we're put together, how to operate and be comfortable in both love and sex. Of course, everybody has to work out this union. But for gainers and encouragers, love and kink are more difficult to reconcile—especially when some people may not even realize that their desires are actually deeply sexual. After all, we hear most of our lives that Fat is definitely not sexy, so how could our attraction to Fat be sexual? I sometimes compare it to growing up with two languages—love and kink. Children who grow up in bilingual households generally take longer to speak their first sentences; they've got two languages to sort out. So maybe it's not so surprising that it takes us longer, too. Among younger gainers and encouragers, it's common that love or lust eclipses the other.

Part of the passage into adulthood for anyone, not just gainers and encouragers, is experiencing the difference between fairy-tale romance, sexual conquest, and authentic love and intimacy. I suggest that another reason it takes gainers and encouragers a bit longer to sort love and sex is that we experience our sexuality so overwhelmingly. You might recall that I described it as a pressurized sexuality, an overwhelming force. Think about it. Only a pretty overwhelming force could make a person ignore convention, morality, and even self-preservation to fatten themselves until they were a behemoth or a mockery. Why else would an encourager put himself in the position, again and again, of dating socially stigmatized partners and fantasize about serving them to increase that stigmatization? Basically, when hormones rage at that blinding intensity…well, it's blinding. Some people simply can't see love or spiritual affinity because what's happening in their body is so intense, and they haven't learned to handle it yet. It would be like asking someone to appreciate poetry being read to them while they were skydiving. To be fair, not all men and women are present to this kind of intensity. They may even go to great lengths to bury it or suppress it. But even that suppression is itself another reason gainers and encouragers seldom speak of love. Love can't flourish in a bed of denial, fear, and doubt.

Two Trains Running

A way that I've come to explain how romantic love differs for gainers and encouragers is by making an analogy of a train on a track. If you have a normal (i.e., non-kinky) sexuality, then sex and love for you probably run along a single track. For example, you're perfectly capable of loving someone so much that they become sexually attractive to you. In time, that love may even form the basis of orgasm and sexual ecstasy. The train that started at one end of the track comes to travel to the other end, and it can move freely back and forth between the two ends, stopping at many stations in between. Similarly, a relationship that may have started as purely sexual may develop into deep romantic love. Here we see the train in motion along that same track but in the opposite direction. The train-track analogy demonstrates that love and lust are not opposites, but are two forms of intimacy, which are sometimes held in tension. Normal folks are free to move easily between the two, stopping at many points in between at various points in the relationship.

Gainers and encouragers (gay or straight, male or female), however, have a different rail system. We have two trains running on parallel tracks. We have a train on a love track and a train on a sex track. The two tracks never intersect. We are biologically incapable of uniting the two, or of ridding ourselves of one track or the other. This has lead to the inaccurate and debilitating conclusion that a kink is trivial or wrong, and that someone with a kink is incapable of sustaining a relationship while indulging the kink. The people who put forward this conclusion assume that we have some other supposedly real sexuality, which has been marred to some degree by our kink. They believe we are less capable of love to the degree that we practice acts that derive from our kink. Again, we see a kink mistaken for merely an act or ideation, and only normal sexuality is credited as legitimate. This is similar to how homosexuality was viewed in the last century. Indeed the whole argument against gay marriage is based on the idea that a same-sex attraction is just a set of sexual acts that cannot embody true love, or that it is an inferior sexuality that cannot serve as the basis of a marriage. Those of us with a kink often hear the same charge from friends and even therapists.

This is of course nonsense and flies in the face of many who have deeply loving and satisfying relationships with others who share their kink. Our kink is not the only feature of our relationships any more than being gay or straight is the only feature of other relationships. Yet it is true that we do not fall in love as others do. Our love for someone can never grow into sexual fulfillment, nor can our sexual fulfillment grow to include love. These are separate tracks for us, and we ride them in separate trains. However, the two trains may run in tandem. We are capable of loving someone and becoming completely consumed by our desire for them. It just happens differently for us. Again, this makes perfect sense once we regard the kink as our sexuality, not an unfortunate feature of something better. Being gay is a sexuality just as much as being straight. But almost no one today tells a gay man to marry his favorite gal pal, with the advice that "The sex will come later" or "You have to get beyond that fetish you have for a partner with a penis."

Because kink is seldom granted the legitimacy of being a sexuality, I often meet people seeking my advice on how to make their relationships work. For example, I counsel many encouragers who adore their "normal" partner and can't imagine life without them. But the sex really doesn't work, and they are increasingly tormented by this fact as the years go by. Similarly, I've talked to encouragers who can think of nothing more erotic than to devote their life to the fattening of a particular man or woman to whom they are hopelessly drawn, but they worry that an attraction so strong could not be based legitimately in romantic love. They ask me how to fall in love with someone "for real," fearing that such an all-consuming desire to fatten a partner can't be "true love." Indeed, these dilemmas make sense from the perspective of the normative, one-track model of love and sex.

Often, their fears that they are not experiencing "true love" are compounded by fat fundamentalism, which implies that a relationship based on gaining or encouraging is actually the opposite of love since it must lead to death. After all, if Fat = Death and for the gainer or encourager

Love = Fat, then in such a relationship Love = Death. This conclusion seems reasonable until we begin to question the premises of this syllogism.

We already dealt with the Fat = Death fallacy in Section 2, and now we're uncovering a similar complexity in the fallacy that Love = Fat. Most gainers and encouragers have a subconscious sense of their two-track nature and tend to see romantic love and gainer sex as dichotomous. They are correct. However, that does not mean that love and lust are not possible for us in a single relationship. Yes, the two qualities move along different tracks, but there is no reason they cannot operate in tandem and even reinforce each other.

When Kink Meets Normal

Many gainers or encouragers, feeders or feedees, are in loving, committed relationships with normie partners—partners who don't find weight gain erotic. Despite being close and intimate on so many other levels, both we and our normie partners are often dissatisfied with sex. When we talk to our normie friends about the problems we're having in our relationships, they don't seem to understand us. We feel guilty that we can't make it work because, according to all our normie friends, we're "so great together." Or it doesn't matter if the sex doesn't work because "after all, it's only sex." Again, in a one-track normative model of sexuality, there is a flow back and forth between love and lust. Normies with enduring relationships often find that more of one can suffice for less of the other. Besides, as people often tell us, sex in a relationship fades as we get older anyway.

So for those of us with a kink, hearing that sex is not "the most important part" of a relationship means that our dissatisfaction must not really be all that important. The tacit assumption is that love is always more important. Everyone knows this, right? Love conquers all, Love will find a way, All you need is love, and—of course—If you really love someone... These aphorisms simply fall miserably short for those of us with a kink. We have a two-track system of love and sexuality. One does not evolve into the other. For us, love and sex are completely independent variables, which may operate to reinforce or contradict each other. So when normies counsel us that love is more important than sex, it's rather like hearing that water is more important than food, or that if we drink enough the food will come. That's why so many gainers and encouragers starve in our relationships, and we don't even know why.

However, even for people with a normal sexuality, arguing the relative importance of love versus sex seems to me to be a dead end. The topic comes up a fair amount in my seminars and couples counseling, and this is what I tell people: When we speak of a romantic relationship, sex is like the gas in your car. I don't know if gas is the most "important" part of your car, but I do know that your car won't run without it. There is a name for an intimate relationship that does not include sex: It's called friendship. We don't have to sacrifice the most important people in our lives to express our sexuality. Sometimes, all that's needed is to redesign our relationships to include those dear to us in a different way.

Going Over the Rainbow

What happens when someone who has a kink strikes up a relationship with someone who doesn't? Everyone has sexual fantasies, but I'm talking about something far more primal and powerful. If you have a kink, you'll find that sex when the kink is present is like leaving Kansas and going over the rainbow. Eventually, having sex without it is like being stuck in a world without Technicolor. Before I had sex with a gainer, I thought sex was okay, but…well, honestly it felt more like a performance I was giving for an eager audience. What was worse was that the performance usually got lackluster reviews. Like Dorothy living in black-and-white Kansas, I thought that was how sex was. I never expected it could be anything more. But if you have a kink and distinguish it, it's like Dorothy opening that door and seeing Oz for the first time. Many people tell me they enjoy sex in and out of their kink, but they admit that sex in their kink is always more powerful. In most cases when I check back with these people in five or ten years, they confess that sex with people who don't share their kink has become increasingly less interesting. One guy told me that he hardly ever has sex anymore because partners who share his kink are rare where he lives and normal partners just aren't worth the effort. "Normal guys are just too much work for too little reward," he said.

Most gainers or encouragers have their first relationship with a norm-ie—someone who doesn't have a sexual kink. Some continue dating normies even though they know such relationships can't fulfill their sexuality, at least not entirely. Here's what that looks like.

Gainers with Normies

Chase is a devastatingly handsome young man who just happens to have an attraction for superchubs. He's a happy-go-lucky guy, around five foot ten with a lean body, perfect hair, and absolutely no trace of conceit or arrogance about how men and women are instantly charmed by his presence. He seems completely unaware of it, which makes it all the more devastating. Chase is also quite open about the fact that he likes fat guys, which makes him a candidate for a serious relationship with one. No doubt about it, Chase is a catch for some lucky fat guy. And indeed, he is in an idyllic relationship with an equally handsome superchub named Doug. They could be on the cover of the welcome brochure for the Round World.

Unfortunately, there is an apple waiting to be bitten in this Eden. Chase has recently been thinking about getting fat. Just a few pounds, he assures his partner—nothing drastic. Doug actually loves the idea of his little stud growing a cute belly to play with. Successive bites at the apple, however, will come to reveal to Chase that he does not just want a little belly. But he could be satisfied with that, he thinks, so he says nothing about it to his boyfriend. Actually, he fantasizes about getting as fat as Doug—even fatter, actually. It thrills him to think that his 380-pound boyfriend would be the thin one in the relationship. He fantasizes about being fattened, and thinks how great it would be if Doug were into doing that to him. For his part, Doug doesn't have much problem with feeding his boyfriend a bit or seeing him get chubby. After all, Doug is a well-adjusted chub who has no malice toward his own fat body, so none toward Chase's either if he were to get fat.

They're still together and still happy. What goes unsaid, however, is that Chase has never had sex with a true encourager who shares his kink. Doug can put food to Chase's lips and say all the things he's supposed to say to sound like an encourager, but he's not a native speaker of the kink. And to be fair, Chase really doesn't know the difference, because he's never known sex to be anything else than what he's always had. But he knows that he can't stay away from gainer websites. Even if he never meets anyone from those sites in person, he knows that this is a part of him that aches to be expressed…somehow. He also knows that he would never disrespect or cheat on his partner. That's why he insisted that his partner be on the sites with him, even though Doug doesn't feel much affinity for the guys there. Nevertheless, everything is aboveboard.

So what do we make of Chase and Doug? Is this a success story of a relationship that has survived a personal discovery and adapted? Is it a testimony to mediocrity and settling for what you know, rather than going after what you want? Or is it the story of how love triumphs over lust, and a lesson in what's really important in life? That's not for me to say. There's no Truth here, no right answer. When I counsel people, I present all of those options and interpretations, but I leave it to the person or the couple to decide which fits best.

Here's another story from a gainer I've known for decades. Tommy knew from an early age that he longed to become obese. A former athlete and gymnast, he desperately wanted to bury his incredibly beautiful body in hundreds of pounds of blubber, especially if it were at the hands of some hot, dominant guy who loved what Tommy was becoming. Like many people, however, Tommy lived his life so that other people would be happy. His strategy for being liked was to please others and make their expectations and desires more important than his own. Whether he was a child pleasing his father by going out for another sport, or pleasing his friends by adopting their tastes and preferences, or pleasing a handsome, successful lover who wanted to make a life with him, Tommy's own desires and needs were never very important to him.

To date, Tommy has been with his partner for over 20 years. They own property together, have friends together, and have made a life together. However, Tommy says they're more like roommates than romantic partners. They stopped having sex years ago. The desire to express his sexuality has raged in Tommy for decades. Its only fulfillment has been in the scant number of times he's cheated on his partner. Tommy recognizes that he's had many opportunities to leave the relationship over the years. But for people like Tommy, his own happiness is secondary to other people's expectations. If he ended his relationship, the disappointment of his partner, of his family, of his friends, of his entire community would be unbearable. Not to mention the effort it would take to divide assets, disassemble their financial links, and live on half the resources. Besides, he says, it's a good life they've made together. But more and more Tommy has come to regret his decision and think about what might have been. He says he feels hollow a lot of the time, like he's just going through the motions of life. "It's like there's this whole other part of me that I've ignored or tried to shut out all these years. I feel like I'm living half a life."

Tommy's story illustrates why I encourage people to deal with their sexuality with some urgency. No matter how unpleasant they think that task will be, it'll only get more unpleasant later. The two points I'd like to highlight about Tommy's story are these: First, you can see again the parallel between Tommy's life and the lives of so many gay men who force themselves to marry women. Second, this kink, this sexuality, does not assert itself only in the bedroom. It touches every part of a person's life. Similarly, every part of a person bears on his sexuality and how he will or will not express it. This is why I can frequently help people with their sexuality by helping them deal with some other aspect of their lives that seems unrelated.

Encouragers with Normies

Parker is an encourager who avoids his sexual desires, which he describes as "dark." He's a bit apprehensive that these desires don't fit with the sunny, quirky intellectual that he projects to the world. In relationships, he's a thoughtful boyfriend, an excellent cook, a homemaker, and the tasteful wit you'd gladly bring as your date to the company holiday party. Parker is definitely relationship material, and he's usually in one.

However, Parker has never been in a relationship with a gainer. Though his greatest sexual fantasy is to be with a huge, obese man who loves being fat and wants to get even fatter, Parker instead finds himself in relationships with fat men whose loathing of their obesity is buried under decades of resignation about their bodies. They hope for no more than to be less fat one day. Parker is one of those encouragers who chooses to distract himself by dating chubs rather than face the depth of his desires by getting into a relationship with a gainer. Chubs have the form of obesity, but not the dark lust for obesity that would match his. Now, Parker really does fall in love with these guys despite the seeming mismatch in sexuality. But even if he's not ready to explore his encourager nature, why doesn't he find a sunny, happy fat man to fall in love with? Why does he always seem to take up with sad sacks? Parker and the self-loathing fat boyfriend are actually perfectly aligned: they both see themselves as fundamentally flawed because of Fat.

A mutual friend who knows about Parker's desires teased him after his last break-up: "So have you got the next self-loathing superchub lined up?" But Parker doesn't get mad at such remarks. Instead, he does what he usually does about his sexuality—he avoids and deflects. He pretends not to hear the friend's comment and moves casually on to talk about how much he'll miss his ex and what a shame it was that they had to break up.

Rodrigo is another encourager who could make some gainer extremely happy. He is masculine, dominant, and possessed of the sober calculation required to fatten and care for a man who would love to be in his thrall. Many gainers seek guys like Rodrigo and ask where his like can be found. I tell them that guys like Rodrigo can often be found in the company of bodybuilders. Bodybuilders and gainers share a similar desire for size, mass, weight, and freakishness. Bodybuilding can also express psychological dysmorphia known colloquially as *bigger-exia*, the feeling that big is never big enough—similar to gainers and their desire to gain fat. Also, slabs of muscle are also seen as hyper-masculine, which is a powerful lure for a Power Chaser or Power Encourager. But bodybuilders are less stigmatized, even in their freakishness, than the extremely obese, which makes them easier to date. Rodrigo, like many encouragers, claims to be fascinated by both superchubs and freakishly huge bodybuilders. However, I know from experience that guys like Rodrigo almost always find their way back to gainers.

Unfortunately it may take many years or even decades for their authentic desires to assert themselves powerfully enough to overcome the admiration of friends and approval of society that being the boyfriend of a bodybuilder offers. This distraction is not unique to encouragers.

As we saw with Chase, gainers can get distracted by chubs. Though the chub doesn't share the gainer's sexuality, the particular chub may be the gainer's ideal, his goal, his role model. Usually the gainer doesn't know this, because, developing 10 to 15 years behind the curve, he hasn't worked all this out yet.

Love and Abuse

There are of course abusive encouragers too, I'm sorry to say. These are the proverbial bad apples who ruin our collective reputation. Instead of finding gainers who share their kink, these encouragers go after partners who have no desire to be fatter. They subtly trick their partner into gaining weight or actively sabotage their attempts to lose weight. They feign innocence, claiming they didn't actually force the food into their victim's mouth. It's the same defense mounted by a person who slips a drug into a potential partner's drink but then claims he never forced the person to accept the drink, much less drink it.

I call this *abuse* because for the encourager, fattening his or her partner is sexual. For the normie partner, the weight gain is non-consensual. And non-consensual sex is abuse. It's no different from a guy who is into sadomasochism hitting his partner when the partner is asleep and feigning innocence when the partner wakes up with bruises. Silence is not consent. Again, it's common to think of men as the abusers here, but I've heard from women seeking my advice on how to talk their partner into gaining weight or techniques to make their partner fatter without them noticing right away.

Some of these encouragers do it out of an insecurity that if they made their true sexuality known, they would be condemned and disdained. Ironically, by fattening their partner covertly, they incur the very contempt they had hoped to avoid. But of course, this sort of encourager has contempt even for their own desires. And, as in the case of Parker, they'll seek out a partner who would most loathe getting fatter because it matches their own feelings of being flawed by Fat. We don't end up in relationships by accident and certainly not by mistake.

I should also say that some encouragers fatten their partners abusively (that is, non-consensually) because it is simply more erotic to them.

For example, I've heard from a few women that they've deliberately overstocked the fridge with junk food in hopes that their fit boyfriend would succumb. I've heard from men who tell me that they cajole their fat partner to indulge in a grand dinner and then suggest dessert, even though their partner complained that they ate too much at lunch. Other men and women who've admitted to fantasies of abusive (non-consensual) weight gain have also told me that they've never actually done it. They think it's hot, but they have too much respect for their partner to deliberately fatten them without consent. Since the erotic power of gaining or encouraging comes from the distress of obesity, trickery or non-consent heightens the distress.

To be fair, however, many gainers have a corresponding abusive fantasy: to be kidnapped, tied down for months or years, and fattened mercilessly against their will. Again, they tell me that giving their consent would lessen the erotic thrill. Just as some men and women have rape fantasies, so too do gainers and encouragers. But this is what a rape fantasy looks like when sex revolves around getting fatter and weight gain becomes sexual violation.

"I'd Love It if You Gained Weight."

Certainly, most encouragers I meet are not abusive. It's true they may have sex with or even be in committed relationships with someone who isn't a gainer. However, any encouragement of their partner to get fatter is hardly covert. In such cases, the encourager tells his or her normie partner about their desires, though perhaps not their true depth. He or she might tell their partner plainly, "I'd love it if you gained weight." For some people, hearing such a declaration would curdle their blood. These people usually exit the relationship quickly.

Other people might interpret that statement as "You're not good enough as you are," which is usually not how the encourager means it. It reminds me of the time when my boss came to me for advice on bodybuilding. He is reasonably fit and very lean, but his wife told him, "I'd love it if you had more muscle." He felt no offense at her remark and simply wished to please her.

Indeed, for many fat partners, "I'd love it if you gained weight" offers freedom. Many fat people have spent their whole lives worrying about crossing a line past which they would be unattractive or even unlovable. For them, "I'd love it if you gained weight" is an assurance that the pressure to stay on the right side of that line is gone, that in fact there is no line. That's actually a pretty big deal. Imagine being told your whole life that you weigh too much and you eat too much. Then you find someone who adores you, and they say, "Eat all you want. Just more to love."

Two consequences follow from such a declaration. First, the fat partner realizes that his weight loss is his own affair, and not a requirement for love or happiness. And second,…well, be careful what you wish for. For many fat people, the guilt of obesity is the only thing that holds their weight in check. Fear and shame are their diet plan. So when that's gone, and they are free to enjoy food, sex, and the devotion of their partner, many men and women end up much fatter than they really feel comfortable being. Were they duped? Sabotaged? No, they just lost track of what they wanted. This is not unique to being with an encourager. Such weight gain can happen just as easily with a chaser or any loving partner who makes it clear that their partner's obesity is not inherently a problem.

Finding Our Match

I don't think that people end up in relationships at random. Even less do I believe that they end up with the "wrong" people. Affinities and commonalities bring us together. We each find the best relationship we are capable of at that time in our lives, the one that fits what we think of ourselves and the world. When these affinities for people are based on emotional needs and insecurities, what results is an entanglement. An entanglement is my name for a relationship that is held together by matching baggage, a union in which one person's imagined lacks and insecurities are a perfect complement to his partner's. "He completes me" is a common phrase in such relationships, the implication being that each person alone is incomplete. This is distinct from a relationship based on love, in which each partner sees himself and the other as already whole.

My own dating history has included many chubs, as well as gainers. I always state up front that I'm an encourager, but that I don't foist my kink on anyone who's not into it. Nevertheless, a fair number of chubs try to solicit my attention by claiming to be gainers or by mentioning that they've gained weight recently. Some even say explicitly that they'd be willing to gain weight for me. It's been said that men will say anything to get in your pants—well, that's how this adage shows up in my world.

For my part, I'm not interested in acting in such a charade. I think that for most chubs, the lure to gain weight for me is just a tactic. They figure there's no harm in pretending to be a gainer for a night if it means some hot fun with a muscular guy. Others, however, may pretend to be a gainer as a desperate act to get attention and love. They may even enter a relationship with an encourager under this pretense. Often they don't see it as much of a betrayal of who they are because who they are doesn't seem to them to be worth much. For me, going through with sex on these terms would be degrading for both of us. I think it degrades the chub and affirms his low opinion of himself if he's willing to give up his sexuality to please me. Moreover, it shames me and betrays my true sexuality to let him fake it for me.

There's another reason I don't allow chubs to pretend that they're gainers with me, and I tell this to young encouragers a lot. I've been with real gainers—guys who sincerely want me to make them obese. We've both had our respective desires for as long as we can remember. We are not abuser and victim. We're not accommodating each other's differences. We are equal partners—consenting and conscious participants in an act that is mutually and intensely erotic. So the empty pantomime of the chub who is just trying to gratify my encourager fantasies pales in comparison to the ecstatic intimacy of a gainer who truly shares what's at the core of my sexuality.

Integrating Love, Life, and Kink

Most readers will find this obvious, but I talk to so many gainers and encouragers who quite honestly have no idea what I mean by the word *intimacy*. Many young gainers and encouragers think that *intimate* is a code word for a penis penetrating an orifice. Alternatively, they sometimes guess that I mean emotional vulnerability, which they then associate with weakness, powerlessness, and being taken advantage of. In contrast, I define intimacy as emotional openness, honesty, and a feeling of being physically connected to another human soul. It's a rather difficult thing to put into words. Intimacy seems meaningless or even absurd to many gainers and encouragers with whom I've talked, yet they long for it as much as they fear it. In this section, we will shed some light on some of those dark corners and the fear of intimacy.

The Kinky Path to Love

The intention of all my work is to leave people free to be who they've always been, and free to love what they've always loved. With gainers and encouragers, this work typically has three phases. You might even think of them as acts of a play.

Making Friends with the Monster

As with a play, the first act of my work with people involves distinguishing and articulating a person's conflicts. In many cases, this is the first time they have ever said these things out loud or admitted to them. For me, it feels like helping someone untie the knots they've made of their fears. I don't try to take away the fear. Usually these men and women don't even know what they're afraid of. They live in a morass of scary thoughts, erotic images, and crushing self-recriminations.

Seeing Life as Whole

In this second act, we look at expressing these sexual desires in a way that is mindful, empowering, and integral to a whole life. "Just do it" would be irresponsible advice for many gainers or encouragers whose circumstances won't allow them to get fat or to fatten someone else. We work toward workable solutions that allow their sexuality to flow without washing away the rest of their lives. Most people get stuck in looking at their lives as a collection of elements (people, things, ideals) that they are driven to pursue or afraid to lose. The intent of my work is for people to discover a freedom from lust and fear that allows them to authentically choose and create their lives. Where there is fear, there is no authentic choice. In all cases, we look to sexuality and relationships not as millstones of shame and secrecy but as sources of enrichment and vitality.

Creating Partnership

This third and final act involves transcending sexual acts and roles, and moving toward a relationship that realizes the inherent symbiosis of kink, which is physical, emotional, and even spiritual. Even many therapists relegate kink to a sort of second-class sexual status. Again, it's all too similar to how homosexuality has been treated in the past—as deviant, narcissistic, unnatural, and incapable of supporting love. As we saw in "Two Trains Running," this results from a misunderstanding of how kink operates. When two people are in love and they share the same sexual kink, the experience is transcendent. It reverberates throughout every part of their lives.

It would certainly be convenient if people showed up asking for things in the proper order. More often than not, however, a gainer or encourager might, for example, ask for help in a relationship but still be deeply uncomfortable with—or even unaware of—their deeper sexual desires. It's a challenging conversation, to be sure, and it's tempting to catch them up, as you would catch someone up who's walked into the middle of a play. However, that never works very well. I've learned to engage people where they are.

Those three *acts* of this work are vast and complex, perhaps enough to merit their own book. But a simple and clear example can be seen in the case of an 18-year-old high school senior named Toby who was tortured by whether or not he should get fat. As we've seen, this is a very common dilemma among gainers—maybe even the most common.

Toby had known since childhood that he wanted to be immensely fat, just as he had known for at least as long that he was gay. You might expect that being gay and wanting to be hugely obese would put Toby off sports, but not at all. He enjoyed sports, running, and weight lifting. But the more he thought about sex, the more he thought about giving up that life and starting to become the beautiful out-of-shape blob he always knew he'd be one day. But then he saw Eric, who was blond, fit, and into cross-country running. Toby wanted to be with Eric so much, but he feared that Eric would be repulsed if he started getting fat. In fact, he wondered if instead of getting fat, he should ask Eric if he wanted to go running together. He conjured images of running with Eric side by side on the beach against crimson sunsets until they collapsed into each other's arms in the sand. Toby knew that all he wanted in the world sexually was to be fat, but how could Eric return his love if Toby were fat? How could he be true to himself and still win the affection of this amazing guy?

In case it's not obvious, I should point out that almost all of what Toby told me was fears and fantasies. They had no physical reality—it was all in his head. Toby had actually never even spoken to Eric; he was just a guy in his math class. They'd never even met. In fact, Toby wasn't even sure the guy was gay, though he assured me there were "signs." This is a case of coming into the middle of the play.

As I listened to Toby paint the picture of this exquisite crush, I thought about what I could say that would be useful. Platitudes such as "Get over it. It's just a crush," "Be true to yourself," or "Go for it" fail on so many levels. And although it might seem a good idea to send Toby back to Act 1 to deal with his fears and fantasies around being alone or unlovable, none of that would be heard over the din of the crush that was roiling in his body. Toby needed coaching that would be useful and empowering, so here's what I told him:

Be where you are. Gaining will be with you forever, but jogging on a beach with your high school crush won't be. Take advantage of what you have in your life now. Gaining will always be there. Naggingly so. But don't let it stop you from experiencing your life. It's true: there are a hundred delights you can experience only when you're 500 pounds. But there are also a hundred delights that you can experience now only as a fit young guy. It's okay to want other things in your life besides being fat. That's not a betrayal of self. You don't have to give up who you are. You just need to acknowledge that at this point in your life you want other things, and right now, they are more important. Right now, running, weightlifting and sports are not things you're willing to give up. Fine.

You may feel differently when you're 25…or 45. But that's not now. Be where you are.

Fat chance: risk versus reward

When I go into a bookstore these days, there's almost always a section labeled Gay and Lesbian. Occasionally, when I'm in a more contumacious bookshop, I find a juicy section labeled Alternative Sexuality. In years of getting my hopes up that I'd find a book like this one, I have always been disappointed to find that Alternative Sexuality is really just one alternative: BDSM, which stands for bondage, discipline, and sadomasochism. This is where you find all the books on how to build your own dungeon, tie up your beloved in a macramé cocoon, or keep someone breathing while you're sweating them out in a rubber body suit. Useful skills to be sure, if you're into that sort of thing.

Far be it from me to cast aspersions on someone else's kink. Even folks who aren't into BDSM can find it titillating—almost like gawking tourists who wish they could be cool or daring enough to be into such mad passion. On the other hand, many people are appalled that a person might crave being encased in rubber, or that another begs to be pissed on and humiliated. But then maybe you're part of the set who thinks meting out air for your lover to survive during sex brings the two of you to ecstatic levels of sacrifice and trust.

Other People's Sexplay

No matter what you're into sexually—missionary position or fire play or plushy stuffed animals—everybody else's unusual sex acts show up on a spectrum. There's a tiny gap in the middle where so-called *normal* lies, or what is perhaps better labeled *commonplace*. However, the farther away we move from that unremarkable center, the more we tend to deride sex acts as silly and ridiculous or condemn them as sick and dangerous. And if these acts are central to our sexual identity, then we ourselves are placed on this spectrum.

What we think of other people's sexplay

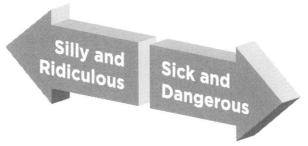

On one end are the people who dress up as horses and riders, or the panty sniffers, or people who like to rub themselves with balloons. This is the "Silly and Ridiculous" side of the spectrum—unless of course you're actually turned on by one of the things I've just mentioned. Then it's not silly and ridiculous at all—it's just hot as hell. On the other end of the spectrum we have "Sick and Dangerous." This is for the people who play with lighting parts of their body on fire to reach orgasm, or the people who weep at the erotic beauty of seeing their blood staining their partner's hands. That's way sick and dangerous, right!? Sure, unless you're into that sort of thing. Then you hasten to explain how it's actually not that dangerous, that you take strict precautions, and that life with no risk isn't worth living. One man's reason for living is another man's deluded rationalization—a charge that has been leveled at me more than a few times. I'll accept that. I've found that telling people that I enjoy making a man fatter by his own consent definitely elicits responses more toward the Sick and Dangerous side of the spectrum. I don't hope to persuade anyone about what's right or wrong. I simply offer a view from inside, and a reminder that wherever you are on the spectrum, you've got your own justifications and insecurities about being there. So on we go.

Edge Play

Gainers, encouragers, feeders, and feedees are not alone in our pursuit of sex that might be risky. Some people's sexual play regularly involves blood, fire, pain, or a potentially lethal use of chemicals. This sort of practice is called edge play; it involves risking your own or someone else's life for the sake of sexual gratification. (This is not the same as edging, getting someone close to orgasm and then backing off before it happens.) Edge play is far more widespread than people seem to think. And yes, it is potentially fatal, which is why the people who practice it have a system of apprenticeship and even take workshops and seminars to make sure that their partners don't die. And they don't die—mostly. Accidents are rare, but do happen. If you believe that weighing 500 pounds makes you a ticking time bomb, then perhaps gaining to this extreme is, as my friend Brian once put it, a form of "long-term edge play." For some of us, the expression of our sexuality is worth the risk. Your opinion may vary.

But we can't have this conversation and pretend that risking one's life is always wrong and never okay. The people who risk their lives on behalf of others are called heroes. Risking their lives is noble. What about people who risk their lives purely for their own gratification? What about skydivers, spelunkers, or people who ascend the world's tallest peaks merely for the accomplishment and the telling of the tale? Although we may not consider their efforts noble, we seldom decry them as selfish and stupid. This is surprising since surely these thrill seekers have children and spouses and families who would be bereft if things went wrong. Thrill seekers are aware of the potentially fatal nature of their play, yet they engage in it anyway. Moreover, these are expensive sports. Surely that money could be better spent on something that would benefit people. At best, that money goes to self-gratification; at worst, it goes to finance an elaborate death. This may sound harsh or unfair, but it's the same argument that the fat fundamentalists make against gluttony in general and gaining in particular.

> # Find what you like and let it kill you.
> **-Richard Samet "Kinky" Friedman**
> American singer, songwriter, humorist, and politician

Finally, when thrill seekers injure themselves or get stuck in a remote location, emergency crews and hospitals expend valuable resources on their rescue and resuscitation. And all this is because these daredevils choose to risk their lives for the fun of it, for sheer pleasure. Again, this parallels the fat fundamentalists' concern about the increased health-care costs for the obese, and how it's unfair to burden society with other people's uncontrollable urges. When it comes to Fat, we have an entirely different judgment of cost and responsibility.

If you're a fat fundamentalist, you might argue that dying from sky-diving, skiing, spelunking or mountaineering is rare, but dying from obesity is guaranteed—or if not death, surely physical harm is inevitable. Well, I would point out that bodily harm is even more common for some in peak physical condition. We have only to look at people involved in professional sports, the arts, and entertainment: football players, boxers, rodeo riders, and ballet dancers are known for the pain and damage their pursuits inflict on their bodies. Pain and damage are accepted as common daily occurrences, in fact. And as any fat fundamentalist will tell you, there's a limit to how much abuse the body can take. There's a limit to how long these people can continue in their professions before their body or one of its parts simply ruptures or wears out. Their injuries may not kill them, but they often cripple them later in life. There's no denying that the pursuit of their various professions debilitates their bodies. We pay them for this—to amuse or amaze us—and their careers last as long as their bodies can take it.

People take risks in life—some greater than others—and they take them for reasons they deem worthy. I don't think you can judge the risk until you experience the reward. My friend Tyler says he's tried to communicate the experience of skydiving to people. For me, jumping out of a perfectly good airplane holds no attraction whatsoever. But he tells me that unless I do it, I'll never truly appreciate what it means. He doesn't think of it as a thrill ride, a way to experience a high. He accords it a deep importance in his life. The same is true of gainers and encouragers. It's not just a sexual high for us. Gainers who risk their health do so for the expression of their sexuality—a sexuality that is wired into them from infancy and that they never chose. If you were faced with never experiencing full sexual gratification again, or pursuing sexual acts that might limit your life or health, which would you choose? How much would you risk?

Worth the Risk?

Back when I talked about Fat Fundamentalism, I broached the idea that being fat may not be an automatic death sentence. Yes, everyone who gets fat ends up dying, but everyone who doesn't get fat ends up dying too. Whether it's true or not, most people believe that being obese is unhealthy and that being very obese is very unhealthy. Gainers and encouragers have the same vast mix of opinions, emotions, and prejudices that everybody else does, which I detailed in "You Don't Know Fat." So actually, the question is not about how unhealthy gainers and encouragers believe obesity to be. The far more interesting question is this: If a gainer perceives gaining to be unhealthy, how do they deal with that? If an encourager perceives obesity to be unhealthy, how do they view their role in helping to fatten a partner? And just how fat and how unhealthy are we really talking about?

I've already explained the powerful erotic drive of me and my kind, but for many people (even many gainers and encouragers), the idea of risk is hard to justify. After all, it's only sex, right? Why risk your life for sex? I suppose I'm talking mostly to the Fat Fundamentalists, the Fat = Death people, but so be it. They have a widely held point of view. Well, there are a number of ways gainers deal with these issues. I'm not sure whether you'll agree with any of them, but I hope to offer a view of the issue that is human rather than moral.

Let's meet three men who have different ways of relating to the possible health issues of gaining and encouraging—one who seeks to mitigate the health risks, one who flees from the risks, and one who deliberately pursues the risks.

Health and Hedonism

My friend Justin is a Power Gainer out to minimize the health risks of gaining. Justin is always asking me for advice on how to eat healthfully and how to cook to get fatter. He's a busy student, but he stuffs himself as much as he has the time and money for. Justin hates himself if he drops below 350 pounds. Nevertheless, the prospect of damaging his health is always a looming fear for him. His blood sugar is good, and his triglycerides are normal. His blood pressure is high, but it was high when he was thin, too. Nevertheless, Justin says that he wonders "how long my luck will last." He carries a lot of weight in his belly (visceral fat, typical Power Gainer build), so his back hurts if he's not mindful of how long he stands or of his posture while sitting. Justin focuses a lot on diet and exercise as a way to mitigate what he perceives as the risks of gaining. He sees gaining as a series of challenges and solutions, much like a bodybuilder who has to train around chronic tendonitis or a ballplayer with joint trouble.

Another guy, Alfonzo, wrote me wracked with guilt about the health issues of gaining. He is a Beauty Encourager who wants to be with a hugely obese man. Ideally he'd like to take a smaller guy and turn him into a gorgeous pile of lard. But like many Beauty Encouragers, Alfonso is also a self-described health nut. He watches his own diet and body scrupulously. He knows all the proper foods to vilify and can even hold forth on the chemistry of why they're so bad for you. (Alfonso is young, so he hasn't had the experience of seeing these demon-food lists change and contradict each other over time.) His conscience won't let him feed a gainer, even one begging to be fed. He sees any form of encouragement as contributing to the gainer's demise, and he feels guilty that he experiences pleasure from feeding a man fatter. When he's with a chub, he usually dates someone who's unhappy with his size and trying to lose weight. Alfonso enjoys having sex with fat men, but he's told me that he's not really having sex with the guy—just with his blubber. He puts it out of his mind that his partner is becoming less and less his ideal as he loses weight. He just focuses on the body in front of him. When I point out how empty and objectifying that might be, he says, "I know, but it's better than the alternative. I'm doing the right thing by not hurting anyone." In that way perhaps, he and they are happy.

My friend Mason tells yet a different story. When I first met Mason, he didn't even think he was a gainer. Most gainers he met online talked on and on about how hot it was to stuff themselves and how fat they wanted to get. At six foot four and just over 400 pounds, Mason's love of eating was certainly in evidence. But sitting around and stuffing himself held little allure for him. He'd been doing that all his life, but it never got him off sexually. And he wasn't attracted to other fat guys or going to fill up at buffets like so many of the gainers he met online. He liked fit guys, even skinny guys if they were dominant. Actually, dominance is the common element in the men Mason likes: fit, dominant guys taunting him with food and making fun of how pathetic his enormous body is. He longed to show off for such a guy by eating the worst foods he could find to make his body even more pathetic. Once he spent an entire week deliberately eating nothing but fast food and climaxing over and over again as he bragged about it to appreciative encouragers online. His weight climbed. Breaking 460 pounds was pleasurable, but it was the adulation of the jocks and their mockery of his body that pushed him to eat like a garbage disposal. Right now he's taking a break. He's not looking to gain more until the right guy comes along who can really ruin him. He's looking for a cocky stud whom he can trust to trash his body and still hang around to enjoy the mess they make of it. It scares the crap out of him. Maybe that's why he's not looking as hard as he could for that man.

These three guys—Justin, Alfonzo, and Mason—all have different relationships to health as it intersects gaining and encouraging. What they have in common is their journey to reconcile it within the context of the rest of their lives.

Quality of Life

My friend John is a very attractive fat man: handsome, burly, in his early 50s and well over 400 pounds. Because of his good looks and his pendulous belly, he gets a fair amount of attention from young gainers who wish they could be him some day. Often these young guys are quite handsome themselves, and John (a garden-variety chub, not a gainer) can't understand why a young stud who could get a job modeling would want to bury himself in blubber to become a social pariah who is slow, weak, and probably sick.

"I try to explain to them," he says. "You don't want to be me. I'm pre-diabetic, I can't walk very far because of my edema, and I have to use a machine to help me breathe when I sleep so I don't choke on my fat." At first, John would spend quite a bit of time chatting online with gainers, trying to persuade them to give up their insane fantasy of becoming as fat as him. "But after a while," he said, "I just had to stop talking to these guys. Half of them would argue that they could 'gain healthy' and avoid ending up with my health problems. The other half," he continued, "would just ask me more and more questions about my health or my diet. I came to find out that what I was telling them gave 'em a hard-on! They got off on getting as unhealthy as I am! So now I don't talk to gainers. Let 'em get fat if they want, but I don't want any part of it."

That story brings us back to risk and the kind of life one wants to lead. You might think that no one wants to be sick and hobbled because of obesity, but you'd be wrong. There are men and women who want exactly that—at the very least, the fantasy eclipses all other sexual thoughts. Most gainers and encouragers don't have such extreme fantasies, and those who do rarely actualize them. Our achievements and goals in real life span a wide range. Sometimes it's innocuous, like outgrowing pants or a blouse. Sometimes it's more drastic, like stretch marks or getting out of breath more easily on a flight of stairs. And sometimes it's extreme, like needing insulin injections or oxygen to survive. Every gainer or encourager draws the line at what's too much, too sick, or too awful, and that line usually moves during a person's life. Our kink gives us the biological capacity to get turned on by any aspect of obesity. Our minds, however, may find some ideas too objectionable to indulge.

All gainers and encouragers have to come to terms with what obesity is worth to them. It is indeed a question of the quality of life, but we must ask it from the other direction as well: How much of your sexuality are you willing to give up? Of course, desires don't dictate actions. Gainers don't have to get fat just because they want to. I know gainers who are employed as fitness instructors and dancers. Being fat doesn't fit their career, or at least it doesn't fit as they've imagined it. Similarly, encouragers don't have to fatten their partners to have a workable relationship. I know several who restrict their sexual desires to fantasy or to sex with gainers outside their primary relationships—not by cheating, but by consent of their partner.

There are also workarounds such as writing erotic fiction, drawing erotic art, online fantasy role playing, or approximation. Approximation for a gainer might include bloating his stomach with air to look fat or padding his clothes with pillows. For an encourager, approximation might entail dating a supersized chub who doesn't want to gain, but doesn't want to diet either.

But context is what's most important. When these workarounds are pursued out of fear, they further inculcate the guilt and shame we feel about our desires, and thus further alienate us from ourselves. However, when pursued out of a mindful and authentic choice, these substitutes can preserve other parts of our lives that we do not wish to alter to accommodate our sexuality. As with anything to do with sexuality, the act is not as important as the context in which it occurs.

The Encourager's Role in Risk

It's easy to see how people believe that gainers are risking their lives. What about their encouragers? After stuffing a partner full of food, the encourager can walk out the door and no one need know, but the gainer is left bloated and fatter the next day. It's true, the encourager does not risk his health as the gainer does. However, in a functional gainer/encourager relationship, he risks all the prejudices, stigmas, and stereotypes that the gainer does. Also, the encourager must do more and more as the gainer is able to do less and less, which is as much a burden as it is a source of eroticism. Nevertheless, I can't deny that if something goes wrong in the relationship, the encourager probably has the ability to walk away. The gainer, however, cannot walk away from his body.

But this inequity is perhaps similar to others that you might see in other sorts of relationships. In a BDSM relationship, only the sub bears the scars. In a relationship of vastly different incomes, the richer partner might be able to walk away at any time. In a heterosexual relationship, only the woman gets pregnant. Only the woman goes through hormonal changes before, during, and after the birth (or at least the more drastic change). And of course only the woman will experience that physical nine-month connection to the child. Men try hard and may even come close to that experience vicariously, but no man has ever died in child-birth. If someone decides to walk away from the family, the dad seems to have an easier route to the exit. But despite these inequities, we don't disparage fatherhood or consider it less legitimate than motherhood. The father and mother simply have different roles in a partnership. Moreover, we've taken great pains in our legal system to address such inequities. I've known some gainer/encourager couples who devised contracts and financial arrangements to ensure that no one is left helpless or destitute if trouble develops in paradise.

The fatherhood analogy is helpful in another respect: Babies get made by accident and even by violence all the time, but ideally most parents think of a baby as a joint creation—an act of love made manifest. Gaining and encouraging has a parallel. Just as fattening a partner may come from coercion or even abuse, the ideal for a gainer/encourager couple is that the gainer's obesity is an act of mutual creation born out of their love for each other. It's a mutual care and respect expressed through physical transformation. I know of a cartoon drawing of a fit man fattening up a willing obese partner. The caption reads, "I don't love you because you're fat. You're fat because I love you." A straight female feeder I know says to guys on her online profile, "If you date me, you're gonna get fatter." Fattening our partners is part of how we express our sexuality. Sexuality runs parallel to our romantic love. If you have a kink yourself, then maybe you understand. If you do not, then perhaps this seems intellectually interesting, or self-deluded, or just plain mentally ill. So be it.

LIFE IN THE BALANCE

A woman once wrote to me for advice on dealing with the guilt of wanting to fatten her boyfriend. Telling him her true sexual fantasies seemed too horrible to contemplate, yet she was equally tormented by keeping secrets from the man she loved. In another case, a man desperately wanted to get even fatter but was heartbroken when his doctor informed him that he was pre-diabetic. He despaired of having to lose weight and never again feeling sexual for the rest of his life. Gainers and encouragers often find themselves in conflict, trying to balance what is normal with what is illicit. Many come to me asking for help in striking a balance, in charting a course that would seem to skirt disaster yet leave room for erotic fulfillment. What's at stake in this balance varies from person to person.

The desire to fatten ourselves or someone else can seem overwhelming and extreme sometimes. The more extreme our desires, the more conflicted we may feel. Of course, some gainers and encouragers experience very little conflict, or the intensity of conflicted feelings may lessen or grow over time. However, to the degree that there is an internal conflict, it gets played out in every area of life: health, money, career, dating, friendships, even food. It's often hard to see the cost of this conflict in our lives. Again, if we reduce gaining or encouraging to just a sexual act, it's hard to see how such behavior could affect anything outside the body or the bedroom. But when we properly regard gaining and encouraging as a sexuality, we can see that the degree of conflict we feel about it permeates all aspects of our life to the same degree.

But whether our desires are mild or extreme, every gainer and encourager has to deal with the inherent dichotomy of our nature. In my experience, our sexuality usually turns on one of the following four pairs of opposites. As with the five on-ramps into gaining and encouraging,

FIGURE 21: Four Types of Gainer/Encourager Conflict

there is nothing written in stone about these categories. In fact, they may seem to you to overlap. However, they provide a way of seeing a pattern that gives us tools and insight. Most people would see each of these opposites as a clear choice of good versus bad and simply opt for what's good. However, as gaining and encouraging turns on the distress of obesity, all of us with this sexuality have within us, to varying degrees, a desire for both

elements of a particular pair. Typically we are concerned with one of these four as the central conflict in our lives and sexuality. It's our task as gainers and encouragers to somehow handle both elements of a particular pair as they contend for dominance within us.

One way to handle the conflict is simply to disavow the second element of the pair—the seemingly negative aspect. Many gainers do exactly

4: Fat Kink and the Drive to Get Fatter

this. For example, "I would never want to get so fat that I was gross." This is how the hero disavows the monster. However, even if we disavow one element of the pair, it is still very much present. It simply becomes something to be scrupulously avoided or even banished. The moth who avoids the flame must watch it constantly lest he be consumed by it.

Most gainers and encouragers, however, are well aware that their desire for obesity inherently involves pursuing the second element of a pair. Like the moth drawn to the flame, they fear it as much as it excites them. For example, a gainer might be aroused by the stretch marks that now scar his once lean body. He knows that the fatter he gets, the farther he'll fall from his once heroic physique and come to resemble the monster. This is both scary and erotic to him. He fears that he may go too far and become irredeemably the monster. And yet how wonderful to be the monster. And yet how terrible. Striving to be the hero means upholding the ideals of masculinity/femininity, strength or potency in the world, and beauty or sexual desirability. The monster, by contrast, embodies weakness or the desire to weaken. He revels in being attacked, condemned, and reviled for his grotesqueness.

For many gainers, the hero/monster dichotomy holds no power over them. Instead, one of the other three pairs holds sway. We're usually focused on one pair in particular that we're trying to balance. What's more, that pair of opposites is manifest not only in our sexuality, but everywhere in our lives. Let's look at an example.

Monroe has an intense desire to be enormously obese. In fact, his most erotic fantasies revolve around being so fat that he's a social pariah, bedbound and consumed by an addiction to food that propels him deeper and deeper into isolation and degradation. In his fantasy, there's no encourager, as that would be too much human contact. Instead, anonymous delivery boys leave food at his door or bring it to him before they flee from his grotesque obesity. This is the fantasy, which Monroe holds as a secret part of himself. He's anonymous on gaining websites and takes great care to remain in the shadows. For you see, the reality is that outside the gainer world, Monroe is a highly social and very active member of the community where he lives. He is very well known and highly visible. He volunteers for several non-profit organizations as a public speaker and activist. He's plugged into all the social media platforms. He knows all the latest pop songs, reality shows, and celebrities, including who's hot and who's not. He has over 1,000 friends on Facebook, and he knows what that number is.

In Monroe, we see the dichotomy of acclamation/rejection. In his real life, he is organized around seeking acclamation and attention and being central to his community. In his fantasy life, however, he sees fat as a way to achieve the ultimate rejection. As extreme as one polarity is for him, the other is equally extreme. Gainers and encouragers all hold within us one of these opposites. Monroe is an extreme example; however, many gainers and encouragers may experience acclamation/rejection far less dramatically. Some don't experience it at all, but instead experience one of the other three to some degree of intensity. As we'll see, there is always a symmetry of magnitude in opposing desires.

Whatever the opposite or its degree, the first element of the pair represents an important ideal that a gainer or encourager usually expresses energetically in daily life. The second element forms the bedrock of his darkest fantasies, which may be so dark that they terrify even him. In some cases, he may vigorously repudiate them. However, fear and ecstasy are connected in most kink, and in gaining and encouraging in particular. Again, we're like moths drawn to a flame. We'll look at more examples of these pairs of opposites as we further explore the symmetry of how our kink is constructed.

The Teeter-Totter of Fear and Desire

The conflict between fear and desire is always symmetrical: Imagine a teeter-totter with Fear sitting on one side and Desire sitting on the other. Fear never sits closer to the center than Desire. The two always balance each other. For example, if a gainer has an erotic desire to grow too fat for his pants, he feels proportionate fear that he can't afford another pair. The gainer will not fear bigger issues in response, such as ill-health or the rejection of his friends and family. Those would be irrelevant and out of proportion to a desire to outgrow his pants. Now, gainers certainly do fear rejection and ill-health, but these issues reach a crisis point only for

those who fantasize about becoming out of shape and freakishly fat. Becoming out of shape and freakishly fat is symmetrical to the fear of rejection and ill-health.

In kink, our desires are always linked to our fears; our fears occur in proportion to our desires. In any particular moment, the two provide context for each other. Over time, what we fear, loathe, and repudiate in kink is inseparably connected to what we covet, desire, and acclaim. Again, if we imagine the teeter-totter with fear on one side and desire on the other, we see this clearly. Two other properties of our sexuality derive from this analogy. First is that we require a partner, because you can't play on a teeter-totter by yourself. Second, if you try to sit at the fulcrum to balance the teeter-totter, nothing moves. The game stops. This is one reason that the popular advice given to gainers and encouragers—to find a balance between extremes—seems so unsatisfying and eventually proves ineffective.

However, it's certainly not for lack of trying. The pursuit of balance bedevils many gainers and encouragers. If friends know of our desires, they may counsel, "I understand that getting fat is important to you, but you're really big now. You just have to find a balance with gaining." If a friend in the community is freaking out, we say, "Don't panic, you just have to find the right balance." To ourselves, we say, *I've swung too far out of balance. I need to leave this website, or exercise more, or get my life back under control.* However, balance is as illusive as it is illusory. As with self-esteem, the concept of balance does not offer us any freedom or enlightenment in our moment-to-moment living.

The Illusion of Balance

Although this presentation of balance and dichotomies is particularly apt for gainers and encouragers, people who don't share our kink have told me that the model I'm about to offer has some applicability to anyone torn by two mutually exclusive ideals. So let's talk about the problem with a balanced approach.

The first strategy that many people adopt might be described as a cyclical approach to balance. Many gainers and encouragers rebound between the two opposites, first driven by lust and then retreating in terror. I mentioned that guy who would cancel his gym membership, stuff himself mercilessly, and gain 40 pounds in a month or two. Then he'd break out in hives at the terror that he was destroying his life, and start a strict diet, rejoin the gym, and pummel his body back into the picture of fitness. He's an example of the hero/monster dichotomy. It's like watching someone trying to play on a teeter-totter by sitting on one side, panicking as that side of the plank descends, and then running desperately to sit on the other side. Some people have actually become so inured to this sort of teeter-tottering that it has become their idea of balance. Running from lust to terror to lust to terror might seem like balance, I suppose. I've seen people practice it for decades.

For an encourager, this might look like eating healthfully and having health-conscious friends, but then disappearing for weeks or months, drowning himself in cybersex with gainers, and talking about feeding them bricks of lard or buckets of fast food. Then he deletes all his online profiles, stops returning correspondence, and returns to his "healthy" life, apologizing to friends with a story about how crazy work has been. He might even swear off encouraging (for a while) because even though the gainer is passionately consenting, this encourager cannot allow himself to be responsible for someone's physical demise and the degradation of his own soul. Here the dichotomy to be balanced is virtue/vice.

Another common strategy is the compromised balance. How do you make a compromise between the hero and the monster? How do you get Hercules and Jabba the Hut to compromise and form a single body? You become a 350-pound power lifter with a monstrously huge gut, a hero's steel thighs, strong bloated arms, and a hero's beard grown so monstrous that it effectively covers the face. Of course, most power lifters are not frustrated gainers. Power lifting isn't sexual—gaining is.

How does someone strike a compromise between freedom and subjugation? He maintains an active online fantasy life of gainer/encourager cybersex, talking about his intense desire to be bound to a bed by his own obesity, or his desire to addict someone so helplessly to eating that obesity is all he has left. But this person has no pictures online, no way to be found, and no intention of ever meeting a sexual partner who shares the fantasy. He is a phantom who will be bent to no one. Alternatively, he may be known in the gainer/encourager community, but no suitor has ever been worthy of him. (Or if they are worthy, they are unavailable.) He strives to hold himself free and apart as hard as he strives to find that one person who will conquer and subdue him. In the story of Rapunzel, imagine that Rapunzel and the wicked queen who imprisons her are actually the same person. No prince has a chance.

The main problem with balance is that it never transcends the dichotomy. Instead, it perpetuates a view of ourselves that is fractured and contradictory. Integrity—a sense of wholeness—is impossible when we perceive our life in terms of contradiction. For gainers and encouragers, it's not too much to say that our life force—our sexuality—seems irreconcilably broken. Perhaps there's a way to look at the situation without fracturing ourselves into opposites. We seem able to do it with other things sometimes. Men and women are often frustrated with each other. A lot of relationship advice is predicated on the view that men and women are opposites. As long as that view holds sway, there can be no reconciliation, only trade-offs and compromise. However, when we see the pair as two human beings who share a common aim, new possibilities for harmony emerge.

The other, more practical problem with trying to achieve balance is that balance is not an action that we can take. It is not something we can actually do. Rather, balance is an assessment that we make about ourselves, situations, or even inanimate objects. A rock that lies half on and half off the edge of a cliff is not balancing itself. The rock doesn't know how to balance; it just isn't falling off the cliff. The rock does not fail or succeed at balancing itself. Only when we look at the rock do we ascribe balance to it. We make that determination as outside observers. So balance doesn't happen over there with the rock. It happens over here in our observation of the rock. That shift in perspective gives us some power in a world that seems to lack balance.

Rocks don't try to balance, yet some remain precariously perched for years or even centuries. What if, like the rock, we didn't have to try to balance? What if we could just not fall off the cliff? Gymnasts are quite expert at balancing, but they will tell you that they do not put their mental focus on balancing when working a bar or a balance beam. To our eyes, they seem balanced and poised, but their attention is not on balancing. They do not think, *I must balance. I am balancing now.* No coach has ever advised an athlete to "balance harder!" A football player makes no conscious effort to balance on one foot as his other foot leaves the ground to kick a goal. His focus is on the goal. Balance is something that we see only when we're looking at life from the outside, not when we're living life in the moment. You can't live a balanced life by trying to balance your life. This is true of any state of being—being happy, being in love, or being balanced. You can't *be* it by trying to *do* it. The assessment of feeling balanced is not present in the moment when one is balancing. It's only something that others say when they observe us or that we might say of ourselves upon reflection.

Here's an example of that difference of perspective:

Mom says to her friend at lunch, "Sally learned how to balance on her bike today, and we took off the training wheels."

Sally overhears and says, "Yeah! I rode all the way to the end of the block!"

Mom's experience is of observing her daughter's new sense of balance. Sally's experience is of successfully riding her bike.

If you can ride a bike, you probably ride it without ever thinking about balance. How did that happen? You might remember almost falling over to one side and pulling hard to right yourself, only then to start falling over toward the other side. You were trying to balance.

Or perhaps you remember learning to drive. You might remember how disastrous it was trying to watch the lines in the road, trying to stay in your lane by staying the same distance from the lines to the left and right of your car as you traveled down the road. I can remember my driving instructor saying, "When you steer, aim high. Look up at the road ahead." He told me that the car would go where I was looking, and if I kept looking at the lines on the road, kept trying to balance between them, I would hit something or someone. Indeed it was only when I gave up balancing between the lines on the highway that I was able to really focus on driving. Whether it's riding a bike, or driving a car, or living a life, balance never comes from trying to balance. It comes when we see a bigger picture—transcending the whole dichotomy that balance implies—and focus on where we want to go, on what we want for our life. Let's take a look at how that might apply to gainers and encouragers (or anyone else caught in a balancing act).

Creating a Whole Instead of Balancing Parts

In my work with gainers and encouragers, I try to open the possibility of what life might look like with their gaining or encouraging fully integrated into their lives. It's a scary conversation for most because of the risks and taboos. It's a tough conversation because gainers and encouragers are usually stuck in some sort of cyclical or compromised balance of their particular ideal-versus-fear dichotomy, which they already know isn't working for them. Instead, I help them generate an idea of what happiness might look like. I help them sort out what they want, what they need, and what they fear. We also talk about how this goal might change, and how that's fine. I work by transforming the dichotomy into something more workable: a life.

I start by asking the person to imagine what they'd like life to be like. I should note here how difficult this seems for people, especially when they've come to me with the supposition that they want conflicting things. It may take the better part of an hour to get past sentences that begin with "I want…" or "I don't want…" One client was particularly resistant to letting go of the fear/desire paradigm, so I just started with tangible details:

"If you were designing your life, what would it look like in five years? For example, do you picture yourself living in a house or apartment?"

"Well, I live in an apartment now, and I don't see that changing."

"Sure, but if we're designing your life, is living in an apartment what you'd design? Or is it just something you're stuck with?"

"No, I like my apartment. I mean, I wish it were bigger. I guess that would be nice."

"Okay, so in five years, you're living in a nice-sized apartment. Now what about a relationship? In five years, what would you imagine? Are you hooking up only? Are you dating? Are you dating several people?

Are you in a relationship? Is the relationship monogamous? Do you live with him? Really think about how you'd like life to look."

Another way I get at this topic is by asking questions such as "What do your friends say about you five years from now?" "What does your Facebook page have on it in five years?" "Five years from now, what does your business card say?" Notice that these questions have nothing to do with gaining or encouraging, yet every gainer or encourager I've taken through this process will inevitably mention something about obesity or weight gain in the course of answering these questions. That's appropriate to making a whole life.

LOVE, KINK, AND SYMBIOSIS

Sometimes we hear stories in the media about someone who regretted gaining a vast amount of weight to please a partner who liked and rewarded it. I've seen YouTube videos of a man who claimed to be duped by encouragers and "lured into the gainer lifestyle." It reminds me of the men who were "lured by homosexuals into the gay lifestyle" but who now repent. In other cases, it's a more legitimate misunderstanding of sexuality. Before dealing with some of the more esoteric aspects of gaining and encouraging, I need to address some misconceptions that prevent us from understanding how kink functions in a partnership.

Mistakes and Misunderstandings

"I tried gaining, and it seemed like fun at the time." That's the sort of thing you say about knitting or skydiving, not sexuality. Sure, you might put on a costume or role-play one night for fun, but if it's not part of your sexuality, you can't keep it up for long. Imagine if someone said, "I tried being gay for a couple of years, but it wasn't very satisfying." For a couple of years? Or how about, "I tried being gay for him for the first few years, but then he wouldn't let me stop!" When we understand gaining and encouraging as a sexuality, not just a sexual act, we begin to see the absurdity of claims like this.

Goals

I'm often asked about the endgame of gaining or encouraging. Actually, this question is posed to the encourager far more often than to the gainer: "So when do you stop? Do you just fatten them to death?"

Gaining and encouraging have no endgame. The assumption that it does is again based on the misconception that gaining or encouraging is an act, and that the act has a purpose or goal. You may as well ask, "What's the endgame of being gay?" "Is making a baby the endgame of being straight?" Gaining or encouraging is not about achieving a particular weight or size. It is merely the sexual orientation that perceives the distress of obesity as intensely erotic. Our sexuality revolves around weight gain and fat in general, with all the inherent advantages and disadvantages that the couple can manage and enjoy.

That said, gainers and encouragers often make up games or goals—gaining 50 pounds by the gainer's birthday, for example. On the other hand, there's certainly a point at which a gainer or encourager may decide that the gainer's body or their life together cannot accommodate getting any fatter. In fact, a gainer may gain and lose hundreds of pounds in their lifetime as the circumstances of their life change. Their encourager will understand and accept this. Like the encourager, the gainer is disappointed to see their body shrink and become leaner, no matter what the circumstance, but they may need to do so for any number of reasons. For example, a gainer might want to increase their mobility for a trip abroad, to take a new job that requires a lot of stamina, or to maintain a certain physique for a career in which being lean is paramount. A gainer/encourager relationship can handle these life changes because both partners see the weight loss as an accommodation to a specific circumstance, not a mismatch of sexual desire. It is completely unlike a relationship in which only one finds sexual gratification in obesity.

Sexual Power Dynamics

When I talked about fat/admirer relationships, I talked about the mutual respect and adoration of these two people for each other. This is no less true for gainers and encouragers. However, the five on-ramps to our sexuality all imply a sexual power dynamic, which is not inherently present between ordinary fat people and their admirers. Some people think of it as a dominant/submissive relationship reminiscent of BDSM—basically, that we are a fat/thin variation on the sub/dom model. Although that may be true to some extent, most people who are not in a functioning dom/sub relationship have very little idea what that dynamic is like and even less what it implies.

When people imagine a power dynamic involving a sexual kink, they usually picture a one-way relationship in which one person has power and the other does not. The gainer/encourager dynamic is a symbiosis, not a one-way street. I'll deal with this more fully a bit later. Before I do that, however, we need to uncover the prejudices that come up for people when the power dynamic is based on Fat.

When we hear about a couple that practices BSDM—for example, a couple where one partner regularly flogs the other for their mutual sexual gratification—we might find it unusual, titillating, or off-putting. We're probably more comfortable picturing a woman in black leather flogging her husband, or one man torturing another, than a woman being eagerly beaten by her masked lover. Even if we know it's consensual, certain prejudices about women and men can make us uncomfortable witnessing such a sexual power dynamic. Our prejudices around Fat, specifically our need to blame or pity a fat person, create a similar reaction in most of us. We see the fat partner as a victim to the degree that we pity them. Similarly, we see them as gluttons or addicts to the degree that we blame them. So the fit partner—a partner who admittedly seeks someone who is fat—is cast in the role of either abuser or enabler. You may notice, however, that most people don't have such strong feelings toward the roles in ordinary BDSM. We're far less likely to perceive our friend who likes to get flogged during sex as an addict or victim. Similarly we're less inclined to see his partner as abusive or enabling if he's doling out lashings instead of cookies. We seem to be far more comfortable with a desire to be beaten than with a desire to be made fatter.

We should also remember that gaining need not be the gaining of hundreds of pounds. It might only be 50. But yes, it could be 500. Here's the story of Hank and Russell, a couple who came to me for advice in dealing with their friends.

Outsiders' Perceptions

Russell had never been in shape, but he had also never been what his friends thought of as fat. But then he met Hank, whom Russell's friends referred to as "that cowboy." Hank was lean and quiet, and had a sly smile that told you he was thinking something, but you'd never figure out what. Despite their speculation on the issue when Russell wasn't around, Russell's friends couldn't really figure out the attraction between the two men. Hank was hot, sure, but they didn't consider him to be the kind of guy Russell would ever go for seriously. Russell's most salient quality was his intelligence. Hank's was that he was…well…hot. It's not that Russell's friends considered Hank dumb exactly, but he didn't seem to be a good match for their friend. As time went on, however, Russell's friends noticed an even bigger disparity in the relationship. Russell began putting on weight. A lot of weight. Russell was eating more than they'd ever seen him eat, and Hank would just smile and pat Russell's belly. Hank seemed only too pleased with it. Sometimes, it was like he was actively encouraging Russell to overeat.

As a result, Russell ballooned. Concern turned to desperation one day when Russell admitted that he was starting to need Hank's help putting on his shoes and socks. "It's okay," Russell assured his friends. "Hank doesn't mind." Then he added, in a furtive whisper, "In fact, I think he enjoys it." Finally Russell's friends began expressing their concern that Hank was manipulating Russell, that he was perhaps one of those awful "feeders" they'd heard about on the internet. Yet Russell seemed in denial. Nothing that his friends could say mustered the slightest concern for his health or any suspicion of Hank.

Now let's hear from Hank's friends:

Hank used to have an active social life. He used to go out with his friends most nights, and he was known among his circle as a bit of a pool shark. Then he met Russell, a pudgy, snobbish guy who didn't seem to have very strong opinions on anything that Hank's friends thought were important topics, such as sports, country music, or local politics.

Hank's friends didn't know much about Russell, but they noticed that Hank seemed less able to spend time with them. Hank would be vague about making plans, or he'd say simply that he was "busy." At first they chalked it up to "that couple thing" that causes someone to fall off the planet when they become involved with a new boyfriend. They kidded Hank about how he'd forgotten his old friends to run off with Russell and Russell's rich friends and their fancy parties. It wasn't really a money issue, Hank told me. After all, many of his friends made more money than Russell. They just spent it differently.

However, Hank told me that two things were bothering his friends. First, Russell seemed to be fatter every time they saw him. Second, Hank seemed interested in Russell more than ever despite Russell's increasing girth. Hank's friends had never considered Russell that good-looking to begin with, and now with all the added weight, they could only imagine that Hank was trying to hang in there and be a good sport about it. That was, in fact, the real source of their jibes. What was the point in Hank giving up the high life? After all, Russell could always lose the weight.

After a few years, however, Hank's friends were truly concerned. To them, Russell had grown absolutely enormous. He was out of breath all the time, and it seemed to limit what the couple could do together. To his friends, poor Hank seemed more like a caretaker than a boyfriend. His friends naturally assumed that Hank was trapped in the relationship, either because of money problems or low self-esteem. Maybe both. Hank tried to tell his friends that everything was fine, but his friends accused him of being in denial. One friend even tried to explain to him that in being so accepting of Russell, Hank was actually being a victim, and that his patience with Russell's obesity was only enabling Russell.

Hank and Russell came to me for advice—not about their relationship with each other, but about their friends. Both men were tired of being cast as victims of their partner's abuse. Both were sick of their friends judging them to be defective or their relationship to be abusive. I explained that they had good friends. After all, for most people, no other explanation besides abuse seems rational. I advised them to come out of the closet and help their friends understand their relationship better.

What about the couple themselves? How did they see their relationship?

In the beginning, Hank went out of his way to push food on Russell. He would even wake him up in the middle of the night to have him drink a shake. And Russell loved this. In fact, it was this sort of sex play that made Russell start to take the relationship seriously. He told me later, however, that he worried that the two had so little in common. The sexual chemistry was great, but he feared that he was confusing love with lust—that he would end up with "the wrong guy" and in "the wrong life" for "just a fetish." And yet, particularly after a night of intense feeding, Russell would entertain thoughts that maybe Hank was "the one." Russell loved his sly, lithe cowboy who dispensed with words and just acted. He loved being in the thrall of such a powerful will. He said it was like having a hand on his back, gently but firmly pushing him forward...forward into greater and greater obesity. Russell enjoyed that it was getting hard to tie his shoes, but it also alarmed him. When he mentioned this to Hank, Hank's response was to get up and bring him a pint of ice cream. The smirk on Hank's face said that he had heard, but that he wasn't about to stop. Russell ate the ice cream with even more relish because of that. But the next morning, Hank made sure he was available to help Russell with his shoes and socks. And he did it every morning from then on, without mentioning it or being asked.

I asked Russell what finally allowed him to commit to a relationship with Hank, despite all the concerns he had about love versus lust. He said, "It was actually simple. I realized that I just enjoyed spending time with him—even when he wasn't feeding me. I wanted to invite him to social functions because I enjoyed his company, not just because I wanted to show off a hot guy on my arm. I think the final drop in the bucket was when a friend scolded me for passing on invitations so I could spend time with 'that cowboy and his friends.' That made me really angry, and I realized my feelings for Hank weren't just sexual. There was love."

Understanding the gainer/encourager relationship asks us to move beyond the dichotomy of pity and blame, which is how we usually think of obesity. What's your reaction to those reality shows where they extract some behemoth, bedridden fat person from their home and bring them to hospital for weight-loss surgery? Pity or blame? Disgust or compassion? These shows inevitably feature the tireless efforts of a dedicated team of health-care workers, cleaning and maneuvering the mountains of blubber that encase the hapless person. But just as I talk to men and women who long to be that trapped fat person, I talk to men and women every day who long to be their caretaker. They crave it like nothing else they've ever known. Most gainers and encouragers who have these longings are quite happy to keep them a fantasy. However, many believe that only the reality will ultimately fulfill them. And sometimes people want both—either at different points in their lives or simultaneously in confusion and conflict.

When we imagine feeding someone to the point that he is too fat to survive on his own, we must also imagine their encourager, their caretaker, who sees to everything from paying the internet bill, to buying and preparing food, to toileting and cleaning the immense blob in their care. And they do it all day. In such a relationship—behemoth and caretaker—who is truly the one in submission? Perhaps both, because both are inextricably bound. Perhaps neither, because both experience their bondage as ecstasy. You may argue that the encourager can walk away at any time, but he does not. Just as his obese partner can stop gorging himself at any time, but he does not.

Just like in any normal relationship, needs arise to be met, and gifts are offered to be accepted. For example, in any relationship, someone might offer to take responsibility for paying the bills, and the other agrees, wanting to be free of the drudgery of managing the couple's finances. Abuse or mismanagement is possible; nevertheless, the arrangement is common and raises no suspicions. Wielding the checkbook is a power assumed by one and accepted as a gift by the other. Exchanges like this are part of any relationship, but certainly they are more dramatic and obvious with us. The gainer and encourager exist in a symbiosis, in a dance of give and take in which power is ceded and responsibility is accepted. The gainer gives his body to his encourager. The encourager in turn places his body in the service of his gainer. This arrangement might last for only a night of fun or for a lifetime of devotion.

The Art and Nature of Symbiosis

Contrary to what most people believe, a sexual power dynamic is not a one-way street in which one person is always at a disadvantage. Whether a couple is normal or kinky, if there is a power dynamic in the couple's sex play, the power flows back and forth fluidly and reciprocally. Also, in a truly functional dominant/submissive dynamic, it is always the submissive who is in control. The sub grants power to his dom to feed him, to scare him, to idolize him. The dom is nothing without the sub. Without the gainer, the encourager would be like the host of a party that had no guests. If you require further proof, consider this: The gainer can shut down the game at any point simply by refusing to eat. It is he who has his finger on the on/off switch. In most cases, the encourager takes the role of the dom, but this is not always true and certainly not necessary for the functioning of the sexual dyad.

There are gainer/encourager relationships that cast the gainer in the role of the dom. For example, I know of one couple where the encourager is not allowed to eat until the gainer has been fed, and even then the encourager is allowed to subsist only on what the gainer leaves behind on his plate. In another couple, the encourager gives up his monthly salary to the gainer, who manages the couple's finances and gives the encourager an allowance.

Some might say that the gainer/encourager dynamic is prone to abuse—that a gainer can become dependent and even captive. I've seen this happen. I've also seen the reverse happen, in which the thin partner becomes an unwilling caretaker of someone who secretly delights in being taken care of. Such suffering or abuse is always caused by a lack of integrity: The encourager doesn't tell the truth (or know the truth) about his deeper desires. Alternatively, the fat partner doesn't tell the truth about his desires to get fat or is in denial of the truth that the relationship is leading somewhere he doesn't want to go.

But lying to yourself or your partner is a pitfall in any relationship. It's the same pitfall that gives rise to infidelity, physical abuse, resentment, and even boredom. It has nothing to do with getting fat. That's just the Round World's variation on the problem. The erotic thrill for gainers and encouragers lies in a game in which the dom pretends to have all the power and the sub pretends that he has none. Again, it is the ceding of power and the acceptance of responsibility that sustains the erotic dyad. If you don't have a kink that's bound up in this, the best analogy I can make is watching an engrossing movie. This is a pale comparison, but it'll have to do.

The Play in Sex Play

When you go to the cinema, you know that the images on the screen are simply colored shadows that represent people, places, or even ideas. These images—these shadow people—seem to speak spontaneously, but we know that their words were actually written in advance and rehearsed many times. In the background, a musical score encourages us to feel what the filmmaker wants us to feel in that moment, which they worked out months or even years in advance. We know all this, and yet we choose to forget it. Why else would we scream, or cry, or feel our hearts in our throats? And we feel those things intensely if it's a good movie. We immerse ourselves in the movie because the experience is fun. We grant the filmmaker and his entourage the power to entertain us—to frighten us, sadden us, anger us—and we even pay them money to do it to us. This is no less true for gainers and encouragers.

You might argue that a movie is a harmless illusion; it's over when the lights come up. But obesity is a lasting reality, a commitment, even a bondage in extreme cases. This is true. Yet how many of us have fallen in love with movies? We don't see just any movie. No, we return to our favorite fantasies—science fiction, or romance, or thrillers—over and over again for years. How many of us even see one certain movie over and over again, whether to relive the same experience or to discover new insight and sensations? How many of us bring that cinema experience into other parts of our lives, collecting movie memorabilia, dressing up as characters from a movie, attending conventions with others who share our passion for the fantasy? Look how hard some of us try to live in that movie. What if it weren't just a movie? What if it were our sexuality?

As an encourager, I create an erotic world for the gainer as part of his sexual fulfillment. He steps into it as part of my fulfillment. I array éclairs or cakes, pizza or meat loaf. I arrange the world to suit his tastes.

I talk of what he will become, conjuring images of what I know he most fears and most desires. I listen to him; I listen to his body with an almost excruciating sensitivity that draws us even closer together. The greater my artistry, the greater his fulfillment. The greater his fulfillment, the greater our ecstasy. It is a symbiosis. If we are in a relationship, that sexual context becomes a major part of our life together. It is how we enact our love physically and sexually. As the gainer gets fatter and the encourager gets more involved with his body, that sexual aspect increasingly dominates their lives together. For some couples, the weight gain is a distant erotic touchstone, and the rest of their life isn't much affected. For other couples, the gainer's extreme obesity is part of an active sex life that affects every other aspect of their life as a couple—from how they set up their finances to what furniture they buy.

As with any relationship, both parties have the capacity to use or abuse the other. But in the best of the intimate encounters I describe, the encourager is transformed, too. The more the gainer needs help to cope with the alienation of a world that seems to shrink around him, the more supportive and nurturing the encourager becomes, even extending to becoming the gainer's physical aide or, in extreme cases, his caretaker. The power flows in both directions—my bodybuilding is a response to the gainer's dissipation, and his obesity is a response to my muscularity. For example, many gainers have told me that seeing my body or picturing me working out makes them want to eat and get fatter. Just as the gainer strives to become one polar-

JARED: Sarah, beware. I have been generous up until now, but I can be cruel.

SARAH: Generous! What have you done that's generous?

JARED: Everything! Everything that you wanted I have done. You asked that the child be taken. I took him. You cowered before me. I was frightening. I have reordered time. I have turned the world upside down. And I have done it all for you. I'm exhausted from living up to your expectations. Isn't that generous? [...] Look Sarah. Look what I'm offering you: your dreams. [...] I ask for so little. Just let me rule you, and you can have everything that you want. [...] Just fear me. Love me. Do as I say, and I will be your slave.

—From the film *Labyrinth*

ity of the Fat dyad, I have transformed myself to become the other. In gaining and encouraging, our bodies are part of our sexual roles. The basis of a gainer/encourager relationship (or any dom/sub dyad) is one in which power is granted and responsibility is accepted.

Let's look at the gainer/encourager dyad another way, by recalling the four conflicts I mentioned earlier: hero/monster, virtue/vice, acclamation/rejection, and freedom/subjugation. Often, the gainer or encourager tries to be both halves of the dyad and experiences this as conflict or a need to work out a balance. However, when he or she finds a partner—their other half, so to speak—they feel a new sense of freedom and sexual satisfaction. When seen in the context of an erotic dyad, these pairs of opposites become sexual roles and the source of sexual ecstasy. In the case of the bodybuilder with the fat boy, one person embodies the hero while his partner embodies the monster. Another couple might embody the acclamation/rejection dichotomy with the gainer being social and gregarious, like Father Christmas, while his reclusive encourager operates outside this sphere behind the scenes to fatten and aid him. One gainer told me that his perfect woman would be a girl he could introduce to his mother, who would find her kind, loving, and "sweet as cherry pie." Then in the bedroom, she would push him mercilessly to fulfill every gluttonous desire he ever had, cruelly fattening him until he became weak and dependent on her. This is the marriage of virtue and vice.

However, it's important to remember that gainer and encourager do not represent some sort of one-way power exchange. They are fluid. Like playing on a teeter-totter, the couple sit on opposite sides of the same plank, the same distance from center. One is up while the other is down, but that's hardly permanent. Soon the one who was up descends and the one who was down rises. This mirrors the power dynamic of the kink. Even though the roles are cast, the power or dominance changes. That is our sexual play.

You might recall my discussion of entanglements in a previous section and wonder how a sexual dyad is different. If you remember, I said that an entanglement is the result of two people creating a bond out of a sense of incompleteness, of insufficient self. "She completes me," "I can't live without him," and "I'll never be this happy again" are typical phrases uttered by people living in entanglements. A sexual dyad, however, is created out of sexual reciprocity and compatibility, not a defect or insufficiency. We can see this more easily if we examine the most common sexual dyad that exists: man/woman. Ideally, a straight man does not seek a female for romantic partnership out of a sense of being incomplete. He does so because a woman is the counterpart for his sexuality as a heterosexual male. Of course, he does not seek just *any* woman; nevertheless, not being a woman is a deal breaker for him if he's heterosexual. Other sorts of sexual dyads include top/bottom, pony/rider, master/slave, daddy/boy, dom/sub, and gainer/encourager.

However, we are more than just two opposites standing next to each other. Our shared kink provides a context that makes us somehow more together than the sum of each of us individually. In the regular world, power couples are set apart from others because their combined economic status and career achievements make the couple seem more than they would be as single people. The gainer/encourager couple operates similarly, but in place of economic status and career achievement, our power derives from our sexuality and the hurdles we've had to overcome to pursue it.

Gainers and encouragers thrive on the distress of obesity. We are sexually powered by the guilt and shame that runs as an axis through the Round World. Therefore, as a pair, we each expose the hidden side of the other. As a lean, muscular man, I am seen as the embodiment of strength, virtue, and heroism. But by the light of the gainer, my shadows are exposed: my weakness, my wickedness, my abject subservience to his base needs. This is erotic to me. Likewise my obese partner is usually seen as grotesque, shameful, and pathetic. But by the light of the encourager, the brilliance of the gainer is revealed: his beauty, his pride, his dauntlessness. He feels this in my presence; it is, in fact, part of my role that he feel it. For just as a doughboy is never more beautiful to me than when his blubber yields to my powerful body, I am never more beautiful to him than when I am conquered by the beauty of his obese body. It is an ecstatic symbiosis that transcends dichotomy, a dance in which no one can really tell who is leading and who is following. Not even the dancers themselves.

5

Life Beyond the Round World

What makes us different is what we are; what unites us is what we do.

—Jonathan Sacks

The Home We Build Together

SOUVENIRS FROM THE ROUND WORLD

Many people reading this book aren't gay, aren't fat, and have no attraction to fat people. Maybe the Round World is not your home. But we all live in our own little worlds—bubbles, really—and wonder what life is like outside.

I said at the outset that this book is a travelogue, that we would visit a place where beauty and power are different from how they are elsewhere. We've been talking about the lives of men and women in a place I call the Round World, where Fat forms a strong basis for sexual attraction. We're coming to the end of our tour of that world, coming back to a world that doesn't particularly love Fat. As we begin the journey back, I'd like to stop at the gift shop, so to speak, and talk about what we might take with us when we leave the Round World, either to go visiting or to return home.

You've read my story of coming to understand my sexuality and coming to know myself. I never seemed to fit in with the A-gays in bars and clubs. It all seemed to center on cocks and asses, pop stars and clubs, health and beauty. However, as I grew to understand myself more, I came to understand those gay men better. As I became more open to myself, I became more open to them. And now I'm a veteran of chub/chaser events and big men's clubs, and I am a vociferous advocate and tour guide for the Round World. But I'm not sure I fit in socially in the Round World any better than I did with the A-gays. As I listen to the chubs and chasers, the conversations still tend to be about putting their cocks up the asses of other guys, and the screeching adulation of celebrities, and the ceaseless talk of health, diet, and beauty. But now somehow it all sounds different—the landscape has changed. These people are now my tribe.

Me and My Tribe

I am a man. I am male as a matter of biology. Male is an easy scientific label, for what it's worth. Being a man, however, is another issue entirely.

I am a man. I am masculine as a matter of cultural context—and yet I have no idea what *masculine* means. In other places and times, people might have strict gender roles to help them sort out who or what is masculine. In some cultures, boys participate in rituals to initiate them into manhood. Usually there are also strict expectations about what a man does and what he is for—perhaps hunting, fighting, or nation building. I do not pine for a code of masculinity. And yet, I seem to be part of one anyway.

Perhaps because gender is so central to the way humans think about ourselves, we insist on tests to help us distinguish between masculine and feminine. Several women have told me that sorting out their femininity has been just as complicated and confusing for them. However, I think as men and women find themselves farther and farther from normal, their tests for masculine and feminine likewise fall further from what's considered normal. For example, in the Round World, obesity can be counted as one of the proofs of manhood expressed as power or beauty. Likewise, it can be considered an embodiment of powerful or beautiful womanhood. Discovering and embracing your sexuality is part of the journey from adolescence into adulthood. Sexual identity comes in part from working out what it means to be a man or a woman, but ultimately it is an act of creation.

More generally, I think that the desires and fears of those of us in the Round World are part of a larger conversation that society is having about what is masculine and feminine. My tribe sees Fat as beautiful and powerful. Your beauty and your power are yours. And they belong to your tribe as well. So when I speak of masculine power or feminine beauty, I haven't really said anything until I can locate the tribal values of power and beauty that I'm talking about.

You'll notice I'm not using the word *community* here. I mean *tribe* because the word suggests something particular. *Community* suggests a communing, a peaceful meditative dwelling in common ideas and rational thought. Community is how we might categorize ourselves or even what we aspire to be as a group of people. And community is a marvelous thing. But *tribe* cuts deeper. Whatever the anthropological definition might be, the word *tribe* has an innate and primal association. Tribes want and fear. Tribes strive. Me and my tribe, that's what we do. You can leave a community, or even get thrown out. But opinions and ideology don't matter in a tribe. Your tribe is your tribe. Tribe is your family. Tribe is your body. You can't walk away from your tribe any more than you can walk away from your foot. You are bound by something intangible that seems innate, biological, or genetic.

Chasers, gainers, and encouragers are my tribe. They are mine even if I say they are not. And we're working out what beauty and power are. And some of us are working out what being a man means, just as some of us are questioning what it means to be a woman—and whether any of that really matters. And we do it mostly by never discussing it, because we're pretty inchoate as a community. In fact, some of us feel pretty inchoate as human beings. But we are a tribe.

Who is your tribe?

How THEY TALK IN YOUR TRIBE

I hope that as you've read this book, it's occurred to you that much—maybe even most—of what I say is not unique to the Round World. Perhaps you see that it could be applied to many communities or subgroups, including your own. In fact, many of my ideas and models have come from having conversations with people who identify as part of some other community.

I'd like to look at our actions rather than our identities. The most basic action that all human beings engage in is talking. Our species defines itself by our capacity for creating our world through language. So in this last section and our journey out of the Round World, I'd like to show how ideas about Fat and the way we talk about it are often parallel to the way we talk about things outside the Round World—perhaps in the place where you live. I'm going to make comparisons between groups of people, not based on identities such as race or obesity or sexuality, but based instead on how we use language.

Fat Lip: Words & Phrases

Imagine you're having a heart-to-heart conversation with a close friend who is talking about a guy they are dating or trying to date. As you listen, your friend says one or more of the following:

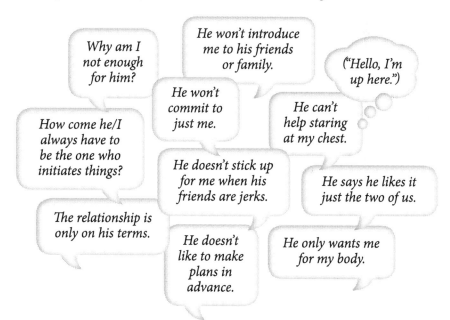

Maybe you have someone in your life whose favorite complaint is included here. Or maybe you're the one with that complaint. Stereotypically, we think of most of these phrases as complaints that women have about men. However, it might surprise you to know that these are among the top complaints I hear from gay fat men about chubby chasers. And I learned from hanging out in A-gay locales that these were the same complaints that fit gay men had about other fit gay men. Furthermore, when I started talking to other chubby chasers, they had some of these same complaints about the fat women they were dating.

Beyond He Said/She Said

So what is the explanation? Are these girly complaints, uttered only by women and girly men? I don't think so. Again, we need to transcend gender and sexual orientation as the primary categories of human identity and sexuality. Once again, looking at the Round World seems to provide an alternate explanation. Rather than being merely feminine or effeminate complaints, they're symptomatic of an internalized power dynamic between partners of any gender or sexual orientation. There seems to be what I call a second-class sexual citizen who makes statements like this. The person may be male or female. She might be a lawyer in New York City or a waitress in Munich. He might be manager in Saudi Arabia or a go-go boy in Dallas. This term I've invented has nothing to do with political oppression or social injustice. I've heard these complaints from people all over the world. Society doesn't designate someone as a second-class sexual citizen—we do that to ourselves.

Second-Class Sexual Citizen

Being a second-class sexual citizen means believing that you have less status than your partners' when it comes to dating, relationships, or sexual appeal. I say *partners* because this is seldom a one-time occurrence for a person. It happens again and again. Some people (gay or straight, male or female) find themselves perpetually pining for people who don't reciprocate their desire for partnership. They find themselves at the effect of their partner's decisions and actions, thus relegating themselves to second-class status. It seems to them as if they have little power in the relationship, or that the decisions about how intimate, formalized, or exclusive the relationship should be lies with the other person. Certainly other people's decisions affect us, but that's different from experiencing a lack of personal power because of other people's actions or inactions. You know you think of yourself as a second-class sexual citizen if you explain your partner's indifference to you with phrases like "He/she could have anyone he/she wants," or "He/she just doesn't see how good we are together." Basically, you're a second-class sexual citizen if you complain that you've granted someone else control of your relationship.

For example, I know a very hot chaser, Randy, who seems perpetually unavailable and aloof. He is very well built, charming, smart, well spoken, and sensitive, with Midwestern, boyish good looks. Chubs wear themselves out trying to pin him down on a time and place to meet or have a second date. One chub in particular, Hugo, told me he felt angry and hurt by Randy's sporadic, non-committal communication, which often consisted of curt invitations such as "Free tonight?" or "I'm in the neighborhood." However, Randy's experience of the situation, as he tells it, is equally frustrating. He feels barraged by solicitations of sex dates, coffee dates, and dinner dates from men who don't really know him but seem to think they are owed a place on his calendar because they sexually arouse each other. Randy feels pressured, controlled, and trapped, so he avoids this perceived domination by withholding communication or communicating vaguely.

If both parties feel pressured and powerless, they can't be communicating very effectively. Actually, they're not communicating at all—they're objectifying each other. (Yes, we're back to that again.) If you recall, I said that objectification is when what you want is more important than who the other person is. In the example above, Hugo wants deeper contact, perhaps leading to a relationship with a man who seems to embody perfection. But Randy doesn't see himself that way at all. Despite his beauty, he mistrusts adoration and is scared of intimacy. He's more likely to see a romantic invitation as domination than as opportunity. On the other hand, Randy wants a good time with a massive fat man. Even better if the guy has a good personality and is fun to be with. But that's not how Hugo thinks of himself. Hugo relates to himself as an amazing human being who just happens to have an enormously obese body, a stigma that he does his best to mitigate. In Hugo's reality, there is a scarcity of men available to him for a serious relationship, and Randy seems like a great catch. Randy, by contrast, doesn't see himself as a catch and doesn't wish to be caught.

You don't have to be a chaser or a superchub to feel like these guys do, or to have their trouble communicating. But so often, we in the Round World think that our situation is unique to us. We seem inclined to blame Fat or our attraction to Fat for all our problems. I hear complaints in my seminars that often start with phrases such as "How come chasers always have to…?" Or "Why don't big girls ever…?" But if we look to the larger world and social media, we can read exactly the same stereotypical complaints coming from people outside the Round World: "Why are women…?" Or "Why don't gay men…?" Or even "How come the men in this website/bar/town/country/society…?" I've found that whatever the trouble in your bubble, the people in the neighboring bubble just have a different version of it.

What's Your Story?

So let's move up the conversational ladder from exchanging phrases to telling stories. As human beings, we tell stories about our lives, about other people's lives, and about the world around us. That means that inevitably we tell stories about the problems we face, whether a problem concerns Fat or an attraction to Fat, or has nothing to do with Fat. Now, when I say story, I don't mean fiction. I don't mean that it's false, but it may not be true either. That's why we frequently ask whether a story is true; it might be, or it might not, or we might have no way of knowing.

Story as Cause and Effect

We believe some stories and disbelieve others. You may recall that I talked about this in "Fat Fundamentalism." There are all sorts of explanations about Fat, and we believe some of them passionately or hopefully or skeptically—or perhaps not at all.

A story isn't just a list of events. It's a way of coherently linking those events together through cause and effect. Cause and effect matter to us: Why did his marriage break up? How did the economic crisis begin? Why am I fat? How can I lose weight? These questions may be deep or trivial, but how we answer them—how we tell the story—operates powerfully in our lives. Consider the stories being told in these two sentences:

> "Rhonda did a great job on that project,
>   so they transferred her to Dallas."

> "Rhonda did a great job on that project,
>   but they transferred her to Dallas."

In both stories, Rhonda ends up in Dallas, but how and why she got there are completely different. Any story is ultimately an explanation; any explanation is ultimately a story. We just prefer not to call it a *story* if we think the story is the Truth.

Stories matter to us because we believe that if we know the cause, we can have some power over the effect. In other words, we think that if we know why something bad happened, then that knowledge will help us fix it or make sure it doesn't happen again. So to solve a problem, the first thing we need is a good story that people will believe, so that they will come to our aid. Any good storyteller knows that the most compelling stories have three essential elements: a hero, a villain, and something worth fighting for.

Stories About Fat

We see storytelling all the time with Fat. To the extent that we see obesity as a problem, we tell ourselves stories to explain it. We talk about "the problem with obesity," by which we mean its causes and effects—forever fighting about which story best fits our beliefs. As in other areas of our lives, when we talk about obesity as a problem, we're often creating a simple fairy tale that includes a hero, a villain, and something worth fighting for. Although we all enjoy being spellbound by a good story, we don't agree on how to tell the story of Fat. So we can tell the story of Fat at least three different ways:

The Tale of the Good Doctor

Once upon a time, there was a poor woman who weighed over 500 pounds and led a small, miserable life (the cause worth fighting for). She was held prisoner in the fat of her own body, which had been put there by decades of bad food choices driven by marketing campaigns gone haywire (the villain). But one day, she saw a wandering doctor (the hero), who happened by as she was flipping channels on her TV. She called to him, and he took her to his TV show, where he put her on the road to recovery through a sensible diet and exercise program. He saved her life, and she lived happily ever after.

Or we can tell the story a completely different way...

The Tale of the Fat Ogre

Once upon a time there was a miserable, fat ogre who weighed over 700 pounds (the villain). He spent his time making YouTube videos trying to get on TV so that he could profit from his pathetic lack of responsibility for his own life. He whined about how he hadn't left his house in a year, yet couldn't stop himself from eating over 10,000 calories a day. But one day Blogger Bill (the hero) saw the ogre's YouTube page and made it his business to wreak havoc all over social media and the internet. Blogger Bill took aim at the vile ogre, shooting him with insults, stinging him with sarcasm, and slicing open his disgusting fat innards with mockery to reveal the ogre's base need for attention and his lack of willpower and self-respect. The ogre finally took down his page and retreated into his hovel. Blogger Bill fights a tireless fight to right wrongs and restore self-respect and responsibility (the cause worth fighting for) to people on the internet, in the food court, and wherever personal responsibility is in danger of faltering.

One last story...

The Tale of the Fat Activist

Once upon a time there was a kingdom of people who were all very fat, some even topping 500 pounds. They had fat husbands and fat wives and fat grandparents and fat grandchildren, and they were all reasonably happy with their round little lives (the cause worth fighting for). But one day, an evil dragon (the villain) set upon the kingdom. He scorched their deep fryers, burnt down their sweet shops, and had his lizardy minions post fliers about which foods were good, which were bad, and how much every person was allowed to eat. The evil dragon declared that if the people of the kingdom didn't comply with his diet, they would all die horribly in a fire kindled of their own fat. The king knew he had to do something! So he called on his most valiant warrior (the hero), and she set out to hunt the dragon. When she found the beast, she saw its armoring scales were made of manila folders stuffed with medical studies and sheets and sheets of health statistics. But the warrior found a chink in the dragon's armor, a place where the medical studies had not been properly conducted and conclusions had been improperly drawn. She gathered her own statistics and forced them into the body of the dragon through the chink. The dragon gave a great roar and tried to incinerate the chubby warrior, but his fire had gone out. She had extinguished it! And the kingdom lived happily ever after.

Stories Beyond Fat

Which story matches your experience? Who's your hero? Your villain? Or here's another way to look at it: In each fairy tale, the hero uses something to defeat the villain. Which defeat sounds like the improbable magic in a fairy story, and which one sounds like commonsense reality? The doctor's slimming diet to save the fat woman? The blogger's evangelical fervor to restore people's responsibility? The warrior's re-evaluation of statistics to right the wrong-headed medical profession? To a great extent, this is what we're really arguing about when it comes to Fat. Who are the heroes, who are the villains, and what's at stake?

I'm talking about this in the context of obesity, but we can take any problem in your tribe and examine it as a fairy story. Perhaps you think it would be inappropriate to turn a serious problem or offense into a fairy story. Dare we cast our explanations of rape, racism, injustice, and brutality as fairy tales? If that seems disrespectful or inappropriate, it's probably because the story already being told is The Truth, and no other interpretation is ethical or even logical. This is certainly the case with monsters. As we'll talk about next, monsters are an important part of our world and the stories we tell about it.

Big Fat Monsters

In many stories that we tell about the world, fat people are cast as monsters—not all fat people, of course...just *those* fat people. And for many fat people, encouragers are monsters. I'd like to take a close look at monstrosity and how we use the concept inside and outside the Round World.

In your tribe, I'm sure that you tell stories about "those people" or "that awful man who..." But monsters are beyond alien, beyond criminal or even immoral. Monsters are foul and irredeemable. They might look human, but we know that they have nothing in common with us. So concepts such as fairness, empathy, and mercy don't apply to them as they do to us and the people like us. Now, some monsters amuse us, and they are fun to play with. For example, my friend told me he got in a bar fight with a handsome beefcake because the beefcake was making fun of a young fat guy who was also deaf. People laughed because the deaf fat guy was oblivious to his own ridicule and then so confused by the laughter that seemed to involve him. Who's the monster in this story? The people laughing clearly thought the deaf fat guy was. How ridiculous, they thought, to not know when you're being insulted and to even laugh along. The deaf fat guy wasn't a real person to them, just a funny monster that made for a good joke.

On the other hand, maybe you think the beefcake is the real monster. Anyone who would do something like that clearly has nothing in common with us and needs to be beaten. My friend tried to reason with him, but then he simply started calling my friend names, as monsters are wont to do. After all, you can't reason with monsters. My friend beat the crap out of the beefcake in the bar that night. Does that make my friend the monster, or is he the hero for subduing the monster? Notice how this story seems to need a monster, a hero, and something worth fighting for.

There is a tipping point at which someone different from us topples over into being a monster. It is the point at which our intolerance of them rises to the point that we are incapable of seeing any commonality with them whatsoever; it seems they are not even the same species as we are. We struggle to find language sufficient to express our anger, revulsion, or fear of the monster. In fact, we grow even more aggravated as we talk about the monster, finding that the depths of its monstrosity lie beyond the capacity of human language. There are never words strong enough to condemn the monster's indecency. We hear this when some people talk about child molesters, but we also hear it when some people talk about the extremely obese. I'm not saying the obese are like child molesters.

I'm saying that when we know a monster when we see one, and we treat all monsters the same.

Another clue that you've got hold of a monster is that monsters offend us by their very existence. It may be an evil deed or crime that earns someone the label of *monster*, but a sinner may repent, a criminal can be reformed. But a monster has no humanity, and therefore no past and no future. He is an immortal being, existing forever at the moment of his atrocity. He is a monster for always and by his very nature. A monster not only lies outside humanity, but outside all nature. A monster doesn't break the law; a monster commits "crimes against nature," and we feel the rush to destroy something that has no rightful place in our world. After all, how could anything so vile and despicable be part of a world that plays host to us.

Who Are Your Monsters?

You can indeed find monsters in the real world. You can get a pretty good sampling on the internet whenever you hear someone advocating inhuman treatment for a fellow human being. We read streaming ribbons of it wherever opinion and commentary are welcome: "Those people should be…" Fill in the blank: shot, rounded up, castrated, sterilized, starved, hanged. Who exactly "those people" are varies by circumstance, but popular groups include rapists, Jews, gays, child molesters, pimps, Nazis, lawyers, politicians, welfare mothers, Muslims, and fat people.

Perhaps you object to my including people whom you consider true monsters (e.g., rapists) along with people you consider innocent victims (e.g., Jews). Well, that's my point. If we can create a class of people as sub-humans or even non-humans, undeserving of our compassion or respect, then it seems only a matter of time or circumstance that dictates which group we single out next to be the monsters. I've listened to a close friend argue that pedophiles are monsters, that they are not human because a human could never have such a monstrous desire to commit such a monstrous act. I've listened to a man argue that "we shouldn't respect gays." He happened to be Muslim, and I pointed out that many people think we shouldn't respect Muslims. He was immediately offended by the comparison that the unjust hatred of Muslims was anything like the righteous hatred of gays.

Some people think that fat people are monsters too. They believe that the grotesque corpulence and unbridled, unrepentant gluttony of fat people put them in a category outside the world of normal human decency and respect. Many fat people themselves have an intense hatred of their own obesity, virtually disassociating themselves from the monstrosity of their heavy, pendulous flesh. I've been called a monster once or twice. After all, I talk about the beauty, glory, and sex appeal of obesity. It's one thing to be a monster, but it's quite another thing when people see you as a monster-lover, or even as an advocate for monstrosity.

The Need for Monsters to Die

I was in Starbucks in my gay neighborhood, and a guy was hitting on me. "I think you're really hot," I said, which was the truth, "but you're not really my type." Of course, that prompted the question "What's your type?" I took out my phone and showed him pictures of one of the guys I was dating at the time. "Oh my god," he chuckled. "I'd shoot myself if I ever looked like that. You like that?" What ensued was an interesting conversation. After averring that I did, in fact, "like that," I asked why he said he'd shoot himself.

> When you battle monsters, be careful you don't become the monster. And when you gaze into the abyss, the abyss also gazes into you.
>
> **—Friedrich Nietzsche**
> *Beyond Good and Evil*, Aphorism 146

He apologized, but I told him it was unnecessary. Why should he apologize for wanting to shoot himself if he got enormously obese? I like what I like. I just wanted to know whether he really would rather shoot himself than be immensely fat. He took refuge in Fat Fundamentalism, explaining how being so fat would be so unhealthy and therefore bad. I said, "Maybe so, but I think it would be a lot more unhealthy to shoot yourself, wouldn't it?" He conceded and said finally, "I just couldn't live like that."

We ended up having a long conversation in which he talked about having to watch every little thing he put in his mouth because he was so afraid of getting fat. The monster was him—the fear that he might one day become irredeemably fat. I think all our monsters are things we fear in ourselves, or fears we have about the world that we locate in a particular type of person.

The conversation in Starbucks reminded me of the scene in the movie *The Fly* when the good-looking scientist finds himself turning into a repulsive fly. At the point when he has only a thread of his humanity left, the misshapen creature says, "Kill me." He has become irredeemably monstrous, and the only way out is death. For many people, the obese are such irredeemable monsters. In some cases, only the fat itself is monstrous. We cut it off, starve it off, freeze it off, suck it out—whatever will kill the monster. The guy in Starbucks said he'd shoot himself if he ever got that fat. In *The Fly*, the scientist begs his girlfriend for death rather than to become fully and forever a monster. The noble monster asks to be killed. If he is not so noble, we often take it upon ourselves to kill him.

Hunting Monsters

Once upon a time, a young man in the town of Laramie was seduced by two men in a bar. They took him for a ride in their pickup truck to a remote area, where they stripped him, pistol-whipped him, and tortured him for hours. Finally they strung him up to a wire fence and left him to die in the cold. To the two men who made this young man's death slow and agonizing, the young man was just a monster and deserved to be treated as such. After all, the young man was gay.

Once upon a time, a middle-aged man in India was beaten with sticks, and rods, and canes for an hour. Then he was dragged into a butcher's shop and castrated with a meat cleaver. His bleeding body was dragged outside, and his testicles were thrown into the middle of the road. He was left there as passersby did nothing. He was a monster, and beneath even their contempt. After all, he had just tried to rape a young girl in an alley.

Both men were nothing more than monsters in the eyes of their attackers. The thing that was attacked was not a human being but an idea that was monstrous. The men in Wyoming thought they had beaten in the head of homosexuality. The people in India thought they had taken a cleaver to the violation of innocence. These attackers see no human being beneath their righteous punishment. They see a monster, as inhuman as any fairy-tale creature.

We all seem to agree that there are monsters among us. We just don't agree on who they are. But everyone agrees that they're not remotely like us, not even human, and don't deserve to be treated as one of God's creatures. Instead, we seek to punish them as one of God's mistakes. For those of us who don't believe in God, or who don't find Him to blame, then so much worse is the wrath for the godless monster who has brought it on himself.

There is a reason that the word *fat* is unspeakable. Fat is monstrous to most people. The very idea is illicit, as is every word that points to it: *fat, obese, lard, blubber, corpulent,* and so on. Even a photograph of obesity is regarded with disgust, blame, or pity. In places where these words must not be uttered, monsters roam. I've talked about whether we blame or pity the monster. I've talked about cases in which we attack the monster or his monstrosity. A monster is someone who could never be us, and someone whom we could never be. We each have our own monsters, because the monster is our opposite. If our identity is like the photograph of who we are, then the monster is our negative image. He occurs as monstrous only in the context of our identity. Without that context, he is simply a very bad person, or a person who has done something terrible. His monstrosity—his absence of humanity—is a direct reflection of our humanity, whatever we consider that to be.

Making Our Monsters

During that conversation I had in Starbucks, the man said he'd shoot himself if he ever "looked like that." He couldn't even bring himself to say *fat*. We see ourselves as the opposite of whatever is so monstrous, dislocating it from ourselves, from our identity, from our very humanity. However, if we have learned anything from the atrocities of history and the countless genocides that have swept through our times, it is that there is no such thing as "I could never do what he has done. I could never be the thing that he is." How else does a child learn to execute families of enemy tribes? How else does a nation turn against an entire race? It might seem a melodramatic exaggeration to compare genocide to fat-shaming. It might seem offensive to compare a crime of senseless hate in Wyoming with a mob's righteous retribution in India. But really, I think our humanity depends on our making exactly this comparison.

There are monsters indeed. They are the outcast parts of ourselves, and we give them no quarter. A monster is any part of the whole that is unlovable, beyond redemption, and so must be destroyed. The whole may be a society or one's own body. The problem is that you can't kill a monster without creating another one, or discovering even more monsters. Again, this is as true for a society as it is for one's own body. I'm not suggesting that we pity the monsters, excuse them, or cater to them. Rather, my work is about unmasking the monsters that seem to have corrupted our sexuality or our bodies. My work is about meeting the monster as an equal and becoming whole. While there may be people who do bad things, monsters are our own creation.

Chewing the Fat: Conversations of Taboo

I've said before that the Round World spins on the axis of guilt and shame. It's not that we in the Round World are a community of ashamed or guilt-ridden people. That's just one possible way to feel about Fat, and it's not even unique to Fat. But there are issues, such as Fat or race or religion, that we don't feel we can talk about openly. They seem too charged with emotion for casual or even civil conversation. These conversations derive their charge from the fact that their topics are taboo.

Talking Around Taboo

Fat is taboo. As I've said, the word *fat* is literally unspeakable in polite company, as are any of its synonyms. It's not the word that is offensive to people—it's the very idea of Fat. Even photographs of fat people elicit disgust, shame, or embarrassment. A taboo is not just something we don't talk about. Most of us don't talk about the physics of quantum charge or the reign of Henry V, but these subjects are not taboo. A taboo is something that we don't talk about even though it's the thing that's there to talk about. A taboo conversation is the words on our tongue that don't get said because we'd be hanged for them. To say them would be to commit heresy in the public discourse.

Taboo conversations take place even when no one is speaking, like when a fat man waddles up to a buffet and people try to get a look at what's on his plate. A taboo conversation can be the unspoken words between the spoken ones, like when a woman is told she has "such a pretty face." Are we concerned that if we said simply, "You're pretty," she might become confused, thinking we mean her pretty elbows? No, we say that she has a pretty face because we feel obligated to stress that in no way is her fat body pretty. Finally, a taboo conversation might be the tacit rules of engagement, such as when I'm affectionate with my 400-pound boyfriend in a gay bar, and the muscle stud next to me passes me his phone number. A fit man with a fat boyfriend is a relationship he need not take seriously.

I'm interested in taboo conversations. As with monsters, a taboo conversation is like the photographic negative of authentic conversation. In a photographic negative, what's brightest appears darkest. Similarly, in a taboo conversation, what's unspoken becomes the loudest. The contents of a taboo conversation are secrets, the thoughts and feelings that we mean not to share. We keep taboos alive by keeping those secrets. We keep secrets, as individuals and as communities, out of fear, usually the fear of what we are or what people will think of us.

Whether or not others agree, we always believe that our fear around a taboo conversation is justified. In the Round World, someone might have a secret such as "I'm sexually attracted to obese men." That's a secret I might keep from my boss, because he might not like me if he knew, and he holds power over me. It's a secret I might keep from my partner, because he might feel belittled or humiliated to be adored for something he dislikes about himself. It's a secret I might keep from my friends, because I know they would ridicule me or even ostracize me for liking something so loathsome. It's a secret I might keep even from myself, because I don't believe that I'm such a shallow person as to chase after someone because of a physical characteristic, especially a characteristic that evokes such disgust and disapproval from the world.

Taboo Versus Inappropriate

Of course, there's a difference between a taboo conversation and an inappropriate conversation. Certainly there are things that are not taboo, but we still stop ourselves from talking about them. For example, it's not taboo to discuss a raise with your boss. However, it's probably inappropriate to bring it up at the office holiday party. Also, not all secrets are taboos. You could certainly invite your friend to a party, but it would be inappropriate to invite her to a surprise party that her husband is throwing for her.

What makes taboo even more complex is that sometimes what we don't say depends on whom we're talking to. Around some people, we watch what we say for fear of treading on some sensitive topic. Around others, we feel free to talk about almost anything—even taboos. So where's the dividing line between a taboo conversation and an inappropriate one? Well, as I see it, whether a conversation is inappropriate depends on circumstance. By contrast, whether a conversation is taboo depends on identity. Our identity, how we define ourselves in relation to the world, is at the center of a taboo conversation.

I know from experience that the only thing more taboo than talking about Fat is talking about Fat as sexual. I'm comfortable liking Fat. Many people in the Round World are comfortable being fat. Their obesity and my attraction to it form a positive part of our identities. For that reason, we may even seem proud of it. So we can talk together about Fat like it's the weather. But for other people, discussing Fat might be as dangerous as discussing politics at a big holiday meal with all the family gathered around the table.

Violating a taboo leads to upset and resentment, as happens at so many holiday dinners. And the upset may last for years, lying buried until something reminds us of it and off we go again. I could be talking about Fat, politics, race, or religion. Upset on that level happens when the taboo is not respected, when the unspeakable is spoken. That's when our identity is threatened.

But if a taboo conversation is really about identity, then the topic is just camouflage for what's really at stake—oneself. We feel free to talk about our fear of cancer, as long as we're sure no one dying of the disease can hear us. What about race or religion? If everybody in the conversation seems to be the same as you, it makes things less dicey, doesn't it? That's because these things are deeply personal. These are more than topics. They form our identity, our interface with the world. We perceive our world through these identities; we go about our lives inside them. And to the extent that some of us have identities linked to taboos, we live in a taboo conversation.

I live in a taboo conversation. The language that gives form to my thoughts and feelings, the reality of my world, is a taboo to most people. This book is an authentic conversation about a taboo conversation. Seen from one point of view, this book is about the tangle of upset that occurs when two taboos—Fat and sexuality—are not just allied, but merged into a singular distinction.

Do you live in a taboo conversation? More than one? Living in a taboo conversation is not the same as being a member of a minority or a marginalized group. It's not about one group's power over another. Rather, it's about the secret that we hold unsaid, the secret that someone else isn't good enough—or we ourselves aren't.

So-Called Stupid Questions

One way to tell whether you live in a taboo conversation is to see whether an honest question about the taboo upsets you. Have you ever been upset by a question even though it was not intended as hostile? For example, many chasers get asked, "What do you like about fat guys?" Even though we know the question is born of curiosity, we often find the question offensive and condemn it as being "stupid" or "ignorant." But don't all honest questions seek to cure ignorance? Nevertheless, the intent of the question doesn't seem to avoid the offense. On the other hand, many chubs will ask a chaser, "What do you like about fat guys?" in order to understand our attraction to them. In this case, no offense is taken— presumably because one of our own tribe is asking.

Similar questions include...

Why are you so fat?

Is it weird working with so many Muslims?

What do you think made you gay?

How much do they pay you for that?

How come you only/never get with white guys

Is that some sort of fetish you have?

Notice the various reactions you have to these examples. They all ask about something taboo—Fat, religion, sexuality, race, and money. We may not react to such questions with the same degree of dislike, but that just means some are more central to our identity than others. However, all of these questions are similar because they seek information while transgressing a taboo. Although it's common to punish the person asking such questions, I've found that treating their curiosity as legitimate is far more productive and empowering for both of us.

I've spend a lot of time answering so-called stupid questions—questions on the tip of the tongue that don't get asked because they provoke upset and embarrassment. Many activists seek to eliminate ignorance about Fat or some other taboo topic, yet their immediate response to a question is often condemnation.

Who Wants to Know: Intent and Identity

I'm sure you have very good reasons that prove that a question is rude or inappropriate or even offensive. You may even be in favor of silencing such questions, believing that they should be left unasked precisely because they are offensive. However, since taboos are about secrecy and silence, censoring questions about a taboo only helps to keep the taboo in place—and perhaps even strengthens it.

We soon come to find that any question about Fat—or any other taboo—creates upset no matter what the intent of the person asking. In fact, questions and comments about a taboo are never more cutting, more damning, than when they come from the voice inside our own head:

How did I get so fat? Why do I chase after fat guys? Why do I have this weird fetish? These are the conversations that offend us when they come from strangers and disgrace us when they come from the voice inside our head. We condemn or deflect these questions, because we think that will take away the shame and guilt they elicit. But these questions are at the heart of who we are if we live in a taboo conversation.

So how do we answer such questions? As Susan Sontag wrote, "The only interesting answers are the ones which destroy the questions." Our answers have the power to destroy such questions and leave the questioner transformed, rather than vilified. Even when we are the questioner.

Of course, not all questions are quite so innocent. I couldn't do the work I do and not encounter some hostility politely couched as questions. With taboo comes upset. For example, I've been asked questions like "Don't you think it's shallow of you to target fat guys to date?" Or "So you fatten them up until you're done with them? Then what?" These are not innocent requests for information, clearly. They are accusations masquerading as questions. The question or comment is intended to wound or shame me. However, even interactions that are meant to insult us can be turned into transformative moments. We can do more than merely survive them. These taboo conversations can empower us, when we look at their construction and how they operate.

Talking Taboo

Let's look at some other taboo conversations besides Fat. Imagine you see a thin woman on a bus with a scarf covering her head. You see no hair peeking out from under her scarf, and you suspect she has none or very little. It occurs to you that she might have cancer. A child who just lost her mother to cancer might go up and ask the woman what happened to her hair. The child might ask whether what happened to her mother is what's happening to the woman on the bus. An adult should know better, we say. Even if that adult had just lost her mother to cancer days before, the risk of upset and offense is too great to ask such things of a perfect stranger. Cancer is a taboo conversation. Death or any extreme loss is also a taboo conversation.

Another woman gets on the bus. She has some difficulty because her body is not formed like other people's, and her feet don't quite face a direction that would make walking easy, especially as the bus lurches before she can find a seat. You know it's not your business. You know it's not a good idea to talk to strangers, yet the woman with the awkward gait intrigues you. Maybe you even find her attractive. Would you let it occur to you that her gait is beautiful? Would it be all right to find her walk beautiful in the privacy of your own mind? It might be perfectly fine to find someone with a disability attractive, but it's quite another matter to find a person's disability attractive. Would you allow yourself to tolerate such a thought, even as a possibility?

The woman with the funny walk is blonde, and she smiles easily at people she makes eye contact with. Would you compliment the woman and tell her you think she's pretty? Would you tell any woman you've never met that you think she's pretty? Would it occur to you that telling a woman with a disability that she's pretty would sound like you pity her, that she might think the only reason you're complimenting her is to spread some goodwill to someone less fortunate? You haven't spoken a word to the woman, but you're having a taboo conversation inside your head.

The woman on the bus could be my friend Kari. She has cerebral palsy, a disability she's had since birth, which gives her an unusual, asymmetrical walk and a sometimes curious way of handling objects. Now, I don't presume to put Kari up as a representative for all disabled people. Like everyone in this book, she's simply a particular person who lives in a taboo conversation. You see, whether or not anyone speaks to her, she is part of that conversation that I described above. Other people are having silent dialogues and imagining her responses. Even though she may be unaware of the conflicted chatter inside someone else's head, it affects her nonetheless. The chatter about her in someone else's head closes down certain possibilities. For example, "You're quite pretty" could lead to a romance, or a friendship, or a conversation about a shared hobby. Or it could inspire someone overhearing the conversation to call his sister, because Kari looks like his sympathetic sister, and the bystander has gone through a tough divorce and could use a sympathetic ear like Kari seems to have. And all these thoughts could just as well be Kari's assessments of herself reflected in the faces of all the people who are looking or not looking at her as she makes her way to an open seat on the bus.

I asked Kari what her reaction might be if she found out that a guy she was dating was sexually attracted to her disability. I don't find that so hard to imagine, actually. Kari's gait has a crooked poetry to it; there's a sort of graceful syncopation in how she moves and holds herself. "What if a guy thought your walk was sexy, that what most call a disability he called a seduction?"

This was Kari's response: "At one time, that would have really bothered me. But I've worked through a lot since then, and now I think I'd be fine with it." I was expecting (hoping?) that her reaction would be somewhat more enthusiastic than "I'd be fine with it." Many people, especially chasers, don't understand why it's not good news to find that someone loves something about you that the rest of the world thinks is unfortunate.

Kari and I have had a lot of discussions, and we've talked about something I mentioned earlier in this book—about the parts of ourselves that are off-limits to affection or sensuality. We talked about the taboo conversation many of us have about parts of our bodies, about keeping them camouflaged or concealed, or simply refusing to acknowledge that these parts exist at all. She told me that her scars represented that for her.

"I had a lot of operations when I was an infant to try to fix and straighten my limbs. The operations probably gave me more mobility, but I never had a choice about whether I wanted to be 'fixed,' and I've never known my body without these scars. I have very mixed feelings about them and what they represent."

I asked her how she'd react if a guy paid attention to her scars or was obviously attracted to them.

"Oh wow, I don't know," she said. "I wouldn't want them to be the focus of his attention."

"So you'd prefer he avoided them?"

"No, that would be worse, I think."

"So he shouldn't like them, but he shouldn't avoid them?"

"Yes, because liking them or avoiding them, he still notices them. He's still reacting to them. I'd just like to forget about them."

That reminded me of many fat people I've talked to who just wanted their fat to be ignored, who wanted to be loved and not reminded of that part of themselves that they find unlovable. That desire is at the core of "Why can't he love me for me?"—where *me* means *the me who isn't fat*. Of course, fat people in my seminars are quick to point out that their objection is to being loved *only* for their fat. "Well," I respond, "who said anything about *only*?" No one who is truly loved is loved for only one thing.

We seem to worry about praise only when it's directed at something that conflicts with how we wish to be seen. I said before that objectification is when what you want is more important than who the other person is—how they want to be seen. But from the opposite side, objectification occurs when the way we want to be seen is less important to the other person than the part of us they find attractive. We feel most objectified when what we've tried our best to banish from our identity is what calls the loudest to another person. In fact, it calls so loudly that we imagine it's the only part of us they see. All the rest of who we are must surely be mute if that single, disregarded crumb of our being can raise in someone a call so clarion.

The Taboo Conversation

I don't think that being disabled is similar to being fat, or that being black is like being gay or having cancer. It's our conversations—not our identities—that are similar. What if our salient commonality is not our identities, but rather that our identities give rise to the same conversation? What if the reason we sometimes feel allied with or alienated by Fat, sexuality, race, gender, disability, or religion has nothing to do with those labels? Suppose that these taboo topics are not topics of different conversations, but rather all manifestations of one conversation: the taboo conversation.

Regardless of the taboo topic or who is discussing it, there is a single conversation that we have when we interact with any taboo. For some of us, that taboo is central to who we are. It's part of our conversation because it's part of us, part of our lives. The disabled woman on the bus, the fat man on the stairs, the black girl at the convenience store, the chubby chaser at the bar—there are those of us who live in a conversation that is taboo. What's more, we all live in the same taboo conversation.

As we've seen, the taboo conversation can encompass any topic that a community regards as socially dangerous or transgressive. I've met people who said that being fat was no big deal where they grew up. By contrast, I've met people who said being fat has ruled every waking moment of their lives. Religion is a taboo topic. A conservative Christian may be admired in some parts of the country, but derided in another. So, too, the atheist. Rather than focusing on untangling the particular taboo topic, perhaps our energies are better spent focusing on the universal properties of the taboo conversation and how it works. Regardless of the taboo—race, Fat, money, disability, religion, and so on—the taboo conversation seems to possess at least three components that affect our relationships with people. Not surprisingly, since a taboo is built on identity, these three components are elements of our identity. In other words, they are how we identify with the taboo, why it's personal to us, and why we get so upset in conversations that touch on it.

Components of the Taboo Conversation

These three components of the taboo conversation are our membership in the taboo community (inclusion/exclusion), our standing within the taboo community (ignorance/authority), and our sense of righteousness (injustice/justification) with respect to issues surrounding the taboo community.

Membership: Inclusion/Exclusion

Since a taboo relies on identity, the taboo conversation always considers whether we identify with the taboo—whether we claim inclusion. Membership in the taboo of Fat is based on body composition. Membership in the taboo of race is based on skin color and physiognomy. For religion, membership is based on religious beliefs or practices. Whether we are included in or excluded from the taboo (and whether the other person identifies the same way) seems to affect the conversation and how we relate to each other. For example, many fat people have no problem using the word *fat* because they consider it accurate. However, most thin people feel unauthorized to use the word because they have no membership in the taboo. They're afraid that they will be seen as insensitive or even bigoted.

This is why euphemisms are always a part of the taboo conversation. They are a code that substitutes for what we mean to say. In a taboo conversation, there are always euphemisms to assign someone membership. For example, "He's heavyset," "She's well off," and, "They're expecting" are ways to designate inclusive membership in the taboo conversations about Fat, money, and sex, respectively.

Since a person's membership status is vital to the taboo conversation, so too then are the credentials of membership. For example, on a website that caters to chubs and chasers, some guys have been told by other members to leave because they weren't fat enough to be considered a chub. Basically, some of the other members didn't think they qualified for membership in the taboo.

Standing: Ignorance/Authority

Another element of the taboo conversation is whether the participants in the conversation have the standing to speak or contribute to the conversation. Experience, visibility, or credibility with respect to the taboo are determiners for one's standing in the conversation. For example, my friend Brian weighs 500 pounds and is in a long-term relationship. He was at one of my seminars when another man, around 300 pounds, said that fat people have a harder time dating and finding relationships than regular people. "We're at a huge disadvantage," he said. "Even if we can come to love ourselves this way [fat], most other people won't."

Then my friend Brian spoke up: "I can't say that I've ever had any trouble dating that I can tell. I've always been huge, so I have nothing to compare it to, but even before I met my partner, I was never hard up for a date." The room was flat—no dissent or rebuttal, not even from the man who'd initially spoken. Brian seemed to have settled the matter completely. Though he and the other man both had membership in the taboo of obesity, Brian's size gave him more credibility in the conversation. In the Round World, being fatter grants more credibility in matters relating to Fat.

My friend Damian says that his black friends who are darker than him claim more authority on matters of racial discrimination. He tells me that they seem to think that his lighter skin makes his opinions or experiences less representative or valid.

Unlike membership in a taboo, which is a static feature of one's identity, one's standing is not necessarily fixed, because it is determined by the other people present who also have membership.

Righteousness: Injustice/Justification

The last element of the taboo conversation involves our judgments and explanations of the particular taboo in question. Most of us living in a taboo conversation claim some sort of injustice visited on us personally and a justification for why we have a right to feel wronged. We are inevitably met by an opposite justification for why our suffering is reasonable, and perhaps even by the charge that we are perpetrating some sort of injustice on others. We see this abundantly in the Round World when talk turns to health care, fashion choices, and even airline seats. In fact, the whole second section of this book, "You Don't Know Fat," is an exploration of the injustice/justification element around the taboo conversation about Fat.

In the taboo conversation about money, we might hear of the injustice suffered by the poor: "The poor lack basic necessities, which are denied them by a system that is designed to exploit them." Conversely, we might hear of the injustice suffered by the rich: "The rewards earned from someone's talent and hard work are taken from them and given to others who've done nothing to deserve them." Each claimed injustice is met with equal fervor by justifications from the other side. Again, such a discussion quickly becomes heated. What seems abstract economics somehow becomes a very personal matter.

It may be hard to see economic disparity as an example of the taboo conversation. After all, isn't that a social justice issue? Isn't it really an issue to do with equality, responsibility, and integrity? Perhaps, but it's also a taboo called money. If it were only a social justice issue, we wouldn't need euphemisms such as *well off* and *underprivileged* when we talk about rich and poor. Contrast this to another social issue: smoking laws. There are no euphemisms to talk about cigarettes or smokers.

The words we use and the people to whom we apply them stake out the injustice and justifications of the taboo conversation. The same dynamic of injustice/justification weaves through any taboo topic, just as inclusion/exclusion and ignorance/authority do. They're the stakes holding down the tent under which we hold the taboo conversation.

Transcending the Taboo Conversation

At its heart, the taboo conversation is not about any particular taboo. It's about whether who we are is acceptable—acceptable to others or even to ourselves. It always entails leaving something or someone out. Seen in the context of its three components, the taboo conversation questions our membership in what's acceptable. It contests our standing—our validity—relative to others in the taboo. And it attacks our notions of what is fair and demands that we justify ourselves. No wonder the taboo conversation is so upsetting! And worst of all, it can take place even when no one is speaking, even when we're alone with our own thoughts. The taboo conversation is really about ourselves, and it feels as though our survival is at stake.

Have you ever argued someone over to your side of an issue? Did you give such compelling reasons that the other person came around to your way of thinking? If so, then you weren't participating in the taboo conversation. Reasons and evidence make no difference in the taboo conversation. Reasons and evidence have absolutely no power to persuade in the taboo conversation because you cannot argue someone out of their identity, which is where the taboo conversation is based.

The taboo conversation feels personal because our identity is bound up in that taboo. It appears to happen between one person and another, but it may be between our group identity and another group's identity. And some of these groups include millions of people. And all these taboos are being expressed in a single archetypal conversation. A single conversation is going on right now, everywhere, by all people in all cultures of all times about whatever topic is considered too fearful or shameful to talk about openly. In that sense, it is a conversation that humanity is having with itself.

The opposite conversation, then, would be about inclusion and acceptance. The taboo conversation becomes authentic communication only when we can get beyond our view of ourselves: beyond our membership in a group, our standing in that group, and the righteousness that we attach to our point of view. I was talking before about the stories we tell about the world and about ourselves. Well, we're in those stories. In fact, usually we're the main character. In the stories we tell about ourselves, we claim membership in a group, and a certain standing, and the power of righteousness. In the stories we tell about other people, we assign them membership—including them in or excluding them from our own group. We listen for their standing, and we judge their point of view. The joke, of course, is that everyone else is doing that to us too.

The Round World is my tribe. Being a gay man who is attracted to fat men is not just my particular taste, or even a desire that I must satisfy. It's part of my identity; it feels as much a part of me as my hands or my voice. It's home. Nevertheless, if I'm to be more than just a point of view among seven billion other points of view, if I'm to be able to make a difference with my life, I need to see beyond the garden walls of my identity. When I mistake my community, my authority, or my point of view for who I am, then I am diminished.

We are more powerful than the labels and points of view we adopt. When I am offended, I know that it is my identity that has been wounded, not me. When someone insults my taste in men, or questions the morality of my desires, my identity is wounded. And in many instances, it is the intent of the speaker to do so. My identity seeks then to annihilate the attacker utterly. I can sense the biochemical changes in my body. My blood pressure goes up. I can feel my adrenaline surging. My body responds as if I'm being attacked because my mind perceives the conversation as a threat. Biochemically, when something we care about is under attack, there's no difference whether it's our leg, our loved one, or our deeply held belief. But why would I feel hurt or upset if an idea or a characteristic is attacked? I get upset only to the extent that the idea or characteristic is part of me. I'm not saying that I don't have strong opinions. I just know that my opinions are not who I am. That comes in very handy when I have conversations with people about Fat.

That's what happened in the case of that guy who said, "If I looked like that, I'd shoot myself." I could have taken that remark as a personal insult to my taste in men, but the remark had nothing to do with me. It didn't even have anything to do with fat people. Instead, what we saw in our conversation was that fat people triggered a lot of issues that he had with his own body. Does this happen all the time with people? I'd say it happens about two-thirds of the time. One third of the time, the person just thinks I'm a disgusting pervert. Another third of the time, the person doesn't have strong feelings about Fat, but is fascinated that someone like me is actually attracted to it. And the final third of the time, we end up making a discovery about each other. It's those second two-thirds that led me to start giving seminars and to write this book.

I've been surprised by the number of offensive remarks that I've turned into authentic conversations by simply refusing to mistake an attack on my identity for an attack on me. If there is no wound to redress, there's no need to return fire. I'm free instead to smile, walk away, or even to engage my would-be attacker in conversation. My answer can destroy the question without destroying the questioner.

> **It's not hard to understand a person; it's only hard to listen without bias.**
>
> —**Criss Jami**, *Killosophy*

My friend Carla is straight, but she was with some gay male friends on the patio of a local gay bar enjoying some drinks on a pleasant Sunday afternoon. The tables were close, and there was a minor upset when Carla and a guy became annoyed with each other over bumping chairs and invaded personal space. It ended with the guy leaving in a huff and his friend running after him saying, "C'mon, it's okay. Who cares what some fat cow thinks?"

Carla went to hide out in the restroom. "I'm not sure why," she told me later, "but the guy got to me, ya know? I'm a big girl and I should be used to that, but I'll admit I had myself a little cry there in the bathroom." She said she thought about a better way to handle the situation than hiding and crying in the bathroom, a better way than simply striking back.

When she eventually returned, she saw that the guy who had run off after his friend had returned to the table next to hers. She went over to him and said, "I just want to ask you something. How would you feel if someone called your sister or your mother a fat cow? What would you do if someone said that to one of them?" The man looked horrified and took off running. "It was hardly the reaction I anticipated!" Carla said. But what happened next was even more surprising. Carla went back to her friends, but the man who had insulted her came back a while later. "He'd obviously been crying," Carla said. "He told me over and over again how sorry he was, and how he'd been made fun of for being gay so many times, and how he was ashamed of himself for saying that about me. Then his friend came over, too, the one who'd been such a jerk in the first place, and he apologized. The next thing I know, we're all laughing and having drinks together. It was absolutely bizarre!"

When I tell this story, I'm often accused of making it up. It sounds too perfect, too good to be true. Nevertheless it did happen, and it demonstrates what's possible in the world. It's not that mysterious or complicated, actually. If someone says something insulting, I can say, "Really? What do you mean?" "Why is that important to you?" "How come you said that?" Or even "Have you always felt this way?" It's astonishing where that sort of conversation can lead. If I leave my identity out of the conversation, I'm free to listen or respond to anything. Listening, authenticity, and curiosity about the other person lead outside the taboo conversation. Membership, standing, and righteousness lead back into it. Outside of the taboo conversation, people are able to listen, find common ground, and yes, sometimes disagree. However, the disagreement is born of mutual respect rather than rancor. Even in that disagreement, we feel closer for having heard one another.

Homecoming

When you and I met, I was sitting in a bar in an affluent, gay neighbor-hood. That seems so long ago. Maybe it has been years. I am so different now from when I started my journey.

I said that this book is a travelogue, a book that leads the reader into a foreign land with strange people and curious customs. But before the reader of any travelogue may take such a journey, it is the author's jour-ney first. The writing of this book has taken me many years. The living of this book has taken me even longer—my whole life, so far. As I finish the book, I can see that I am not the same person who started writing it. I never felt myself changing. I just know that the man who started writing this book is not the one typing this now. And the man I will be years from now perhaps will not recognize these words as having been his own.

One of my concerns in writing a book like this is that I can't shake the feeling that in ten years, I will see how much more there is for me to see. There is an art to this, an art to delving into and discovering what truly matters to us, our lives becoming more and more aligned with it, our selves becoming more and more the embodiment of it. We are the art of becoming.

So now as you and I come to this stopping point, the end of the book, I see my words as an artifact of where I am. An expression of myself thrown clear from a life in motion and coming to rest, frozen in time, for other travelers to examine. Throughout the book, you may have dis-agreed or agreed with me at various points, but it is not my intent for the book to find agreement, or debate, or even understanding. Now that you're back from your armchair tour of the Round World, my greatest hope for the journey we have taken together in these pages is that you will chart the lands of your own undiscovered country. I believe that as members of a species, we want to know each other. We have no way to step outside ourselves as human beings to examine what it means to be human. Our only tool is sharing ourselves to glimpse the totality of who we really are. To paraphrase the poet Warsan Shire, my home is not where I came from. Perhaps home is somewhere I'm going and never have been before.

To join the conversation and hear
about my upcoming seminars,
join my mailing list by visiting my website at
www.danoliverio.com

Printed in Great Britain
by Amazon